Pandemic Injustice

Confronting Systemic Omissions and Impacts in Educational Policy

An iMPACTS Partnership Publication

Shaheen Shariff
Series Editor

Vol. 2

Pandemic Injustice

Navigating legal and policy lines during the COVID-19 pandemic

Christopher Dietzel and Kimia Towfigh, Editors

PETER LANG
New York - Berlin - Bruxelles - Chennai - Lausanne - Oxford

Library of Congress Cataloging-in-Publication Control Number: 2023027122

Bibliographic information published by the Deutsche Nationalbibliothek.
The German National Library lists this publication in the German
National Bibliography; detailed bibliographic data is available
on the Internet at http://dnb.d-nb.de.

Cover design by Alyssa Jetha

ISSN 2834-6939 (print) ISSN 2834-6920 (online)
ISBN 9781636674810 (paperback)
ISBN 9781636674827 (hardback)
ISBN 9781636674834 (ebook)
ISBN 9781636674841 (epub)
DOI 10.3726/b20951

© 2024 Peter Lang Group AG, Lausanne
Published by Peter Lang Publishing Inc., New York, USA
info@peterlang.com - www.peterl ang.com

All rights reserved.
All parts of this publication are protected by copyright.
Any utilization outside the strict limits of the copyright law, without the permission of the publisher, is forbidden and liable to prosecution.
This applies in particular to reproductions, translations, microfilming, and storage and processing in electronic retrieval systems.

This publication has been peer reviewed.

Dedication from Shaheen Shariff, PhD
To my iMPACTS graduate and undergraduate researchers for their unwavering commitment, passion, resilience, and strength. I have learned much from you.

Dedication from Christopher Dietzel, PhD
To the many people who overcame incredible challenges and exercised strength during a period of great uncertainty.

Dedication from Kimia Towfigh, BCL/JD
To healthcare workers, educational professionals, and front-line workers who collectively demonstrated resilience and hope during the COVID-19 pandemic.

Acknowledgment of Funding

This work was supported by *iMPACTS: Collaborations to Address Sexual Violence on Campus*; Social Sciences and Humanities Research Council (SSHRC) of Canada Partnership Grant Number: 895-2016-1026, Project Director, Shaheen Shariff, PhD, James McGill Professor, McGill University.

Contents

Preface by the Series Editor   xi

Part I   Rights and Safety

Chapter One: Striking a Balance: An Assessment of Anti-SLAPP Litigation in Canada   3
Kimia Towfigh

Chapter Two: Are We in This Together? A Foucauldian Analysis of Canada's Response to the COVID-19 Pandemic   21
Iradele Plante

Chapter Three: Danger Inside and Outside the Home: Domestic Violence During the COVID-19 Pandemic   41
Safia Amiry

Part II   Education

Chapter Four: Making Sense of Zoombombing in the Context of COVID-19 and Mandatory Online Learning: An Exploratory Study   61
Amanda Couture-Carron, Michele Pich, and Nawal Ammar

Chapter Five: "What Will Happen to Us?": Policy Barriers and International Student Marginalization in Canada During the COVID-19 Pandemic   81
Shannon Hutcheson

Chapter Six: Exploring Educational Issues During the COVID-19 Pandemic: A Focus on Students, Teachers, and Families in Ontario, Canada   101
Laurie Higgins and William T. Smale

Part III Health and Well-Being

Chapter Seven: Sex Work as Public Health: A Critical Discourse Analysis of Canada's COVID-19 Pandemic Response for Sex Workers   119
Sarah Towle and Alexandra M. Zidenberg

Chapter Eight: Neo-Vagrancy Laws in Media Discourses During Canada's First Wave of COVID-19   139
Elliot Fonarev, Ravita Surajbali, and Joe Hermer

Chapter Nine: Flow of Inequity: Period Poverty and the COVID-19 Pandemic   159
Lisa Smith, Rim Gacimi, Neal Adolph, and Jane Hope

Appendix   177
Notes on Contributors   181

Preface by the Series Editor

SHAHEEN SHARIFF

The World Health Organization's (WHO) declaration of a global COVID-19 pandemic on March 11, 2020, brought the world as we knew it to a screeching halt (WHO, 2021b). Concerns about transmitting the novel coronavirus have pushed governments to respond in innovative and unprecedented ways. They halted international and local travel, implemented lockdowns, and mandated physical distancing and isolation—all of which have compounded complex, pre-existing societal and economic issues. As the virus was spreading, COVID was often described as the "great equalizer" (Galasso, 2020; Mein, 2020), implying that it would affect all individuals the same, without differentiation between gender, race, age, or socioeconomic status. This, of course, was not the case.

According to the WHO, the COVID-19 pandemic has had a disproportionate impact on members of society who occupy the most vulnerable social groups (WHO, 2021a). In healthcare, government mismanagement and lack of permanent staff, caregivers, and resources have compromised the lives of immunosuppressed people and those needing urgent care. The elderly, along with Black people and people living in low-income neighborhoods, experienced disproportionately high rates of infection and death (Rocha et al., 2020; Statistics Canada, 2021). Border closures trapped international students in countries where they were temporarily studying, which resulted in suspended work permits, expired visas, and minimal access to healthcare or insurance. These challenges are only the tip of the iceberg when it comes to the impacts of the pandemic—and all of this takes place within the backdrop of a pre-COVID world that was increasingly violent, hostile, anti-immigrant, and racist (Shariff, 2020). For example, police brutality has targeted visible racial minorities, especially Black people, as society was reminded of with the murder of George Floyd. The repeal of *Roe v. Wade* has removed rights of bodily autonomy from women, girls, and other people who seek out safe, legal abortions. Moreover, the number of anti-LGBTQ+ laws and policies has grown in recent years (ACLU, 2022). These are only some of the many problems in North America that disproportionately impact people from marginalized and vulnerable communities.

This edited collection, which is the second volume in the *Confronting Systemic Omissions and Impacts in Educational Policy* series and the first volume focused on the COVID-19 pandemic, sheds light on how the pandemic has exacerbated pre-existing legal and policy issues, and it stresses the importance of understanding, analyzing, and critiquing law and policy decisions during times of crisis. The collection offers multi-disciplinary scholarly insights, legal and policy analysis, and educational guidelines to address unprecedented socio-legal and psychological impacts on society that have evolved since the onset of the pandemic. Further, these chapters add to the ongoing dialogue about how North American society can improve by examining dilemmas and highlighting opportunities for positive change. Thus, this collection aims to give a different perspective on how we can move forward and create more justice in a post-COVID society. As Principal Investigator and Project Director of iMPACTS,[1] I gladly present this rich compilation of chapters written by academic colleagues and students.

Chapter One, written by Kimia Towfigh, identifies strategic lawsuits against public participation (SLAPPs) legislation that intends to censor, intimidate, and silence defendants as a threat to procedural fairness, freedom of speech, and democratic process. Drawing on Supreme Court of Canada decisions *1704604 Ontario Ltd. v. Pointes Protection Association* and *Bent v. Platnick*, in which the Court interpreted and applied Ontario's anti-SLAPP legislation, Towfigh provides a comparative overview of anti-SLAPP mechanisms in British Columbia, Quebec, and Ontario. In addition, Towfigh calls attention to how SLAPP plaintiffs and other stakeholders, like government representatives, have applied provisions from the COVID-19 pandemic to stifle objectors and protests. Censorship tactics are not only used in the legal sector, as the pandemic has worsened delays in the Canadian justice system and briefly shut down courthouse operations across the country. These cases serve as a significant reminder that published assertions still need to be adequately supported, regardless of expectations of anonymity and despite the widespread shift of public dialogue online. The process of finding the truth is becoming more and more endangered when incorrect information is spread through online sources and social media platforms. As a result, Towfigh's chapter promotes responsible journalism, communication, and fact-checking, especially when questioning the character of identifiable individuals.

Chapter Two focuses on the legal strategies used to advance public health and safety while protecting civil liberties. Specifically, Iradele Plante's chapter consists of three parts that explore how state powers have grown in the wake of the COVID-19 pandemic. In the first section, using Michel Foucault's "plague town" archetype as a guide, Plante examines how the destruction left behind by a pandemic can be used as a political tool to strengthen state powers. As such, she draws from Foucauldian philosophy since the study of power relations is strikingly similar to legislative discourse. Plante also explores how Foucault's ideology maps onto the Canadian reality of the COVID-19 pandemic. The second section of this chapter examines how the scope, intent, and delegation of power align with the Foucauldian plague town. The last section of the chapter looks at how democratic safeguards can increase well-being while limiting the encroachment on civil freedoms. Overall, Plante's chapter serves as a tool that could help policymakers and legal professionals better understand how authority can be transferred in emergency situations, as well as how to prevent abuse and minimize the potential for abuse.

Chapter Three explores the widespread concern of how government-mandated lockdown restrictions during the COVID-19 pandemic have contributed to increased rates of domestic violence. Safia Amiry examines how and why a pandemic can exacerbate domestic violence as she considers questions such as: Which demographic groups are more at risk? What policies have been implemented? What strategies have been taken by governments and non-government institutions to address domestic violence? In reflecting on these questions, Amiry recognizes what work has been done to address domestic violence and what is still lacking. This chapter examines the advancement and shortcomings of these policies and approaches by applying critical feminist theory to investigate the power dynamics of domestic violence and consider which factors exacerbate these problems. The final section of Amiry's chapter examines how domestic violence during the pandemic may have short-term and long-term policy effects. This chapter can help educate policymakers on the implications of rising rates of domestic violence both during and after the COVID-19 pandemic.

Chapter Four investigates the novel phenomenon of *zoombombing*, which refers to unwelcome and uninvited intruders who join a virtual meeting on Zoom and perpetuate online harm by verbally shouting, making racist comments, showing graphic pornography, and/or sexually assailing audience members. Amanda Couture-Carron, Michele Pich, and Nawal Ammar examine how zoombombing could fall under the purview of current university policies that address harassment and/or cyberbullying. As such, they explore the similarities and differences between zoombombing, harassment, and cyberbullying. The authors also investigate whether zoombombing is a distinct phenomenon that requires its own focus and analysis within legal and policy frames. Such an understanding is important as it helps university administrators and policymakers identify whether their institutions could respond to zoombombing by using the same reliefs, laws, statutes, and services they have applied to respond to existing instances of harassment and cyberbullying. The authors conclude that zoombombing cannot be categorized as either harassment or cyberbullying since doing so would ignore important differences that make zoombombing and its effects distinct from other forms of online harm.

Chapter Five investigates how international students have been marginalized by policies in international education before and during the COVID-19 pandemic. Specifically, Shannon Hutcheson focuses on the pandemic context of international higher education by examining various policies and actions taken by universities as well as the Canadian and U.S. governments, and she exposes how neoliberalism and policies have affected international students' experiences at universities abroad. To do so, Hutcheson analyzes social commentary, media articles, and academic literature to expose some of the concerns that international students have with higher education. Acknowledging the pandemic's novelty as well as a variety of policy challenges that have arisen and worsened by the pandemic, Hutcheson ends the chapter by suggesting crucial recommendations on how institutional change must occur for there to be equitable education.

Chapter Six focuses on the educational issues resulting from the COVID-19 pandemic and its impact on students, teachers, and families in Ontario, Canada. Laurie Higgins and William T. Smale take their readers back to the beginning of the pandemic when governments were considering various methods of teaching. They examine how the pandemic-related uncertainty that permeated schools created anxiety for educators as they became responsible for a variety of issues ranging from health considerations to educational practices. Higgins and Smale also consider how online learning may impact students differently, especially students with disabilities. Moreover, they reflect on how the roles of educators and parents shifted during the pandemic as these groups had to adapt to different educational scenarios, such as learning from home or going back to school. This chapter also discusses how the pandemic has affected pedagogical practices and methods, thereby offering a critical analysis of what happened during this time of crisis in schools and the Ontario educational community.

Chapter Seven delves into the needs of sex workers in Canada both generally and during the COVID-19 pandemic. Sarah Towle and Alexandra M. Zidenberg aim to answer the following research questions: How were sex workers represented in official governmental and community-based publications that aimed to provide support to this population during the pandemic? What supports and/or resources were offered to sex workers during the pandemic? To answer these questions, the authors conducted a critical discourse analysis of how sex workers were represented in select publications during the COVID-19 pandemic. Specifically, Towle and Zidenberg examined three provincial publications and juxtaposed them with an analysis of a more comprehensive community guide, jointly released by two organizations that serve sex workers. The chapter draws on both a public health ethics framework from the Public Health Agency of Canada (PHAC) that was released during the pandemic and a legal framework from the United Nations' Advisory Group on Sex Work. The authors assert that, due to the Canadian government's pandemic-related approaches, sex workers may have been discouraged from utilizing vital health and social services during this critical time. They conclude that it is essential for vulnerable groups, including sex workers, to have access to comprehensive information and services—without creating additional hurdles or barriers.

Chapter Eight, written by Elliot Fonarev, Ravita Surajbali, and Joe Hermer, demonstrates how the media presented neo-vagrancy laws as an approach to address homelessness during Canada's first wave of the COVID-19 pandemic. The authors present findings from a content analysis of 22 Canadian news articles published between March and August 2020, which were the first five months after the implementation of emergency and public health measures related to COVID-19 in Canada. Through their examination of changes, amendments, and proposed changes to neo-vagrancy laws during the pandemic, the authors suggest that neo-vagrancy laws were reified as an effective approach to disputes over how to use public places in a way that disregards the rights of those who are homeless and puts the needs of the consumer-citizen first.

Chapter Nine explores the issue of period poverty, a term used to refer to the barriers that women, girls, trans men, and non-binary people confront when trying to access menstrual supplies and other resources that support their reproductive health. Specifically, authors Lisa Smith, Rim Gacimi, Neal Adolph, and Jane Hope review available literature in this field and analyze how two organizations, United Way of the Lower Mainland and Aisle International, worked to address period poverty in Canada during the COVID-19 pandemic. First, they found that more people sought assistance during the pandemic, which strained the non-profit sector that was already working beyond capacity. They also noted that these two organizations provided goods and services in local areas, thereby allowing them to address period poverty while still following government-mandated social distancing guidelines. Lastly, the authors found that the pandemic exacerbated supply chain issues and that period poverty impacted people's health, safety, and mobility during the pandemic. The authors argue that it is important for organizations to reflect on the challenges they encountered during the pandemic because understanding those issues will allow them to better address period poverty in the future.

Overall, this edited collection brings together a diverse array of scholarly work that highlights various legal and policy-related topics, including litigations, zoombombing, international students' experiences, violence against women, sex workers' health, governmental crisis responses, neo-vagrancy laws, period povery, and educational issues. This research sheds light on how vulnerable communities have been disproportionately impacted by governments' policies and laws since the onset of the COVID-19 pandemic. In many cases, these effects were exacerbated and compounded by pre-existing legal, societal, and political systems that disadvantage marginalized populations.

The WHO declared an end to the COVID-19 pandemic (WHO, 2023), but the effects of the pandemic still linger. As we reflect on this critical period and look ahead, it is crucial to understand how pandemic-related law and policy issues have impacted society and how they may contribute to future problems. Many issues examined in this edited collection already existed pre-COVID, and they are likely to continue to be an obstacle. Thus, as we look to the future, we must recommit ourselves to leveraging law and policy to protect the most vulnerable members of our society. The practices we implement today must be evidence-informed and provide in-depth solutions rather than a temporary fix. As the COVID-19 pandemic has shown us, legal and policy responses and interventions may end up being a matter of life or death for people in marginalized communities.

Note

1 iMPACTS is a multi-sector, multi-disciplinary partnership project funded by the Social Sciences and Humanities Research Council of Canada (SSHRC) to better understand and address sexual and gender-based violence in universities from the perspectives of law, education, and media. To learn more, visit the website: https://www.mcgill.ca/definetheline/impacts.

REFERENCES

American Civil Liberties Union. (2022, July 1). *Legislation affecting LGBTQ rights across the country.* https://www.aclu.org/legislation-affecting-lgbtq-rights-across-country

Elmer, G., Burton, A. G., & Neville, S. J. (2020, June 9). *Zoom-bombings disrupt online events with racist and misogynist attacks.* The Conversation. https://theconversation.com/zoom-bombings-disrupt-online-events-with-racist-and-misogynist-attacks-138389

Galasso, V. (2020). COVID: Not a great equalizer. *CESifo Economic Studies, 66*(4), 376–393. https://doi.org/10.1093/cesifo/ifaa019

Mein, S. A. (2020). COVID-19 and health disparities: The reality of "the Great Equalizer." *Journal of General Internal Medicine, 35*(8), 2439–2440.

Rocha, R., Shingler, B., & Montpetit, J. (2020, June 11). *Montreal's poorest and most racially diverse neighbourhoods hit hardest by COVID-19, data analysis shows.* https://www.cbc.ca/news/canada/montreal/race-covid-19-montreal-data-census-1.5607123

Shariff, S. (2020). Sexual violence: Impacts on and implications for the intersections of law and education. *Education & Law Journal, 29*(2), iii–viii.

Statistics Canada. (2021, October 18). *Impact of the COVID-19 pandemic on Canadian seniors.* https://www150.statcan.gc.ca/n1/pub/75-006-x/2021001/article/00008-eng.htm

World Health Organization. (2020, June 29). *Listings of WHO's response to COVID-19.* https://www.who.int/news/item/29-06-2020-covidtimeline

World Health Organization. (2021a). *COVID-19 and the social determinants of health and health equity: Evidence brief.* https://www.who.int/publications/i/item/9789240038387

World Health Organization. (2021b, September 17). *Considerations for COVID-19 surveillance for vulnerable populations.* https://www.who.int/publications/i/item/considerations-for-covid-19-surveillance-for-vulnerable-populations

World Health Organization. (2023, May 5). *WHO chief declares end to COVID-19 as a global health emergency.* https://news.un.org/en/story/2023/05/1136367

PART I
Rights and Safety

CHAPTER ONE

Striking a Balance: An Assessment of Anti-SLAPP Litigation in Canada

KIMIA TOWFIGH[1]

Abstract: This piece provides a historical overview of strategic lawsuits against public participation (SLAPPs) in Canada. An examination of the jurisprudential development across the provinces of British Columbia, Ontario and Quebec demonstrates that SLAPPs invoke a nuanced balance between rights of free speech and the protection of one's reputation, and often raise concerns regarding procedural fairness, access to justice, and the democratic process. Furthermore, this piece examines the current landscape of SLAPPs in Canada by drawing on recent Supreme Court of Canada decisions *1704604 Ontario Ltd. v. Pointes Protection Association* and *Bent v. Platnick*, which both invoked an analysis of section 137.1 of the Ontario Courts of Justice Act (colloquially known as Canada's anti-SLAPP legislation). Overall, these landmark decisions provide a nuanced balance between dismissing unfounded and meritless claims, while also permitting legitimate cases to proceed at court. The context of the COVID-19 pandemic has also presented novel developments of the application of Canada's anti-SLAPP legislation. Specifically, the level of public interest regarding the accuracy of public health guidelines has been challenged. Overall, this contested issue demonstrates that striking an appropriate balance between free speech and the protection of reputation is a multifaceted exercise, particularly in the midst of a global pandemic.

Keywords: strategic lawsuits against public participation, SLAPPs, anti-SLAPP laws, freedom of expression, public health misinformation

INTRODUCTION

> Laws are spider webs through which the big flies pass and the little ones get caught.
> —Honoré de Balzac

For decades, access to justice has been a matter of increased concern within the legal community across jurisdictions. Challenges surrounding this issue have amplified since the COVID-19 pandemic began. Access to justice is not only related to fundamental rights of legal representation and access to the courtroom, but it is also intrinsically linked to procedural processes in the legal system. When vexatious litigants disproportionately abuse legal processes by instituting frivolous and unfounded claims in court, the overall integrity of the justice system is jeopardized.

This piece will frame strategic lawsuits against public participation (SLAPPs)—which are often intended to intimidate, censor and silence defendants—as an overall threat to procedural fairness, freedom of speech, and the democratic process. To carefully balance rights of free speech and the right to sue to protect one's reputation, courts must distinguish between frivolous lawsuits and legitimate defamation claims. While freedom of expression is a cornerstone of democracy and a protected *Canadian Charter of Rights and Freedoms* ("*Charter*") value, it is not absolute—thus, some circumstances may justify its inhibition. Paradoxically, unfettered free speech that unduly causes harm to minority groups may undermine the very values and principles that the *Charter* endeavors to protect.

This chapter draws on the Supreme Court of Canada decisions *1704604 Ontario Ltd. v. Pointes Protection Association* (*Pointes*, 2022) and *Bent v. Platnick* (*Bent v. Platnick*, 2022), in which the Court interpreted and applied Ontario's anti-SLAPP legislation. Though each case had a different outcome, the Supreme Court's guidance provides a nuanced balance between dismissing unfounded and meritless claims, while also permitting legitimate cases to proceed at court. Lastly, this chapter frames the topic of SLAPPs within the context of the COVID-19 pandemic and draws on contemporary examples, such as the advent of public health misinformation campaigns. Overall, this chapter aims to provide the reader with an overview of anti-SLAPP legislation and examine the implications of SLAPPs in the context of the COVID-19 pandemic.

PROCEDURAL FAIRNESS AND ACCESS TO JUSTICE IN CANADA

In Canadian jurisprudence, various policy initiatives and legislative reforms have gained widespread influence to address growing access to justice challenges for stakeholders in the legal community (Farrow, 2014). Noting the increasing costs, delays, and complexities inherent within Canadian courts, former Supreme Court Chief Justice Beverley McLachlin stated, "we do not have access to justice in Canada" (2012, p. ix). Indeed, the number of self-represented litigants (SRLs) across the country has increased exponentially, with 37 % of parties representing themselves in court in family law matters, compared to 14.2 % of litigants who were self-represented in similar matters in 1999 (Macfarlane, 2013, p. 35). Since the COVID-19 pandemic has drastically shifted conventional ways of social interaction and exacerbated socioeconomic inequalities, access to justice is sought out now more than ever which, in turn, brings additional attention to the need for access to justice reform (Chiodo, 2021).

While access to justice is conventionally recognized as the right to appear in court and the financial ability to afford adequate legal services, procedural rules are intrinsically linked to access to justice. As an integral function of the court system, procedural rules reflect and impact both legal culture and basic values of society; indeed, civil procedure has been described as "a mirror held up against the legal system itself" (Bramberg et al., 2013, pp. 67–68).

An essential tenet of procedural fairness and access to justice stems from the proportionality principle to ensure the affordable, timely, and just adjudication of claims (*Hryniak v. Mauldin*, 2014). As such, abusive claims brought forward by vexatious litigants may not only cause undue prejudice and financial distress to parties, but also jeopardize the administration of justice. Nonetheless, this concern must also be balanced to accommodate individuals with legitimate claims to access the legal system and seek redress from harms.

STRATEGIC LAWSUITS AGAINST PUBLIC PARTICIPATION IN CANADA

Often presented in the form of defamation claims, SLAPPs are legal proceedings designed to silence and censure the public participation of an individual or organization. Often, plaintiffs do not intend for their claims to succeed on the merits, but rather aim to intimidate defendants, exhaust limited resources, and gain economic advantage (Donson, 2000). As such, SLAPPs are often recognized as a form of frivolous and abusive procedural behavior for disproportionately curtailing freedom of expression and unduly limiting participation in debates on matters of public interest (Salama & White, 2017). Indeed, the potential impacts of SLAPPs on civic society are concerning. Legal proceedings of such a nature risk creating a chilling effect on the exercise of public discourse, thereby deterring civic participation while also undermining the fabric of democratic society (Biché, 2013).

On the other hand, defamation lawsuits are a mechanism to redress harms to one's reputation and temper free speech based on unsubstantiated claims that may cause undue reputational harm to an individual. As the Supreme Court of Canada recognizes, "the right to free expression does not confer a licence to ruin reputations" (*Grant v. Torstar Corp*, 2009, p. 688.). Indeed, the Court has likened one's reputation as a "plant of tender growth [whose] blossom, once lost, is not easily restored" (*Botiuk v. Toronto Free Press Publication Ltd.*, 1995, p. 92). The countervailing considerations of free speech and the protection of reputation are thus at the crux of anti-SLAPP legislation, and courts are faced with the challenging task of striking a balance between individual rights to protect their reputation against false claims with critics' right to free speech.

Due to the increased proliferation of SLAPPs, some provincial legislatures have enacted legislation to mitigate the detrimental impacts of these lawsuits and other abusive litigation tactics. The following section will provide a comparative overview of anti-SLAPP mechanisms in British Columbia, Quebec, and Ontario.

British Columbia

Following *Fraser v. Saanich*, one of the first Canadian cases to recognize the existence of SLAPPs in Canada, British Columbia became the first province to pass anti-SLAPP legislation, though it was repealed five months later (Wilkins et al., 2010, p. 10). Due to the necessity to demonstrate malicious intent, the initial legislation was problematized for its narrow application and high threshold (Scott & Tollefson, 2010, p. 54). Moreover, critics noted that the nature of the legislation could impede a plaintiff's right to access the justice system or be misused by defendants (Scott & Tollefson, 2010, p. 51).

In 2018, the *Protection of Public Participation Act* (PPPA) was proposed by the British Columbia legislature with the intention of preventing SLAPPs from being used to censor public opinion, intimidate people, and silence critics (Ministry of Attorney General, 2018). Compared to the previous legislation, it is broader in scope, as the defendant is not required to demonstrate that the plaintiff had an improper purpose in commencing the proceeding (Pointes Protection Association [PPA] s 4). This legislation provides a screening mechanism for cases that may limit public debate on a significant issue by allowing a defendant to apply to dismiss a lawsuit if it unreasonably impinges their ability to speak freely on a matter of public interest. However, critics contend that the broad nature of anti-SLAPP legislation may have the residual effect of deterring individual plaintiffs from bringing forward defamation claims made in good faith due to the anticipation of anti-SLAPP measures (Randazza, 2012). Despite these concerns, the legislation provides a nuanced framework to assess several factors, including the substantial merit of the case and the anticipation of the applicant's defense in the proceeding. As such, prospective plaintiffs with legitimate defamation claims should not be unduly deterred from accessing the justice system.

Quebec

In Quebec, judicial responses to anti-SLAPP legislation were addressed with the amendment of the *Quebec Code of Civil Procedure* (2014). While other provinces have passed specific anti-SLAPP legislation, article 51 of the *Quebec Code of Civil Procedure* is broader in nature, as it not only applies to SLAPPs, but also encompasses a wide range of other abusive procedures, thereby enabling plaintiffs to sanction pleadings that are "unfounded, frivolous, or intended to cause delays" or conduct that is "vexatious or quarrelsome"—particularly if it operates to restrict another person's freedom of expression in Canada (*Quebec Code of Civil Procedure*, 2014, article 51). This section can be invoked by the court itself, and it has been applied in a variety of different scenarios (*Klepper v. Lulham*, 2017; *Savoie v. Thériault-Martel*, 2013).

Ontario

In 2015, the Ontario Legislature introduced section 137.1 of the Ontario *Courts of Justice Act* as a mechanism to encourage freedom of expression, promote participation in public discourse and curtail proceedings that limit freedom of expression on matters of public interest. In effect, this legislation is not an adjudication of a claim's merits, but rather a screening mechanism that allows defendants of SLAPP suits to dismiss frivolous proceedings. Nonetheless, plaintiffs must not be "unduly deprived of the opportunity to pursue [claims]" (*Pointes*, 2020, p. 21). In 2018, the Ontario Court of Appeal heard six cases before a single panel to provide a cohesive interpretation of the section 137.1 framework.

First, the Court of Appeal clarified that a defendant must prove that the proceeding concerns an expression (including non-verbal and private communications) relating to a matter of public interest ("the threshold burden"). As clarified by Justice Doherty in the Court of Appeal *Pointes* decision, the expression of "public interest" is a broadly defined concept, with a determination to be made "objectively, having regard to the context in which the expression was made and the entirety of the relevant communication" (*Pointes*, 2020, p. 24). Moreover, the subject matter must be one "inviting public interest" or that a segment of the public has "substantial concern for the welfare of citizens" (*Pointes*, 2020, p. 24). Despite the large and liberal interpretation of "public interest," it is significant to note that there is no qualitative assessment of the expression at the stage of a section 137.1 claim, as a section 137.1 motion is not a determinative adjudication of the merits of the proceeding.

If the defendant satisfactorily meets the threshold burden, the onus then shifts to the plaintiff who must demonstrate that (a) the proceeding has substantial merit; (b) the defendant has no valid defense in the proceeding (the "merits-based hurdle"); and (c) the public interest in permitting the proceeding to continue outweighs the public interest in protecting the defendant's harmful expression (the "public interest hurdle").

Overall, section 137.1 seeks to weed out frivolous claims, while also allowing plaintiffs to bring forward proceedings that are merit-based and in the public interest. Nearly two years later, this legislation was interpreted for the first time by the Supreme Court of Canada in *Bent* and *Pointes* to rearticulate the test provided by the Ontario Court of Appeal and provide further clarity regarding the purpose and interpretation of section 137.1.

1704604 ONTARIO LTD V. POINTES PROTECTION ASSOCIATION

In the case at hand, a land development company ("170 Ontario") wished to develop a subdivision in Sault Ste Marie. To do so, approval from the city's Region Conservation Authority and City Council was required. The development was opposed on environmental grounds by the PPA, a non-profit corporation created on behalf of affected residents in the neighborhood.

While 170 Ontario obtained the Conservation Authority's approval, the PPA contested by filing an application for judicial review of the Conservation Authority's decision. 170 Ontario's application to the City Council was later rejected and it appealed to the Ontario Municipal Board (OMB), which granted Pointes standing to participation. The parties later settled the judicial review by signing a settlement agreement, which explicitly imposed limitations on Pointe's future conduct. As per the agreement, the PPA could not institute further court proceedings regarding the Conservation Authority's decision or condemn 170 Ontario's behavior as contrary to the provisions of the *Conservation Authorities Act*.

At the OMB hearing, the president of the PPA testified that 170 Ontario's proposed development would cause environmental damage to the wetland region. The OMB dismissed 170 Ontario's appeal and upheld the City Council's refusal of its development plan. Consequently, 170 Ontario instituted a breach of contract action against Pointes for $6 million because the defendants sought the same relief as their judicial review application and implicitly gave evidence regarding the wetland issue. In response, Pointes brought a motion under section 137.1 of the *Courts of Justice Act* (1990) to have the action dismissed.

Judicial History

At the Ontario Superior Court, the motion judge dismissed PPA's section 137.1 motion and allowed 170 Ontario's action to proceed. While the PPA's threshold burden was met, the judge concluded that 170 Ontario met the merit-based and public interest hurdles. The Court of Appeal allowed the PPA's appeal, granted its section 137.1 motion and dismissed 170 Ontario's lawsuit. With regard to substantial merit, the Court found that the motion judge erred by not considering principles of contractual interpretation and that 170 Ontario could not meet its burden on any of the section 137.1(4) prongs.

Legal Reasoning

The Supreme Court in *Pointes* unanimously agreed with the Court of Appeal that the section 137.1 motion should be granted, and that the plaintiff's underlying action should be dismissed as a SLAPP. Before analyzing the facts of the case at hand, Justice Côté provided a thorough and extensive analysis of each section of the 137.1 framework. She emphasized that additional factors that may prove useful in the public interest assessment include the importance of the expression, the history of litigation between the parties, broader or collateral effects on other expressions on matters of public interest, the potential chilling effect on future expression by a party or by others, any disproportion between the resources being used in the lawsuit, and the possibility that the claim might provoke hostility against an identifiable group or group protected under section 15 of the *Charter*. This clarification ultimately provides a nuanced framework for the judiciary to contextualize future 137.1 claims and assess matters of public interest.

Moreover, Justice Côté provided further clarity about the standard of review for the merits-based hurdle. When assessing the merits-based hurdle at section 137.1(4)(a), the burden of proof is a "grounds to believe" standard. As such, when examining whether the underlying proceeding has substantial merit and that there is no valid defense, the standard is "something more than mere suspicion, but less than proof on the balance of probabilities" (*Mugesera v. Canada*, 2005, p. 145). In effect, this relaxed standard of proof reminds litigants that the likelihood of an outcome is to be adjudicated during a preliminary assessment, and not the overall outcome itself.

Importantly, Justice Côté also clarified that the Court of Appeal erred by favoring a theoretical assessment by the "reasonable trier" under section 137.1(4)(a), which should instead be made from the motion judge's perspective to support the finding that a plaintiff's claim has substantial merit, and that the defendant has no valid defense to the claim. Indeed, deference to a trial judge's findings is an essential tenet of the Canadian court system. While trial judges are tasked with resolving disputes based on facts, appellate judges must delineate legal rules to ensure their universal application (*Housen v. Nikolaisen*, 2002). Findings of fact cannot be reversed unless a trial judge made a "palpable and overriding" error. The purpose of this distinction is to limit the length of appeals, while also promoting both the autonomy and integrity of trial proceedings.

In applying the section 137.1 framework to the case, Justice Côté concluded that the PPA easily meets the threshold burden, as the testimony constitutes an expression made publicly that relates to a matter of public interest; namely, the environmental impact of a proposed private development which impacted a significant number of residents in the region.

When turning to the merits-based hurdle, in which 170 Ontario must prove that its action has substantial merit and that the PPA has no valid defense, Justice Côté concluded that 170 Ontario fails the former criteria. By drawing on rules of contractual interpretation, she emphasizes that the plain language of the agreement did not prohibit Pointes from advancing an argument that does not pertain to the Conservation Authority's decision. As such, the submission that Pointes breached an implied term of the agreement extends the reasonable parameters of contractual interpretation and thus did not result in a breach of contract. Ultimately, as Justice Côté did not find substantial merit to 170 Ontario's action, it consequently failed to satisfy section 137.1(4)(a) and is thereby categorized as a SLAPP.

In her judgment, Justice Côté demonstrates that environmental degradation in association with large-scale developments are significant matters of public interest, with recognition that the express purpose of section 137.1 is to encourage and promote public participation in debates on such matters that invite public attention. Indeed, encouraging truthful and open testimony is fundamental to public participation in public forums without the fear of retribution or vindication from powerful corporations.

Analysis and Implications

This decision is significant in many respects. First, it constitutes an unequivocal statement by the Supreme Court that frivolous claims lacking legal merit will not proceed within the court system. For activists, civil society groups and non-governmental organizations who are often advocates at the forefront of public debate, the judgment reflects the importance of public participation in the democratic process and condemns baseless lawsuits that are aimed to silence dissenters and stifle free speech. Indeed, this case attracted several interveners, including Greenpeace and CBC, who have both been subjects of SLAPPs due to their advocacy and activism in matters of public interest.

During the COVID-19 pandemic, many mass demonstrations mobilized across jurisdictions, even though physical distancing measures radically challenged the public's ability to practice civic engagement. Throughout rapidly evolving state-imposed lockdowns, several movements embraced digital technologies as a primary means of taking action, allowing large numbers of people to efficiently mobilize in large groups without risking the spread of infection (Courage, 2020). One example includes the worldwide mobilization for racial justice and against police brutality following the murder of George Floyd in Minneapolis, United States in 2020 (Ferrari, 2022). Despite this, censorship concerns have also increased among activists as they reckoned with the increase in use of online platforms during government-mandated lockdowns. For example, the use of online platforms allows for data collection and traceability, which can be leveraged against activists who critique large corporations or powerful individuals (Koeze & Popper, 2020).

Moreover, communication tools such as Zoom and Slack that are often used to engage large groups have been condemned for weak privacy policies and poor encryption practices (Oliver, 2020). With a rapidly expanding consumer base during lockdown measures, Zoom users reported a surge of meeting disruptions and hijacks from uninvited individuals who often shared explicit content and racial slurs at the expense of participants, a phenomenon later coined as "zoombombing" (see Chapter Four). In particular, activist groups are frequent targets of xenophobic attacks and racial harassment, and these occurrences have only intensified within the digital realm (Bresge, 2020). Although Zoom quickly strengthened its default security measures in April 2020 after alarm from the public, inherent vulnerabilities of digital platforms nonetheless remain. Studies also suggest that zoombombing across the United States intensified during the pandemic lockdown (see Chapter Four). Overall, issues of harassment and surveillance threaten the security of activists who participate in online mobilization efforts, particularly those from marginalized communities.

Moreover, as the COVID-19 pandemic has increased delays within the Canadian justice system while courthouses temporarily ceased operations across the country, censorship practices are not only limited to the legal realm. These efforts also transcend to online spaces, where mobilization efforts may be sabotaged to impede meaningful discourse and dissenting opinions. And since the COVID-19 pandemic has amplified judicial delays, proponents of SLAPP lawsuits may strategically institute baseless claims to deliberately drag out proceedings and increase litigation costs for defendants.

Beyond SLAPP plaintiffs, other actors including government officials have also utilized the conditions of COVID-19 as a means to silence dissenters and quash protests (Henderson, 2020). Emergency powers meant to curb the spread of the virus may impede fundamental freedoms and civic spaces (see Chapter Two). Moreover, many human rights activists express concern that governments may use the crisis as a pretext to infringe on people's fundamental rights and freedoms. As UN Special Rapporteur Fionnuala Ní Aoláin explains, "states and security sector institutions will find emergency powers attractive because they offer shortcuts" and that such powers tend to "persist and become permanent" (ICNL, 2020). For instance, many countries have instituted tracking tools and surveillance apparatus to monitor the spread of the virus, and these measures may be disproportionately used against dissidents (Henderson, 2020). Moreover, many governments censored government critics by curtailing freedom of assembly and banning all mass gatherings in the midst of the ongoing public health emergency (Henderson, 2020). Overall, several government-imposed safety measures adopted and enacted during the COVID-19 pandemic curtailed fundamental rights and freedoms, which may have lasting effects long after the current public health crisis.

Additionally, the *Pointes* judgment demonstrates that anti-SLAPP legislation in Canada is not necessarily limited to defamation claims, but may also encompass breach of contract proceedings, as was the case in *Pointes*. As such, this broadened conceptualization may allow litigants to bring forward anti-SLAPP motions in a variety of different contexts deemed in the public interest, including sexual assault claimants who may be under a confidentiality provision or non-disclosure agreement within an employment context.

From a broader perspective, the implications of this case are also of great significance. When less powerful members of society face financial barriers, this judgment encourages the use of the court system in good faith and condemns abusive litigation tactics that risk exacerbating access to justice in Canada. These concerns are heightened in the context of the COVID-19 pandemic, as marginalized groups are disproportionately impacted by lockdown measures, risking an even wider disparity of resources between litigants (McLachlin, 2012). However, in applying the *Pointes* decision to *Bent v. Platnick*, the Court asserts that plaintiffs with a legitimate and well-founded defamation claim should not be unduly deprived of the opportunity to pursue their claim in court and protect their reputation.

BENT V. PLATNICK

The case of *Bent v. Platnick* involved a lawyer, Ms. Bent, who was also a partner at an Ontario law firm and president-elect of the Ontario Trial Lawyers Association (OTLA). Following two insurance coverage disputes involving a medical doctor, Dr. Platnick, who was independently hired to review a personal injury claim, Ms.

Bent sent an email to a Listserv of approximately 670 OTLA members alleging that Dr. Platnick had altered multiple doctors' reports. Despite the confidentiality of the Listserv emails, Ms. Bent's email was anonymously leaked by a member of the OTLA and was later reproduced and published in a magazine. Consequently, Dr. Platnick commenced a defamation lawsuit against Ms. Bent and her law firm, claiming damages of $16.3 million.

Judicial History

In response to Dr. Platnick's defamation lawsuit, Ms. Bent filed a motion under section 137.1 of the *Courts of Justice Acts* (*CJA*) to dismiss the proceeding. The motion judge dismissed the defamation proceeding as a SLAPP, since Dr. Platnick failed to discharge his burden under the public interest hurdle at section 137.1(4). At appeal, the Ontario Court of Appeal dismissed B's motion and remitted P's defamation suit for consideration, as the judges believed that the motion judge erred in his analysis of the public interest hurdle in section 137.1(4). Overall, the Court of Appeal judges unanimously agreed that the harm against Dr. Platnick outweighed the public interest in protecting Ms. Bent's defamatory expression.

Legal Reasoning

With a narrow 5–4 majority, the Supreme Court agreed with the Court of Appeal's judgment and dismissed Ms. Bent's section 137.1 claim, allowing Dr. Platnick's defamation lawsuit to proceed. In her analysis, Justice Côté writing on behalf of the majority of the Court accepts that Ms. Bent met the threshold burden under section 137.1(3). Although the email was not verbal in nature, it nonetheless arose from expressed communication and thus falls under the statutory definition of "expression" as per section 137.1(2). Moreover, the nature of the expression itself sufficiently meets the "broad and liberal" interpretation of the public interest threshold for a variety of reasons. First, Ms. Bent's email was directed at a large number of individuals with an interest in the OTLA. Secondly, the expression itself raised concerns about truthfulness, reliability and the integrity of medical reports filed of insurers in the arbitration process, which relates to the administration of justice and the public confidence in the rule of law that flows therefrom.

Next, the burden shifted to Dr. Platnick to demonstrate that the defamation proceeding has substantial merit and that Ms. Bent has no valid defense to it under section 137.1(4)(1) (the "merit-based hurdle"). The Court found that Dr. Platnick's defamation proceeding met the "substantial merit" criteria: The impugned words were defamatory in the eyes of a reasonable person and published with direct reference to the plaintiff. Indeed, allegations of professional misconduct would lower a doctor's reputation in the eyes of a reasonable person. Evidence also demonstrated that the plaintiff suffered substantial financial losses and incurred mass cancellations from clients shortly following the publication of allegations.

To assess the second prong of the merit-based hurdle, the Court considered Ms. Bent's defenses of justification and qualified privilege and concludes that neither of the defenses are valid. The former defense requires a defendant to demonstrate that the statement as a whole was substantively true. The Court found that Ms. Bent's allegations of dishonesty and professional misconduct was not supported by evidence. Next, the defense of qualified privilege requires a party to establish that they have an interest or duty to publish the information at issue and that the recipient has a corresponding duty to receive it. As president of the OCLA, Ms. Bent argued that she was educating her colleagues practicing as personal injury lawyers about the integrity of the arbitration process. However, the Court rejected this defense, as the specific references made were not necessary to the discharge of the duty giving rise to the privilege, and also constituted a gratuitous and inaccurate attack on Dr. Platnick's character.

Finally, the Court assessed the public interest hurdle at section 137.1(4)(b) which is at the core of the section 137.1 analysis. It concluded that Dr. Platnick's harm suffered arose as a result of Ms. Bent's expression and was sufficiently serious that the public interest in permitting the proceeding to continue outweighed the public interest in protecting B's expression.

By employing a contextual analysis, the Court noted that the extensive reputational and financial harms suffered by Dr. Platnick from the personal attack against him was sufficiently linked to Ms. Bent's expression. Consequently, the public interest in permitting the defamation proceeding to continue outweighs the public interest in protecting Ms. Bent's expression. Indeed, within days following the Listserv publication, Dr. Platnick suffered a direct financial impact and incurred mass cancellations from insurance companies using his services, as well as psychological and emotional harm. Though Ms. Bent did not republish the Listserv, the Court claims that she can nonetheless be held liable for republication, as the republication of alleged fraud was at least reasonably foreseeable, given the gravity of the allegation.

The dissenting judgment penned by Justice Abella concludes that the defamation suit should be dismissed under section 137.1 of the *CJA*. While the matter of public interest as per section 137.1(3) was not disputed, the minority of the Court assesses that Ms. Bent had a valid defense of qualified privilege and concludes that Ms. Bent is entitled to the dismissal of the defamation action as per section 137.1(3).

Justice Abella noted that as president-elect of the OTLA, Ms. Bent had the duty to inform OTLA members about misleading expert reports and protect clients' interests against unfair practices by experts. Overall, as a practicing lawyer, Ms. Bent also had the professional duty to uphold the administration of justice, and her colleagues had a corresponding duty to receive the communication to protect the interest of their clients. Ms. Bent also had the reasonable expectation that the Listserv members would keep the information strictly confidential, as the Listserv members were bound to a confidentiality clause as well as their professional duties in the *Rules of Professional Conduct*. While the defense of qualified privilege can be defeated if the motive for publishing is "actual or expressed malice," Justice Abella found no basis to conclude that Ms. Bent acted with carelessness or reckless disregard in publishing her email.

Finally, in her analysis of the public interest hurdle (which requires making a causal connection between the defendant's expression and the alleged corresponding harm), Justice Abella noted that the harm alleged by Dr. Platnick occurred because of the *leak* of the email, not the initial email itself. Moreover, due to the undertaking of confidentiality from each Listserv member, the reproduction of the email and the harm that arose therefrom was not reasonably foreseeable by Ms. Bent.

Overall, the dissenting judgment that divides the court reflects the complexity of anti-SLAPP legislation and the administration of justice, as well as the professional obligations that manifest from a lawyer's occupation. Whether or not Ms. Bent had the reasonable expectation that her colleagues would keep information distributed in the Listserv confidential, the majority of the Court affirms that Dr. Platnick is deserving of the opportunity to potentially vindicate his reputation in court, allowing the defamation claim to proceed.

Implications

While the Court in *Pointes* unanimously allowed the section 137.1 claim to proceed and condemned abusive litigation tactics that aim to stifle public participation, the divided judgment in *Bent v. Platnick* highlights the complexity of anti-SLAPP litigation and demonstrates that the section 137.1 test may continue to raise issues in the courts. Ultimately, the majority of the court affirms that legal proceedings may be a legitimate means of restoring harm when the effects of unfounded defamatory speech cause significant financial and emotional distress to an individual.

The implications of the *Bent* case and the continuation of Dr. Platnick's defamation proceedings in contrast to the *Pointes* case are significant. First, the judgment stresses the importance of acting with due diligence when attacking an individual's professional integrity. In this context, even the perceived expectation of confidentiality and privacy of communication is not an adequate defense. As such, we are reminded that freedom of expression is not absolute—indeed, defamatory attacks lacking substantiation are hardly matters of public interest and paradoxically antithetical to the values that ground section 2(b) of the *Charter*, including the search for truth, democratic discourse, and self-fulfillment.

Moreover, this case importantly highlights that despite the widespread shift of public discourse to the online platform, published claims must be accurately substantiated, regardless of expectations of confidentiality. When false information on online sources and social media platforms is propagated, the truth-seeking process is increasingly at threat. As such, this case encourages responsible journalism and communication, as well as the accurate substantiation of facts, particularly when attacking the integrity of identifiable individuals. Moreover, in an era of proliferated internet usage, misinformation is increasingly likely to be rapidly disseminated—a phenomenon often dubbed as an "infodemic" (Lewis, 2020). Due to social media algorithms that sort and customize content based on individual user preferences (Kitchens et al., 2020), networks of conspiracy theories grounded in government distrust have recently propagated, including claims that dispute the severity of the virus and the effectiveness of mask-wearing, as well as allegations that the coronavirus was deliberately engineered by the Chinese government (Lourenco, 2020). Such beliefs ultimately impede public efforts to control the spread of the virus, as health officials have prescribed mask-wearing, physical distancing, and handwashing as effective prevention measures.

The proliferation of misinformation during a public health crisis presents novel implications and distinct legal issues in the realm of SLAPP litigation, including the balance of free speech with consequential effects of the deliberate spread of misleading information, including endangerment of public health. For example, in the case of *Gill v Maciver*, three plaintiff doctors actively critiqued public health advice regarding the prevention of the spread of COVID-19 on Twitter by questioning the risks of COVID-19 and the efficacy of vaccines, while also purporting hydroxychloroquine as an effective treatment for infection caused by the virus (*Gill v. Maciver*, 2022). The plaintiffs sought $12 million in damages for reputational damage against a group of over 20 defendant physicians that publicly condemned the plaintiff physicians for spreading information that could potentially misinform or mislead the public (*Gill v. Maciver*, 2022). Specifically, the defendant physicians denounced the stance of the plaintiff physicians in response to the COVID-19 pandemic on Twitter, warned against the dangers of misinformation regarding risks of COVID-19 transmission and urged individuals to follow public health measures based on factual evidence in response to the pandemic.

In applying the *Bent* and *170 Ontario* decisions to this case, the Ontario Superior Court of Justice ("the Superior Court") ruled that the expressions complained of by the plaintiffs directly related to a matter of public interest, namely, promoting discourse about matters of public health. Moreover, the Superior

Court emphasized that public health information in the context of an unprecedent global pandemic greatly outweighs unsubstantiated claims of conspiracy, while also noting the defendant physicians' good faith efforts to protect the public from misinformation in the context of a global pandemic.

Moreover, the Superior Court also considered the defenses of qualified privilege and fair comment with respect to tweets that the plaintiffs alleged to be defamatory and held that such defenses have a real prospect of success in the circumstances. Specifically, as physicians, the defendants had a moral and professional duty to educate the public regarding the accuracy of medical knowledge and to facilitate disease prevention. Moreover, the alleged defamatory statements were: (i) of public interest; (ii) based in fact; (iii) recognizable as opinion; (iv) could honestly be made by any person; and (v) lacked malice. As such, the plaintiffs could not meet the burden to demonstrate that there were grounds to believe that the expressions were defamatory. Finally, the Superior Court also noted a lack of a causal link of harm arising from the impugned expression and the plaintiff's reputations, asserting that the plaintiffs themselves were the most obvious causes of damage to their own reputations.

Overall, the *Gill v. Maciver* case demonstrates that the accuracy of public health information is paramount to actively prevent the spread of infectious disease and support the welfare of citizens, thereby meeting the public interest threshold in section 137.1 of the *CJA*. Moreover, this case illustrates that the search for truth, a core value underlying freedom of expression, is afforded high weight in the section 137.1(4)(b) weighing exercise. Indeed, the Superior Court notes that "a public health emergency in which informed, knowledgeable experts are stifled from commenting publicly to combat misinformation is a significant threat to the general public interest" (*Gill v. Maciver*, 2022, para. 218).

Alternatively, another SLAPP case that emerged in the context of the COVID-19 pandemic failed to meet the threshold burden in section 137.1. In the case at hand, the defendant left a negative online review of the plaintiff's company, claiming that the plaintiff missed all agreed-upon shipment dates for the delivery of medical masks (*Dent-X Canada v. Houde*, 2022). The plaintiff company subsequently launched a defamation suit against the consumer. In applying the section 137.1 framework of the *CJA*, the Court of Appeal for Ontario held that although the quality of masks may be an issue closely connected to the public interest during a global pandemic, the statement overall entailed a private dispute between businesses and thus did not sufficiently relate to a matter of public interest. This case is distinct from *Gill v. Maciver*, which directly entailed expressions regarding matters of public health during the COVID-19 pandemic.

In its recent decisions regarding anti-SLAPP legislation, the Supreme Court clarifies the application of anti-SLAPP legislation in Canada, providing further guidance on a complex area of the law. Yet, the strongly divided judgment in

Bent leaves room for judicial discretion and may provide uncertainty for future litigants. The provincial courts in *Gill v. Maciver* and *Dent-X Canada v. Houde* subsequently apply the Supreme Court's guidance to public health information, which is an issue of increasing relevance during the COVID-19 pandemic. Overall, these decisions suggest that there is heightened public interest in protecting expressions relating to public health information during a global pandemic.

Overall, this contested issue demonstrates that striking an appropriate balance between free speech and the protection of reputation is a multifaceted and nuanced exercise, especially when matters of public health are concerned.

CONCLUSION

SLAPPs, often designed to silence individuals and stifle dissenting speech, have been increasingly condemned for wasting court resources, jeopardizing access to justice and threatening the democratic system as a whole. Moreover, these concerns are even more significant in the midst of a global pandemic, as marginalized groups are disproportionately impacted by lockdown measures and state-imposed restrictions (McLachlin, 2012), while the capacity to influence public perception regarding public health measures is heightened. To mitigate conflicting rights of free speech and the right to sue to protect one's reputation, courts must distinguish between abusive lawsuits and legitimate defamation claims. In *Pointes*, the Supreme Court of Canada unequivocally affirms that the section 137.1 framework is not only limited in application to defamation lawsuits, but also to matters of contractual breach, thereby widening the scope of the legislation.

However, this unanimous judgment is tempered in *Bent*, as the Court asserts that free speech is not absolute and that certain circumstances warrant its limitation. Indeed, unfettered expression that unduly harms an individual's dignity is paradoxically antithetical to the very values that the *Charter* seeks to protect. In the context of the pandemic, the public interest of accurate health guidelines also present novel implications in interpreting anti-SLAPP legislation. Thus far, the application of the Supreme Court of Canada's decisions in lower provincial courts suggest a strong public interest regarding the accuracy of public health information, particularly in the midst of a global pandemic. Nonetheless, the strongly divided judgment in the Supreme Court of Canada's *Bent* decision leaves room for judicial discretion and demonstrates that the interpretation of anti-SLAPP legislation is a complex and nuanced exercise, reflecting a contested debate about the appropriate balance between free speech and the protection of reputation.

NOTE

1 Associate Attorney, EY Law LLP.

REFERENCES

1704604 Ontario Ltd v. Pointes Protection Association 2020 SCC 22 (Can.).
1704604 Ontario Ltd v. Pointes Protection Association 2018 ONCA 685 (Can.).
Bent v. Platnick 2020 SCC 23 (Can.).
Beverly Mclachlin. (2020). "As courts reopen, let's focus on creating equitable access to justice for all" The Globe and Mail, https://www.theglobeandmail.com/opinion/article-as-courts-reopen-lets-focus-on-creating-equitable-access-to-justice/
Biché, T. D. (2013). Thawing public participation: Modeling the chilling effect of strategic lawsuits against public participation and minimizing its impact. *Southern California Interdisciplinary Law Journal, 22*(42), 420.
Botiuk v. Toronto Free Press Publications Ltd., [1995] 3 S.C.R. 3 (Can.).
Bramberg, D., Farrow, T. C., Karayanni, M., & Knutsen, E. S. (2013). Learning the "how" of law: Teaching procedure and legal education. *Osgoode Hall Law Journal, 51*(1), 67–68.
Bresge, A. (2020). *Activists targeted in "Zoom-bombing" attacks call on big tech to boost security.* The Canadian Press. https://www.blueline.ca/activists-targeted-in-zoom-bombing-attacks-call-on-big-tech-to-boost-security/
Chiodo, S. E. (2021). Ontario civil justice reform in the wake of COVID-19: Inspired or institutionalized? *Osgoode Hall Law Journal, 57*(3), 801–833.
Courage, K. (2020). *Activism in the era of COVID-19.* Colorado State University College News.
Courts of Justice Act, RSO 1990, c C 43.
Dent-X Canada v. Houde 2022 ONCA 414 (Can.).
Donson, F. (2000). *Legal intimidation: A SLAPP in the face of democracy.* Free Association Books.
Farrow, T. (2014). What is access to justice? *Osgoode Hall Law Journal, 51*(3), 957.
Ferrari, E. (2022). Latency and crisis: Mutual aid activism in the Covid-19 pandemic. *Qualitative Sociology, 45*, 413–431.
Gill v. Maciver, 2022 ONSC 6169 (Can.).
Grant v. Torstar Corp., 2009 SCC 61, [2009] 3 S.C.R. 640 (Can.).
Housen v. Nikolaisen 2002 SCC 33 (Can.).
Kitchens, B., Johnson, S., & Gray, P. (2020). Understanding echo chambers and filter bubbles: The impact of social media on diversification and partisan shifts in news consumption. *MIS Quarterly, 44*(4), 1619–1649.
Klepper v. Lulham, 2017 Q.C.C.A. 2069 (Can.).
Koeze, E., & Popper, N. (2020). The virus changed the way we internet. *New York Times.* https://www.nytimes.com/interactive/2020/04/07/technology/coronavirus-internet-use.html
Henderson, A. (2020). *Silencing dissent—It's easier in a COVID world.* International Corporate Accountability Roundtable.
Housen v. Nikolaisen 2002 SCC 33 (Can.).
Hryniak v. Mauldin, 2014 SCC 7, [2014] 1 S.C.R. 87 (Can.).

ICNL. (2020). *Coronavirus & civic space*. International Center for Not-for-Profit Law. https://www.icnl.org/coronavirus-response

Lewis, T. (2020). Nine COVID-10 myths that just won't go away. *Scientific American*. https://www.scientificamerican.com/article/nine-covid-19-myths-that-just-wont-go-away/

Lourenco, D. (2020). *Researchers say belief in conspiracy theories poses barrier to controlling the spread of COVID-19*. CTV News. https://www.ctvnews.ca/health/coronavirus/researchers-say-belief-in-conspiracy-theories-poses-barrier-to-controlling-the-spread-of-covid-19-1.5114446

Macfarlane, J. (2013). *The national self-represented litigants project: Identifying and meeting the needs of self-represented litigants*. Treasurer's Advisory Group on Access to Justice (TAG) Working Group Report.

McLachlin, B. (2012). Forward. In M. Trebilcock, A. Duggan & L. Sossin. (Eds.), *Middle income access to justice*. University of Toronto Press.

Ministry of Attorney General. (2018, May 15). *News release: New law to safeguard freedom of expression*. Government of Canada. https://archive.news.gov.bc.ca/releases/news_releases_2017-2021/2018AG0032-000918.htm

Oliver, L. (2020, March 19). *What you should know about online tools during the COVID-19 crisis*. Electronic Frontier Foundation. https://www.eff.org/deeplinks/2020/03/what-you-should-know-about-online-tools-during-covid-19-crisis

Protection of Public Participation Act [SBC 2019] Chapter 3, assented to March 25, 2019.

Quebec Code of Civil Procedure [2014] Chapter C-25.01.

Randazza, M. (2012). The need for a unified and cohesive national anti-SLAPP law. *Oregon Law Review, 91*(2), 627.

Salama, O., & White, R. (2017). Dissent, litigation and investigation: Hitting the powerful where it hurts. *Critical Criminology, 25*(1), 523.

Savoie v. Thériault-Martel, 2013 Q.C.C.S. 4280 (Can.).

Scott, M., & Tollefson, C. (2010). Strategic lawsuits against public participation: The British Columbia experience. *RECIEL, 19*(1), 45.

Wilkins, H., Nadarajah, R., & Shapiro, P. (2010). *Breaking the silence: The urgent need for anti-SLAPP legislation in Ontario*. Ecojustice. https://ecojustice.ca/wp-content/uploads/2014/11/Breaking-the-Silence_the-need-for-anti-SLAPP-legislation.pdf

CHAPTER TWO

Are We in This Together? A Foucauldian Analysis of Canada's Response to the COVID-19 Pandemic

IRADELE PLANTE[1]

Abstract: While COVID-19 itself is a novel virus, pandemics are neither unprecedented nor unpredictable. This chapter contextualizes the COVID-19 pandemic with a shared history of how state powers expand during a crisis, and the legal tools that may be used to promote collective health and safety while preserving civil rights. First, the chapter explores the Foucauldian concept of a "plague town" which relies on discipline and punishment to achieve compliance. Next, the chapter investigates Canadian emergency preparedness legislation enacted during the early stages of the COVID-19 pandemic, as well as the mechanisms that allowed for the expansion of governing powers and law enforcement. Lastly, the chapter considers alternative legal principles that distinguish Canadian pandemic preparedness responses from an archetypal plague town that ensures governmental accountability and minimizes the infringement on civil rights.

Keywords: COVID-19 pandemic, emergency preparedness, legislation, Canada, Foucault, plague town

INTRODUCTION

Historically, pandemics have forced humans to break with the past and imagine their world anew. This one is no different. We can choose to walk through it, dragging the carcasses of our prejudice and hatred, our avarice, our data banks and dead ideas. Or we can walk through lightly, with little luggage, ready to imagine another world. And ready to fight for it.

—Arundhati Roy (2020)

Since March 2020, Canadians have been figuring out what it means to be "living in unprecedented times." The emergence of COVID-19 brought waves of panic through the collective psyche and sent governments scrambling to enact emergency responses to address overwhelmed hospitals and monumental job losses, and to minimize the spread of the disease through physical distancing measures. Within a short period of time, the relationship between the state and its people shifted, calling into question the role of the government in pandemic preparedness and the way that emergency measures may justify infringement on civil liberties. For many, living in a pandemic has felt like an entirely new way of "being." Avoiding parks, visiting family through closed windows, wearing masks, and offering hand sanitizer instead of a handshake have now become common social practices in Canada. The way members of society are now instructed to interact with one another *feels* unprecedented.

While COVID-19 itself is a novel virus, a global pandemic like this one is neither unprecedented nor unpredictable. Disease ecologist Peter Daszak estimated that roughly five new diseases emerge each year, with the potential to break out into a widespread pandemic (Vox Media, 2018). Daszak also estimated that researchers are only aware of less than 0.1 % of all viruses present in nature, meaning that emerging pandemics are often viral strains that public health systems are not prepared for (Vox Media, 2018).[2] In the face of such uncertainty, governments are saddled with the nearly impossible task of preparing for a catastrophe without knowing what it may be.

This chapter investigates how state powers have expanded during the COVID-19 pandemic, with an examination of the legal tools employed to promote collective health and safety, while also preserving civil rights. The first part of this chapter, informed by Michel Foucault's archetype of a "plague town" (1996), examines how devastation in the wake of a pandemic can be harnessed as a political tool to expand state powers. Foucauldian philosophy guides this chapter because its analysis on power distribution bears a striking resemblance to the legislative discourse presently unfolding. Through centralized surveillance and a rigid hierarchy of powers, together with decentralized policing, the Foucauldian plague town forges a compliant "model citizen" and punishes deviance in the name of public health. Stated differently, this chapter unpacks the extent to which Foucault's philosophy aligns with Canada's reality.

The second part considers the federal and provincial powers that are triggered when a public health emergency is declared. Specifically, it examines how the scope, intent, and delegation of power align with the Foucauldian plague town. The effectiveness of public health measures in the context of a global pandemic are also discussed. In contrast, the final part of the chapter, safeguards against pandemic responses leading to a reification of inequalities will be examined. Overall, this chapter aims to help legal practitioners and policymakers better understand how power can be delegated during times of emergency, as well as its potential for—and protection against—abuse.

THE FOUCAULDIAN PLAGUE TOWN

Canadian pandemic preparedness is part of a shared history that knows no bounds between borders. An infectious disease can turn from a manageable outbreak to a catastrophe based on a number of factors. The characteristics of a disease, such as the biological virality, mode of transmission, and interaction with the human immune system can have a major influence on its infectiousness. Additionally, the architecture of a city, social inequality, warfare, and global trade have also greatly contributed to the spread of infections (Holmes, 2018). Notably, the emergence of global trade facilitated outbreaks between cities. For instance, rats infected with the bubonic plague were transported onto grain ships arriving to Constantinople from Egypt (Wade, 2010). The Roman Emperor Justinian I pushed trade so aggressively that he was colloquially known as the "leading exporter of the bubonic plague" (Wade, 2010). Similarly, the plague's second wave in the fourteenth century was thought to have originated from a Mongolian attack on the trading posts in the Caffa and Crimean region of Italy, consequently halting the exchange of goods along the Silk Road (Echenberg, 2002). In the early 1900s, the third wave, which remained in Southwest China for several years, eventually spread along steam routes as the global demand for copper increased. The disease was then distributed across 23 countries, including the Californian region in the United States (Bruce, 1898; Randall, 2019).

Prior to scientific empiricism, many medical decisions regarding quarantine were based on religious beliefs or spiritual suspicions. For example, the prevailing theory prior to the eighteenth century was that infectious diseases were caused by miasma (a noxious form of "bad air" or rotting organic matter), which was eventually replaced by the germ theory of disease by the late 1880s (Wisecrack, 2020a). Even the word "quarantine" is a derivative of the Italian word "forty" (i.e., "*la quarantena*"), a number that was often associated with purification in Christian scripture (Wisecrack, 2020). In some cases, these methods were relatively successful for diseases such as the bubonic plague that had a relatively short incubation period.

Foucault's Concept of a Town Under Plague

Public health measures can be developed as a means of controlling urban space. Michel Foucault alleges that many modern power structures were birthed from "plague towns" as European governments realized they could capitalize on moral panic to serve their own means (Foucault, 1996). Citing seventeenth-century French archives, Foucault studied the ways in which a "town under plague" could be used as an exceptional disciplinary model:

> First, a strict spatial partitioning [...] the division of the town into distinct quarters, each governed by an intendant [and surveilled by a syndic]. On the appointed day, everyone is ordered to stay indoors. The syndic [...] comes to lock the door of each house from the outside. [...] Inspection functions ceaselessly. The gaze is alert and everywhere [...] Every day, the syndic stops before each house, and gets the inhabitants [...] to show themselves and declare their status. The registration of the pathological [became permanent] and constantly centralized, where magistrates have complete control over medical treatment. (Foucault, 1996, p. 197)

Foucault contends that the chaos of a plague-stricken town is made orderly by surveillance, hierarchies of power that justify interference with social life, and decentralized policing that each work in a continuous feedback loop to maintain state control (Foucault, 1996). The expansion of the state serves to restrict personal freedoms and prevent the spread of diseases by compromising individualism in favor of a shared collectivity that conforms to a set of health and social standards (Foucault, 2001).

Health surveillance relies on a centralized system of intelligence gathering for standardization purposes. By the eighteenth century, the separation between church and state adapted judicial investigation to an "authoritarian search for the truth observed or attested [overriding] old procedures of oath or [...] the judgement of God" (Foucault, 1996, p. 196). Empirical medical research was popularized at the time, which could segment and classify certain characteristics and symptoms, naturally creating a separation between conformity and deviance (Foucault, 1996, p. 195). Such practices eventually grounded fully fledged disciplines familiar to the administration of healthcare and justice, such as psychology, psychiatry, pedagogy, and criminology. These practices established the construction of empirical expertise (Foucault, 1996, p. 196). Statistical inference and standardization also became a means to model "good behavior" or highlight factors that would exacerbate infection rates.

Informed by findings from surveillance, decision-making became rooted in a tightly knit hierarchy of power justifying intrusion on social life. A Foucauldian hierarchy of power is staffed by those who share empirical expertise in surveillance systems, such as doctors or health authorities. Health became politicized and managed by a long series of regulations concerning not only disease, but also general forms of existence and behavior. The expansion of such a healthcare system also forged health professionals who spent increasing amounts of time tending to general administrative tasks assigned to them by health authorities, feeding back into the centralized surveillance system (Foucault, 2001).

The professionalization of health expertise stretched beyond strictly the medical realm into broader conditions of life, such as nutrition, housing, and environment. Dating back to the 1600s, Italian governments founded "health magistrates" who were granted judicial and executive powers with wide oversight on sanitary standards, such as the regulation of butcher meat and forced animal euthanasia (Snowden, 2019; Wisecrack, 2020). Similar powers were also granted to Italian "sanitary municipal authorities" (colloquially known as "body snatchers"), allowing them to forcibly send those infected—or even *suspected* of infection—to quarantine lazarettos, which were known to be notoriously overpopulated, underfunded, and an almost certain death sentence (Snowden, 2019; Wisecrack, 2020).

An orderly system cannot function without compliance. Foucault's more widely known theories of discipline and punishment described law enforcement as a birth of a network with branched lines of regulation that serve to uphold the sovereignty of the state. As Marinković and Ristić (2019) noted, "policing can be used for different purposes, oscillating in the trihedral legal system, disciplinary mechanisms and regulatory, security apparatuses-dispositifs, and their different technologies of power and management" (p. 355). Policing compliance—in both a health and social context—stems from the delegation of powers within health authorities and is governed by public health guidelines. In Canada, both public health and emergency legislation can expand police powers as part of their pandemic preparedness response, allowing law enforcement to persecute behaviors that could promote the spread of infection or threaten the social fabric of a "healthy society."

More tacitly, compliance relies on the public's trust in administrative institutions. Trust is an expectation placed on a professional power (or agency) in the face of incomplete knowledge of control. Trust is future-oriented and works to reduce complexity and anxiety involving risk or uncertainty (Owen & Powell, 2006). In the face of a widespread pandemic that involves both risk and anxiety, public trust becomes a key lynchpin in expanding administrative directives that infringe on democratic rights. Many of the social restrictions included in Canada's response to the COVID-19 pandemic have necessarily relied on public trust, such as wearing masks, maintaining a respectful distance, and restricting social gatherings. In turn, the public trusts that the government is acting in good faith while accounting for individual interests and social well-being.

Surveillance, hierarchy, policing, and public trust do not function in isolation; they influence one another, creating a feedback loop that expands the administrative state and gives rise to a norm of "good citizenship," while simultaneously stigmatizing those who deviate from it (Owen & Powell, 2006). Social identities are created by their engagement with institutions, forming self-managing citizens. A plague town "[roots the occupant] in a state of conscious and permanent visibility that assures the automatic functioning of power [and] ensures that surveillance is permanent in its effects, even if it is discontinuous in its action" (Foucault, 1975). In the case of a pandemic, health and hygiene practices have implications beyond illness; they speak to the integrity of a person and the extent to which they can be trusted by the state and others. Those who deviate then lose that trust and become a threat to society.

The authoritative power of a Foucauldian plague town opens the possibility for abuse. In Canada, compulsory vaccination measures to curb smallpox were introduced in the early 1860s in the United Canadas and Prince Edward Island, pioneered by the Hudson's Bay Company, which served as the *de facto* public health agency at the time (Rutty & Sullivan, 2007). In 1885, the Ontario Board of Health expanded its authority by deploying medical inspectors to enforce widespread fumigation for freight trains that ran interprovincially (Rutty & Sullivan, 2007). Around the same time in the United States, leprosy outbreaks in the early 1900s compelled federal and state governments to enact measures that deployed "virus squads" to force vaccination and required citizens to publicly report suspicious activity, or even sanction bounty hunting (Board of Health, Archives of Hawai'i, 1867–1941). In the interest of curbing infection, governmental control was able to expand its administration, delegate authorities to private companies, and normalize a culture of whistleblowing.

Benefits of an Expanded Administrative State

Naturally, broad governmental control has many benefits during times of crises; it can institute best practices and efficiently disseminate treatment. Historically, quarantine measures gave rise to the standardization of sanitariums across Europe, which decreased the likelihood of infection between individuals and promoted overall standards of cleanliness (Snowden, 2019).

Nimble governmental powers allowed for the swift allocation of resources, disseminated life-saving treatments, and promoted economic efficiency. Policing compliance was an effective way to ensure individuals stayed apart during time-sensitive periods of disease incubation. Public trust in governmental institutions led to the downfall of feudalism, sparked civic engagement, and gave rise to the fundamental tenets of democratic systems (Snowden, 2019).

Governmental coordination became a formative part of international human rights regimes. Following the second cholera outbreak in 1829, European governments rolled out a series of 14 International Sanitary Conferences between 1851 and 1938 in an effort to coordinate resources and create alliances between countries (Howard-Jones, 1975). After World War II, Canada was central to the creation of the World Health Organization in 1948, championed by Deputy Minister of National Health and Welfare Dr. Brock Chisholm, who served as the First

Director General from 1948 to 1953 (Rutty & Sullivan, 2007; Howard-Jones, 1975). Within the same year, the *Universal Declaration of Human Rights* was enacted, which declared, for the first time on an international stage, the right to a standard of living that takes "all human rights, civil, political, economic, social or cultural as [...] inseparable and interdependent" (Navenethem, 2008). Similar right-to-health provisions were subsequently embedded in the *International Convention on the Elimination of all Forms of Racial Discrimination* (1965) and the *International Covenant on Economic, Social and Cultural Rights* (1996). The modern conceptions of well-being and public health directly resulted from governmental coordination, lobbying and reciprocity between state actors to the betterment of a broader "global" community. In other words, the expansion of the administrative state created the concept that "we are all in this together" and encouraged collaboration across party lines.

EMERGENCY POWERS IN CANADA

Public health in Canada is a shared responsibility between provincial/territorial jurisdictions and federal jurisdictions, whereby each level of government has developed its own respective structures and institutions to carry out essential functions. When a public health emergency is declared by the Minister of Health, as per the advice of the Chief Medical Officer of Health, such measures address a specific medical concern that seriously endangers the lives, health, or social well-being of a population. Conversely, a declaration of a state of emergency is typically made by a minister of Public Safety under a different set of legislation, with the goal of correcting a problem that affects the public's well-being. Declarations of public health and state of emergencies both significantly broaden the scope of legal and operational resources for governments to act upon, while also allowing for coordination in different regulated areas of public and private law that would otherwise function independently (Standing Senate Committee on Social Affairs, Science and Technology, 2010). As made evident by the COVID-19 pandemic, both a public health and state of emergency can be declared in the same jurisdiction and function conterminously.

Public health is a matter of shared jurisdiction. The *Constitution Act* (1867) outlined the division of responsibilities between federal and provincial governments. During the time of enactment, the administration of health and public health was a nascent concept based on the assumption that state assistance was made in exceptional circumstances, but largely self-regulated by citizens themselves (Standing Senate Committee on Social Affairs, Science and Technology, 2010). Because health matters are not specifically assigned to one level of government and deliberately left amorphous when challenged in the courts, both levels of government are free to legislate in the area, depending on the circumstance, nature, and scope of the health concern (Gibson, 2007).

The Surveillance of Federal Powers

The federal government derives its authority over public health from its power over quarantine under section 91(11) of the Constitution, though until recently, it left most of the regulation to the provinces. The federal government's relative impartiality in pandemic preparedness was harshly criticized as a "lackluster response" during the 2003 SARS epidemic, where provinces were ill-equipped to create a unified coordinated response across jurisdictions. This led Parliament to update the *Quarantine Act* in 2005 and create the Public Health Agency of Canada (PHAC) shortly thereafter.

The *Quarantine Act* empowers the federal Minister of Health to designate quarantine stations, appoint quarantine officers to inspect borders, and compel screenings (Gammon, 2006). Although the earliest rendition of the *Quarantine Act* went into effect shortly after Confederation in 1872, it was amended post-SARS with refined powers to designate quarantine facilities, declare emergency conditions to mitigate outbreaks, and impose harsh penalties—sometimes up to $750,000 or six months in jail (*Quarantine Act*, 2005, s 58; Harris, 2020). In March 2020, the *Act* was invoked twice: First, to mandate a 14-day quarantine for Canadians returning from Wuhan, China; and second, for all international travelers arriving in Canada. On the advice of PHAC, the federal government has also imposed mandatory health checks at border crossings and issued medical certificate requirements for travelers who refuse to self-isolate (McQuigge, 2020).

The 2003 SARS outbreak illustrated that leadership could be strengthened through the establishment of a federal agency that created new mechanisms for federal, provincial, and territorial collaboration. The *Public Health Agency of Canada Act* (2006) created the PHAC and established the role of the Chief Public Health Officer[3] who acts as the leading health professional representing the Government of Canada and liaisons with other public health authorities. While standalone provincial public health agencies have existed since 1884 (e.g., National Advisory Committee on SARS and Public Health, 2003), PHAC is the first *federally* controlled agency for emergency preparedness and infectious disease control. PHAC folds into the national health portfolio alongside Health Canada and the Canadian Institutes of Health Research by operating the National Microbiology Laboratory, which provides COVID-19 testing and surveys under-resourced regions (Public Health Ontario, 2020). Taken together, PHAC is positioned as the overarching collection agency where epidemiological data and health education information is funneled into, later to be delegated by medical authorities and disseminated to provinces and municipalities (Government of Canada, 2020a).

PHAC can also be reframed as a de facto clearinghouse for health surveillance. Both explicitly and implicitly, the administrative creation of PHAC has substantially expanded its powers to regulate behavior. Private matters are also at the mercy of Public Health Orders, shared through a variety of news outlets including Dr. Tam's daily address to the nation. Decision-making powers on health have also become decentralized away from elected officials in the cabinet to administrators with specialized expertise, such as epidemiologists, statisticians, and physicians. The recommendations are now rooted in evidence-based scientific methodology that gathers statistics of prevalence rates and mitigating factors that contribute to the spread of COVID-19, evidence which is then used to further make more decisions. The coordinating function of the national body functions precisely as Foucault would describe a centralized surveillance measure, and its statutory authority is intricately connected between various administrative bodies and reinforces what types of research is likely to be acted upon.

Public health authorities are also intrinsically tied to federal enforcement agencies. For example, upon entry to Canada, the Canadian Border Services Agency alerts PHAC of any traveler noncompliance (real or suspicious), who then notify the national operations center of the Royal Canadian Mountain Police (RCMP) in coordination with municipal law enforcement. Between April 10 and May 20, 2020, the RCMP recorded over 2,100 home visits related to COVID-19, which were often conducted in full personal protective equipment (PPE) isolation gear (Aiello, 2020). Home visits have since decreased as restrictions relaxed in June 2020, and now the RCMP has shifted gears to support the Canadian Anti-Fraud Centre with various scams that have increased (Government of Canada, 2020b).

Canada's response to the COVID-19 pandemic can be both collaborative and adversarial. Most notably, the *Quarantine Act* can become a highly powerful and discretionary surveillance measure to track anyone who enters, leaves, and moves within Canada, supported by a national law enforcement system.

The administrative safeguards that stemmed from Canada's response to the COVID-19 pandemic, including mandatory isolation measures for international travelers and non-essential travel bans were found to significantly reduce transmission of the COVID-19 virus during the early stages of the pandemic (Talic, 2021). Specifically, following Canada's non-essential travel ban of foreign nationals in March 2020, the number of COVID-19 cases entering Canada declined ten-fold within a four-week period. However, such restrictions were found to be insufficient to prevent new outbreaks within the community (McLaughlin, 2022). On a global scale, while the application of travel-related restrictions was found to lead to significant reductions in imported cases, the extent of reduction varied by country (Grepin, 2021).

Beyond border restrictions, scientific literature associated personal protective and social measures including handwashing, mask-wearing, and physical distancing with reductions in the incidence of COVID-19 (Talic, 2021).

Notwithstanding the effectiveness of public health measures, the power to search and compel health checks to those crossing borders is also subject to a high degree of discretion restricting civil liberties—mainly people's democratic right to associate and freedom to move—in the name of ensuring regulatory oversight. As such, regulatory measures that aim to curb the spread of COVID-19 must be balanced against social and economic considerations, which will be discussed in further detail below.

Heightened surveillance disproportionately impacts immigrant and racialized individuals, who are more likely to travel across borders for education, employment, or family purposes. Various immigration programs have expanded to accept applicants as a way to jumpstart the Canadian economy, thereby also increasing the flow of those crossing borders during a time of restriction (Bolongaro & Hagan, 2020). Racist incidents from Canadian Border Service employees are not a new phenomenon (Nasser, 2020; Zoledziowski, 2020), but with the increased surveillance, alongside the linkage between public health and law enforcement agencies, these populations have likely been subjected to a higher degree of scrutiny. For those hoping to establish permanent residency or citizenship, their status may be jeopardized as law enforcement becomes increasingly entangled in their affairs as they travel.

Many infectious diseases tend to originate in countries outside of Canada, which further perpetuates racist stereotypes when they present themselves domestically. A May 2020 report by Research Co. found that nearly 20 % of respondents would colloquially refer to COVID-19 as the "Chinese virus" alongside a dramatic rise in anti-Asian related hate crimes (Simon & Chen, 2021; Weichel, 2020). Another recent survey of healthcare workers in Manitoba found that one in five who self-identified as being of Asian heritage reported experiencing racism during the pandemic (Reimer, 2020). Seemingly neutral surveillance measures effectively condone racism by reinforcing the message that international travelers are the cause of domestic difficulties. Anti-immigrant sentiment may increase as unemployment stagnates and immigration programs expand (Bolongaro & Hagan, 2020).

Taken together, two sides of pandemic preparedness can be observed. For some, surveillance functions as a potentially life-saving contact-tracing mechanism. For others, surveillance instills a sense of distrust against those who hope to establish and maintain a livelihood in Canada, during a time of transition. The harsh surveillance of the plague town then disproportionately focuses on those who already face systemic anti-immigration sentiment.

The Hierarchy of Provincial, Territorial, and Municipal Powers

Most legislative authority for public health measures fall on the provincial and territorial governments. Every province has established a Chief Medical Officer of Health or equivalent role tasked with carrying out various functions such as monitoring health of residents, sanctioning hospitals, and further regulating activities in private life.

As mentioned, provinces each have an equivalent "public health" or "emergency" legislation that expands governmental powers. While public health statutes vary across jurisdictions, some contain specific provisions that enable the Lieutenant Governor in Council to declare emergencies. By late March 2020, every province declared some type of emergency either by declaring a "public health emergency" under a provincial public health statute or a general "state of emergency" under an emergency management statute (Block & Goldenberg, 2020; Block, Goldenberg, & Waschuk, 2020; Block, Goldenberg, et al., 2020; Block, Loranger, et al., 2020; Block, Smyth, et al., 2020). Public health emergency powers tend to focus on the management of healthcare, imposing quarantine, and redistributing medical supplies (*Public Health Act*, 2001). Some statutes cover additional elements such as mandatory vaccination, conscription for support services, information collection and the removal of personal items. Emergency orders can vary from province to province to province, but they often regulate the operations of businesses, public events and the number of people who can associate together. Emergency measures may also enforce mandatory mask policies and coordinate regulations in schools and hospitals (see Appendix A).

Provincial authorities are responsible for both the creation and execution of most public health orders. During a public health emergency and/or state of emergency, provincial governments can manage resources, delegate essential goods, and compel private actors such as businesses. Such health authorities now bear the responsibility of collecting statistical information related to COVID-19 infections and deaths, which is then used to inform public health measures and track disease transmission.

Municipalities are responsible for the delivery of most public health services, though they are often acting in accordance with provincial/territorial powers, and other directives and conditions for funding (Standing Senate Committee on Social Affairs, Science and Technology, 2010). The most common model of delivery is the Regional Health Authority/District, where locally or appointed boards are responsible for the provision of health services within a defined geographical area, often in combination with other health or community services.

In many ways, regional health authorities can operate similarly to a Foucauldian syndicate. Syndicates are best positioned to ensure that accurate data is collected and that registered individuals receive appropriate medical treatment. In tow, many municipalities have some regulatory power, particularly in areas that are well-populated so long as their directives must align with the overarching strategies established by federal and provincial governments.

Regional health authorities have a voice in what kind of contact-tracing data is deemed valuable. Typically, when a COVID-19 test is positive, health authorities will ask individuals for their name, address, age, and gender. Many public health advocates, including Arjumand Siddiqi from the University of Toronto, strongly encourage health authorities to also include data on race and ethnicity as a way to ensure equitable service distribution and governmental accountability (Siddiqi, 2020). Studies from the United States have shown that Indigenous, Black, and Latino Americans have a COVID-19 death rate that is double than that of their white counterparts (APM Research Lab, 2021). It is uncertain whether Canada bears similar statistical outcomes, as the data is not captured, or deemed unnecessary.

As such, the Foucauldian syndicate can omit crucial information that speaks to the social determinants of health exacerbating infection rates. Without these indicators in mind, governments are more likely to deploy resources equally among certain regions, effectively ignoring the ways specific groups are more vulnerable to infection over others. Race-based data can be of enormous benefit to racialized communities, both for resource redistribution and governmental accountability against discriminatory practices.

As we can see, a Foucauldian plague operates in two separate worlds. To some, health authorities are tuned into regional concerns and advocate for needs based on the indicators presented to them. But surveillance is a double-edged sword: Nationally, the movements of racialized communities are put under a microscope while their local realities remain ignored. For communities already marginalized by the healthcare system, regional authorities become part of a larger systemic problem that is further compounded as it goes up the chain of command.

The Decentralization of Enforcement Powers

Provincial and municipal compliance measures are also reinforced by the police. Public health and emergency measures legislation both carry significant enforcement powers and penalties. Enforcement measures under public health legislation is typically issued with an explicit goal of public health compliance (e.g., Nova Scotia COVID-19 Directive, 2020). The expansion of police powers under emergency legislation is broadly defined, and enforcement significantly varies across provinces. Generally, the duties of police officers are defined by legislation that allows them to interfere with individual liberty when it is reasonably necessary for the preservation of peace, protection of life, and service to a larger public purpose (*Dedman v The Queen*, 1985, para. 10). When a state of emergency is declared, provincial governments reconsider what can be "reasonably necessary," given that everyday behaviors such as physical contact are reframed as a serious health threat. Because many public health and emergency management statutes remain intentionally vague (e.g., Saskatchewan, Yukon and Prince Edward Island, Appendix A), there is little guidance about the limitations of such powers. The fear of noncompliance, further reinforced by the fear of the COVID-19 virus, feeds into a culture of surveillance among citizens, such that policing one another is expected and encouraged.

Public health messaging that touts that "we are all looking after one another" and "we're all in this together" also tacitly encourages a culture of whistleblowing (Pelley, 2020). Canada has instituted over 30 COVID-19 "snitch lines" across seven provinces to report issues relating to noncompliance (Canadian Civil Liberties Association, 2020). It also encourages a "model citizen" who is always informed of the changing evidence, compliant of new restrictions and has their community's best interest at heart.

There are concerning indications that racialized individuals are disproportionately impacted by enforcement actions. A June 2020 report from the Canadian Civil Liberties Association highlighted numerous accounts of racialized individuals who felt they had been targeted by law enforcement because of their race (Canadian Civil Liberties Association, 2020a). In September 2020, a "telewarrant" system was implemented in Quebec that allowed police to receive warrants remotely so that they could enter the homes of people suspected of hosting illegal gatherings during lockdowns (Banerjee, 2020). Like many minor offenses, such as vandalism or simple possession charges, COVID-19-related infractions can serve as a gateway into the criminal justice system for people who become "known to the police," which increases their chances of further criminalization and social marginalization (Owusu-Bempah et al., 2018).

Deploying a variety of policing tactics that penalize noncompliance is the hallmark of Foucault's analysis on discipline and punishment (Foucault, 1996). Here, policing exists at all levels of government, forming a dense but decentralized network of power serving multiple purposes. Federal police powers largely concern behavior associated with travel that threatens the security of the country, while provincial and municipal powers concern compliance to public health standards. In doing so, policing writ large has fundamentally changed how people personally relate to one another, as now the most innocent of human interactions—a handshake, kiss, or hug—is now surveillance and criminalized.

Again, the Foucauldian conceptualization of policing will focus primarily on those who already experience discrimination from health and social systems and are more vulnerable to infection. If someone is infected, their behavior, risk assessments and sanitization standards are meticulously picked apart in the name of public protection. For those who are already heavily surveyed, a system that further decentralizes police powers intensifies the dynamics of these fraught relationships.

PROTECTIONIST MECHANISMS

Despite ongoing challenges, Canadian emergency preparedness has the potential to differ from a draconian plague town due to other legal tools embedded in its political system. Canadian civil rights protect against discrimination or arbitrariness from governing bodies and grant certain freedoms such as due process, voting rights, and freedom from arbitrary arrest. Since 1982, Canada's constitution has been amended to include the *Canadian Charter of Rights and Freedoms* that preserves basic rights required for a free and democratic country (*Canadian Charter of Rights and Freedoms*, 1982).

Public health legislation in Canada must be consistent with the *Canadian Charter of Rights and Freedoms* and it can be challenged if affected persons believe that their rights have been violated. Many emergency measures relating to pandemic preparedness could be perceived as an infringement of civil rights. For instance, mandatory mask requirements infringe on people's right of expression and limiting social gatherings also encroach freedoms of association. The Charter allows Canadian citizens to challenge these laws if they are deemed grossly disproportionate or arbitrary, challenging the Foucauldian model citizen that requires assimilation in order for society to be healthy (Foucault, 1996).

However, section 1 of the *Charter* allows governments to justify their infringement if their goal is sufficiently pressing, substantial, and rationally connected to protecting the health and safety of its citizens (Ries, 2007). If a Charter challenge is brought forward, governmental authorities must prove why their actions are justifiable in the eyes of the law under section 1, thereby requiring a certain degree of transparency and accountability. This runs counter to Foucauldian models of power, which require the delegation and disbursement of decision-making, dissolving accountability structures in the process (Foucault, 1975). Here, the court system can be a valuable player in ensuring governmental authority is exercised reasonably.

Societal ideologies about health have also influenced the Canadian health administrative system. Many public health laws in Canada were drafted between the 1980s and the 2010s, during a period when "right-to-health" advocacy[4] was folding into the mainstream (Rutty & Sullivan, 2007). By virtue of the democratic formalities embedded in the legislative process, along with overarching *Charter* rights, public health legislation can be drafted with a rights-based ideology, which would consider state accountability and opportunities for judicial review on the allocation of healthcare resources or the disproportionate impact it may have on vulnerable populations. These kinds of proactive mechanisms address hierarchies of power by ensuring governments justify their decision-making processes through internal evaluations, budgeting documents, and reporting.

Most state of emergency legislations have expiration and renewal provisions, requiring the cabinet to formally reconvene every time a declaration is made or extended. While laws made after a declared state of emergency might not be subject to the same degree of scrutiny, most declarations have a set criterion (*Emergency Management and Civil Protection Act*, 2006, s 7.0.1(3); *Emergencies Act*, 1985), require mandatory reporting, or provide "safety net powers" or "vetoing powers" to different legislative actors to disallow motions (*Emergency Management Ent and Civil Protection Act*, 2006, s 7.0.9). Since state of emergency and public health emergency powers exercise a great deal of control, renewal provisions serve as a counterbalance requiring provincial governments to assess the state of emergency day by day and justify why these powers should be extended. It also promotes a message that, even in a crisis, Canadian legislatures are committed to a democratic process and preserves public trust.

Charter rights are particularly important for challenging enforcement measures, supported by the efforts of watchdog organizations like the Canadian Civil Liberties Association (CCLA). For example, on August 17, 2020, the Ontario government ended police access to a COVID-19 database after the CCLA filed a legal challenge prohibiting the blanket disclosure of personal medical information, an unpreceded order that directly flowed from Ontario's emergency legislation (Canadian Civil Rights Association, 2020b). Another 2020 report also published by the CCLA discovered that individuals were getting ticketed for behavior disconnected from the goal of protecting public health or where viral transmission was nearly impossible, such as sitting in a parked car or walking across an empty soccer field. In both cases, both directives were being challenged due to Charter violations on overbroad and arbitrary enforcement, infringing life, liberty and security rights protected by section 7 (Canadian Civil Rights Association, 2020a).

While such legal mechanisms are indeed important to a free and democratic society, it does not make them any less accessible. A study published by Sara Greene from Duke University School of Law found that poor and minority groups are less likely than higher-income counterparts to seek help when experiencing a civil legal problem due to a general distrust of public institutions (Greene, 2015). If legal protectionism remains the main source of accountability against state encroachment, then it remains accessible to some at the cost of others.

No example illustrates this distinction quite like the 1900 California case of *Jew Ho v. Williamson*, which struck down an overly broad quarantine measure that only applied to Chinese people within a condensed San Francisco neighborhood. Without attempting to isolate the houses of alleged plague victims, the city had restricted the movement of Chinese people within 12 city blocks, thereby increasing the danger of infection within its boundaries. People living outside the neighborhood, however, were allowed to roam freely under a more relaxed set of quarantine measures. Ultimately, the federal court ruled that such provisions were deemed unjust and therefore contrary to the laws limiting police powers (*Jew Ho v. Williamson*, 1900). It is unlikely that Canada could—or would—enact similar legislation today; however, the stereotypes that connect infectious disease control to specific populations remains embedded in other forms of emergency preparedness responses.

Overall, I believe that the Foucauldian plague town exists for some and not for others. Despite protectionism measures that temper the effects of a Foucauldian plague town, a democratic system relies on individuals to bring claims, and not everyone has access to the legislative and judicial system in the same way. Combined with increased surveillance and criminalization, and the lack of evidence to support such discriminatory practices, the pandemic preparedness response is experienced in two different ways; for model citizens, the public's trust in the government is retained and their safety is protected. For those who are characterized deviant, the government remains distrustful, and employs various surveillance tactics to ensure compliance. As such, I am left wondering: Who benefits from state expansion? Who remains villainized?

NOTES

1 Attorney at Maclean Weidemann Lawyers LLP.
2 The research conducted by Vox Media was prepared before the COVID-19 pandemic.
3 Dr. Theresa Tam was named Canada's Chief Public Health Officer on June 26, 2017. At the time of publication, Dr. Tam still holds this position.
4 Article 25(1) of the Universal Declaration of Human Rights 1948 stipulates that "everyone has the right to a standard of living adequate for the health and well-being of himself and his family, including [...] medical care." A right-to-health approach will consider the obstacles to health access and attacks of healthcare.

REFERENCES

Aiello, R. (2020, May 21). Police have in on nearly 2,200 quarantining travellers at home. *CTV News*. https://www.ctvnews.ca/health/coronavirus/police-have-checked-in-on-nearly-2-200-quarantining-travellers-at-home-1.4949021

APM Research Lab. (2021, February 4). *The color of Coronavirus: COVID-19 deaths by race and ethnicity in the US.* https://www.apmresearchlab.org/covid/deaths-by-race

Banerjee, S. (2020, October 1). Quebec police given "telewarrant" system to enforce new lockdown orders. *The Globe and Mail.* https://www.theglobeandmail.com/canada/article-quebec-police-given-telewarrant-system-to-enforce-new-lockdown/

Block, E. S., & Goldenberg, A. (2020, March 18). *COVID-19: Can they do that? Part I: Ontario's Emergency Management and Civil Protection Act.* McCarthy Tetrault. www.mccarthy.ca/en/insights/articles/covid-19-can-they-do-part-i-ontarios-emergency-management-and-civil-protection-act

Block, E. S., Goldenberg, A., Feder, M., & Hughes, N. (2020, March 19). *COVID-19: Can they do that? Part III: British Columbia's Emergency Program Act and Public Health Act.* McCarthy Tetrault. www.mccarthy.ca/en/insights/articles/covid-19-can-they-do-part-iii-british-columbias-emergency-program-act-and-public-health-act

Block, E. S., Goldenberg, A., & Waschuk, G. (2020, April 8). *COVID-19: Can they do that? Part V: Roundup: Manitoba, New Brunswick, Newfoundland and Labrador, the NWT, Nova Scotia, Nunavut, P.E.I., Saskatchewan and Yukon.* McCarthy Tetrault. www.mccarthy.ca/en/insights/articles/covid-19-can-they-do-part-v-roundup-manitoba-new-brunswick-newfoundland-and-labrador-nwt-nova-scotia-nunavut-pei-saskatchewan-and-yukon

Block, E. S., Loranger, J.-M., & Goldenberg, A. (2020, March 21). *COVID-19: Can they do that? Part VII: Québec's Public Health Act and Civil Protection Act.* McCarthy Tetrault. www.mccarthy.ca/en/insights/articles/covid-19-can-they-do-part-vii-quebecs-public-health-act-and-civil-protection-act

Block, E. S., Smyth, K. L., Loranger, J.-M., Goldenberg, A., & Fitz-Simon, N. (2020, April 7). *COVID-19: Can they do that? Part IX: Enforcement of emergency measures.* McCarthy Tetrault. www.mccarthy.ca/en/insights/articles/covid-19-can-they-do-part-ix-enforcement-emergency-measures

Board of Health, archives of Hawai'i, series 33–5, "Hansen's Disease, 1867–1941." Retrieved August 21, 2020.

Bolongaro, K., & Hagan, S. (2020, October 20). *Trudeau ratchets up Canada's immigration targets to boost recovery.* Bloomberg. https://www.bloomberg.com/news/articles/2020-10-30/trudeau-ratchets-up-immigration-targets-to-boost-recovery

British Columbia Public Health Act, SBC 2008 c 28.

Bruce, B. (1898). *Reports of the Medical Officer of the Privy Council and Local Government Board, Annual Report, on behalf of His Majesty's Stationery Office.* Darling & Son.

Canadian Civil Liberties Association. (2020, June 24). Stay Off the Grass: COVID-19 and Law Enforcement in Canada. https://ccla.org/wp-content/uploads/2021/06/2020-06-24-Stay-Off-the-Grass-COVID19-and-Law-Enforcement-in-Canada1.pdf

Constitution Act, 1867, 30 & 31 Vict, c 3.

Dedman v The Queen 1985 2 SCR 2.

Echenberg, M. (2002). Pestis redux: The initial years of the third bubonic plague pandemic, 1894–1901. *Journal of World History, 13*(2), 429–449.

Emergency Management and Civil Protection Act, RSO 1990, c E.9, <https://canlii.ca/t/55qnl> retrieved on 2023-07-13

Foucault, M. (1975). *Discipline and punish.* Gallimard.

Foucault, M. (1996). *Discipline and punish: The birth of the prison.* Vintage Books.

Foucault, M. (2001). The politics of health in the eighteenth century. In J. D. Faubion (Ed.), *Power (Essential works of Foucault 1954–1984)* (Vol. 3, pp. 90–106). The New Press.

Gibson, E. (2007). Public health information, federalism, and politics. *Health Law Review, 16*(1), 5.

Government of Canada. (2020a, March 7). *Public Health Agency of Canada*. Government of Canada. www.canada.ca/en/public-health.html

Government of Canada. (2020b, September 8). *COVID-19 Fraud*. Government of Canada. https://antifraudcentre-centreantifraude.ca/features-vedette/2020/covid-19-eng.htm

Greene, S. S. (2015). Race, class, and access to civil justice. *Iowa Law Review, 101*, 1263.

Grepin, A. G., Ho, T.-L., Liu, Z., Marion, S., Piper, J., Worsnop, C. Z., & Lee, K. (2021). Evidence of the effectiveness of travel-related measures during the early phase of the COVID-19 pandemic: A rapid systematic review. *BMJ, 6*, Article e004537. https://gh.bmj.com/content/6/3/e004537

Harris, S. (2020, October 25). *77 fines issued, 7 people charged for breaking Canada's quarantine rules during COVID-19*. CBC News. https://www.cbc.ca/news/business/police-rcmp-fines-charges-quarantine-act-travel-1.5775267#:~:text=CBC%20News%20was%20able%20to,fines%20of%20up%20to%20%24750%2C000

Howard-Jones, N. (1975). *The scientific background of the international sanitary conferences 1851–1938*. World Health Organization. https://apps.who.int/iris/bitstream/handle/10665/62873/14549_eng.pdf?sequence=1

International Convention on the Elimination of All Forms of Racial Discrimination, UN General Assembly (1965, 21 December), 660 at 195 (entry into force January 4, 1969).

International Covenant on Economic, Social and Cultural Rights, UN General Assembly (1966, 16 December), 993 at 3 (entry into force January 3, 1976).

Jew Ho v Williamson 1900 103 F 10.

Marinković, D., & Ristić, D. (2019). Foucault and the Birth of the Police. *Revija za kriminalistiko in kriminologijo/Ljubljana, 70*(4), 352–363.

McLaughlin, A. (2022). Genomic epidemiology of the first two waves of SARS-CoV-2 in Canada. *eLife*. https://elifesciences.org/articles/73896

McQuigge, M. (2020, March 25). *The Quarantine Act explained, as isolation becomes mandatory for some*. CTV News. www.ctvnews.ca/health/coronavirus/the-quarantine-act-explained-as-isolation-becomes-mandatory-for-some-1.4868457

National Advisory Committee on SARS and Public Health. (2003). *Learning from SARS: Renewal of public health in Canada*. Government of Canada. www.canada.ca/content/dam/phac-aspc/migration/phac-aspc/publicat/sars-sras/pdf/sars-e.pdf

Nasser, S. (2020, October 15). *Canadian files complain after CBSA agent allegedly tells him "You're Somalian" as reason for questioning*. CBC News. https://www.cbc.ca/news/canada/toronto/cbsa-racism-complaint-1.5762676

Nova Scotia COVID-19 Directive. (2020, March 30). *Ministers directive*. Government of Nova Scotia. www.novascotia.ca/coronavirus/docs/Minister-Furey-Directive-March-30-2020.pdf

Owen, T., & Powell, J. (2006). "Trust", the professional power and social theory: Lessons from post-Foucauldian framework. *International Journal of Sociology and Social Policy, 26*, 110–120.

Owusu-Bempah, A., Luscombe, A., & Finlay, B. (2018). Unequal justice: Race and cannabis arrests in the post-legal landscape. In D. Weinstock (Ed.), *High Times: The legalization and regulation of cannabis in Canada*. McGill Queens University Press.

Public Health Act, CQLR 2001 c S-2.

Public Health Agency of Canada Act, RSA 2006, c 5.

Public Health and Safety Act, RSY 2002, c 176.

Quarantine Act, SC 2005, c 20, <https://canlii.ca/t/54b27> retrieved on 2023-07-13

Randall, D. (2019). *Black death at the Golden Gate: The race to save American from the bubonic plague.* W. W. Norton.

Reimer, W. (2020, April 14). *Coronavirus: CUPE survey reveals anti-Asian racism towards Manitoba health-care workers.* Global News. https://globalnews.ca/news/6816668/cupe-survey-anti-asian-racism-manitoba-coronavirus/

Ries, N. M. (2007). Legal issues in disease outbreaks: Judicial review of public health powers. *Health Law Review, 16*(1), 11.

Roy, A. (2020, April 3). Arundhati Roy: "The pandemic is a portal." *Financial Times.* https://www.ft.com/content/10d8f5e8-74eb-11ea-95fe-fcd274e920ca

Rutty, C., & Sullivan, S. C. (2007). *This is public health: A Canadian history.* Canadian Public Health Association. https://www.cpha.ca/sites/default/files/assets/history/book/history-book-print_all_e.pdf

Siddiqi, A. (2020, August 19). The post-pandemic future: Race-based data collection can make our city more equitable. *Toronto Life.* https://torontolife.com/city/the-post-pandemic-future-race-based-data-collection-can-make-our-city-more-equitable/

Simon, S., & Chen, J. (2021, February 27). *Anti-Asian hate crime rise dramatically amid pandemic.* National Public Radio. https://www.npr.org/2021/02/27/972056885/anti-asian-hate-crimes-rise-dramatically-amid-pandemic

Standing Senate Committee on Social Affairs, Science and Technology. (2010). Canada's response to the 2009 H1N1 influenza pandemic. *Journals of the Senate.* https://sencanada.ca/content/sen/Committee/403/soci/rep/rep15dec10-e.pdf

Snowden, F. M. (2019). *Epidemics and society: From the black death to the present.* Yale University Press.

Talic, S., Shah, S., Wild, H., Gasevic, D., Maharaj, A., Ademi, Z., Li, X., Xu, W., Mesa-Eguiagaray, I., Rostron, J., Theodoratou, E., Zhang, X., Motee, A., Liew, D., & Ilic, D. (2021). Effectiveness of public health measures in reducing the incidence of covid-19, SARS-CoV-2 transmission, and COVID-19 mortality: Systematic review and meta-analysis. *BMJ, 375*, Article e068302. https://www.bmj.com/content/375/bmj-2021-068302

Universal Declaration of Human Rights, UN General Assembly (1948), 217 A III (entry into force December 10, 1948.)

Vox Media. (2018, May 23). *Explained: The next pandemic* [Video]. Netflix. www.netflix.com/title/80216752

Wade, N. (2010, October 31). Europe's plagues came from China, study finds. *The New York Times.* https://www.nytimes.com/2010/11/01/health/01plague.html

Weichel, A. (2020, May 19). *Canadians strongly opposed to calling COVID-19 "Chinese virus" or "Chinese flu", poll finds.* CTV News Vancouver. https://bc.ctvnews.ca/canadians-strongly-opposed-to-calling-covid-19-chinese-virus-or-chinese-flu-poll-finds-1.4945437

Wisecrack. (2020a, April 13). *How Pandemics Change Society* [Video]. Youtube. www.youtube.com/watch?v=2Rr9b-HMSS4

Wisecrack. (2020b, June 1). *How a pandemic ends—Wisecrack Edition* [Video]. Youtube www.youtube.com/watch?v=k-ONTqMXlrI

Zoledziowski, A. (2020, June 6). *Canadian Border Services fires employee after racist video mocks George Floyd.* Vice News. https://www.vice.com/en/article/ep4xdm/canada-border-services-fires-employee-after-racist-video-mocks-george-floyd

CHAPTER THREE

Danger Inside and Outside the Home: Domestic Violence During the COVID-19 Pandemic

SAFIA AMIRY[1]

Abstract: Since the declaration of COVID-19 as a global pandemic, most governments have implemented public health measures. Quarantine and social isolation were determined as central strategies for curbing the spread of the virus, but these measures have caused many unintended consequences. For instance, isolation measures enabled different forms of violence, including domestic and sexual violence. Caged in violent homes, with no contact or limited contact with the outside world, many victims were caught in situations where they had difficulty seeking help or accessing support. Moreover, the concept of "the home" has changed during the pandemic. While "the home" generally refers to a place that provides pleasure, relaxation, and privacy, this changed for victims of domestic violence during the pandemic. In addition, the home became a workplace for those employed, a school for those taking classes, and a caretaking facility for those needing care. As such, this chapter investigates domestic violence during the COVID-19 pandemic and critically examines strategies and policies put in place by governments and non-government organizations to address this issue. This chapter also analyzes the progress and shortcomings of these programs to highlight what has been done and what can be improved. Findings can be used to inform policies and interventions to address the increase in violence that arose from the pandemic, as well as the pandemic's lingering and long-term impacts.

Keywords: COVID-19 pandemic, lockdown, policy, violence reporting, domestic violence

INTRODUCTION

At the end of 2019, a new viral disease called the coronavirus (COVID-19) emerged in Wuhan, in the Hubei Province of China (Chan et al., 2020). Within three months of the virus outbreak, this local epidemic became a global pandemic (Bouillon-Minois et al., 2020). To tackle this outbreak, governments and other organizations have implemented strict public health requirements. Although lockdowns and social distancing measures, have become central strategies to help slow the spread of COVID-19, new problems have emerged. For example, the pandemic has contributed to economic vulnerability and job losses, closure of schools, universities, and businesses, and feelings of isolation and loneliness.

While many pandemic discussions remain focused on public health issues and faltering economies, there are growing international concerns about an increase in domestic violence and child abuse. Fear, increased stress, and frustration, as well as limited personal time and space are factors that could lead to increased conflicts at home, which could result in more frequent and/or more severe incidents of violence and abuse (Bouillon-Minois et al., 2020). Moreover, since it is not uncommon for perpetrators of domestic violence to isolate their victims and reduce opportunities for them to disclose their abuse or seek help, pandemic-related lockdowns and other social isolation measures enable these behaviors (Campbell, 2020). Furthermore, religious institutions (e.g., churches, temples, mosques) and social institutions (e.g., libraries, schools) are often sources where victims can seek reprieve from their abusive homes and receive emotional support. With social isolation measures in place during lockdowns, these safe spaces are no longer accessible, or they are only available with limited access. As victims interact with fewer people, domestic violence and child abuse may remain invisible and underreported. This is particularly true for children, as teachers, administrators, and counselors are the primary reporters of child mistreatment (Bullinger et al., 2021). Overall, school closures and social distancing measures reduced teacher-student contact, which ultimately prevented children from reporting abuse and mistreatment. Therefore, pandemic-related measures and restrictions may inadvertently hinder victims from seeking help and prolong victims' exposure to violence.

This chapter investigates the widespread concern that government-mandated lockdown restrictions during the COVID-19 pandemic have contributed to increased rates of domestic violence. I examine how and why a pandemic can exacerbate domestic violence and, in doing so, I consider questions such as: Which demographics are more at risk? What policies have been implemented, and strategies have been taken, by governments and non-government institutions to address issues of domestic violence? This chapter also explores the progress and shortcomings of these policies and strategies to highlight how much work has been done to address domestic violence during the pandemic and what is missing. Lastly, this chapter considers long- and short-term policy implications of domestic violence during the pandemic. As such, this chapter aims to inform policymakers on the implications of increased violence during a pandemic, as well as its long-term impact after the current pandemic.

METHODOLOGY

For this study, I apply critical feminist theory to explore the power dynamics of domestic violence and examine which factors exacerbate this problem. Because feminist critical theory make gender the focus of analysis, and it also challenges the existing distribution of power (Rhode, 2018). Moreover, from a critical feminist perspective, it becomes clear that the words "custom," "tradition," and "status quo" signal hegemonic systems of patriarchal privilege (Creedon, 1993). Also feminist critical theory will allow us to understand the understand the importance of the historical context and how can it help us to discern the current implications of the inequitable policies. We cannot ignore the prejudices of the past; the History and historical contexts must be taken into consideration and examined when attempting to understand to current situation (Lawrence et al., 1993).

Policymakers and other decision-makers must be aware of history and these structures when introducing policies that aim to address domestic violence. Like other critical approaches, a critical feminist perspective draws on techniques of consciousness-raising in the contemporary feminist organization, as well as on pragmatic philosophical traditions to make sure the change is translated in both knowledge creation and program implementation. A critical feminist perspective will allow me to focus on experiences, integrate these experiences into theory, and rely on theory for a deeper understanding of the experiences (Rhode, 2018). Therefore, given the deep roots of domestic violence in patriarchal practices and power relations, I will use a critical feminist perspective to unpack the complexity of domestic violence and, in doing so, will situate victims' experiences at the center of policy and programs, which aim to tackle this problem. Moreover, as critical feminist theory highlights the importance of historical context in understanding the current issue, it is important for this study to not undermine the historical roots and foundations of domestic violence in order to highlight the gaps in the current policies.

Domestic violence is an important and relevant topic since, at the time of writing this chapter, we are still living in the COVID-19 pandemic and many people around the world are experiencing domestic violence. Therefore, my goals for this chapter are to shed light on this global problem, suggest strategies to address it, and inspire future research on domestic violence. Notably, this chapter aims to catalyze change and encourage policymakers and other decision-makers to adjust policies that address domestic violence during and after this global crisis.

WHAT IS DOMESTIC VIOLENCE?

Domestic violence is considered as one of the most common forms of violence against women worldwide (Rauhaus et al., 2020). This form of violence includes (but is not limited to) physical abuse, intimidation and emotional abuse, sexual abuse, reproductive oppression, limitation of access to healthcare, financial abuse, neglect, and digital abuse (Buzawa & Buzawa, 2017; Rauhaus et al., 2020). Although heterosexual women are disproportionately affected by domestic violence, men and people in same-sex relationships also experience domestic violence (Bradbury-Jones & Isham, 2020). Children and the elderly can also be victims of domestic violence (Bidin & Yusoff, 2015).

Researchers believe that official assessments of domestic violence rates around the world have been immensely underestimated, since many victims choose not to report being abused for different reasons (Buzawa & Buzawa, 2017). Furthermore, findings from the World Health Organization suggest that: (a) around the world, almost one third of women (30 %) who have been in a relationship have experienced physical and/or sexual violence by their intimate partner; (b) the prevalence of domestic violence varies by regions, with women in Africa (36.6 %), the Eastern Mediterranean (37 %), and Southeast Asia (37.7 %) suffering the highest rates of violence; and (c) worldwide, as many as 38 % of all murders of women are committed by their intimate partners (WHO, 2013). Additionally, the home is identified as one of the most dangerous places for women who continue to suffer from the heaviest burden of fatal victimization, due to inequality and gender stereotypes (Rauhaus et al., 2020).

It has only been few decades that more attention has been given to domestic violence. According to Tracy (2007), when feminism emerged in the 1960s and 1970s, many feminist scholars started assessing the history and impact of misogyny and gender inequality in different realms of life, which led to the first modern work on abuse being published in mid-1970. During this period of early modern feminism, the perspective developed that the patriarchy is the main culprit of abuse against women (Tracy, 2007). "Patriarchy" has been defined as "rule by the male head of a social unit" in which the "patriarch, typically a societal elder, has legitimate power over others in the social unit, including other (especially younger) men, all women and children" (Pilcher & Whelehan, 2004, p. 93). Similarly, feminist researchers refer to the concept of patriarchy as the social system of masculine domination over women and argue that patriarchy is one of the underlying causes of violence against women and children (Tracy, 2007). However, it is important to note that other issues such as mental health problems, alcoholism, and unemployment are also factors that can enable domestic violence.

While domestic violence remains an alarming global concern, victims of domestic violence may choose not to report this violence for several reasons, including denial, feelings of shame, intimidation, fear of retaliation, and/or religious or cultural beliefs and practices (Rauhaus et al., 2020). Additionally, social support systems and law enforcement play an important role in the decision-making process for victims to gain the courage to report incidents of abuse. Because victims often face victim-blaming attitudes, most domestic violence cases remain unreported (Rauhaus et al., 2020). This gap in the system is elaborated in Chapter Seven by Towle and Zidenberg who examine sex workers and the nature of their work, which prevents them from even seeking the help from the police. This further highlight that the inefficiency in the system is one of the reasons for the cases related to violence and domestic violence remain unreported.

Domestic violence is particularly challenging for women from vulnerable groups of society, including women of color, immigrants, and women who are economically disadvantaged. These factors can worsen women's experiences since, for example, they confront overlapping and oppressive structural and cultural barriers, as well as a lack of access to support from the government and other institutions (Sharma & Borah, 2020). Moreover, women who experienced domestic violence prior to the COVID-19 pandemic may confront additional challenges as the pandemic has exacerbated many social and societal problems, as discussed by Towle and Zidenberg in Chapter Seven and Smith et al. in Chapter Nine. For this many reasons, it is important to critically domestic violence and issues associated with domestic violence during the COVID-19 pandemic, while also exploring ways to address the root causes of these problems.

DOMESTIC VIOLENCE DURING COVID-19

Domestic violence is a complex issue, with many intersecting and interlocking barriers and challenges. However, the novelty of the COVID-19 pandemic increased the complexity and nature of the violence, and it presented additional barriers to reporting and accessing support. Though there is limited research on how domestic violence is impacted by health epidemics specifically, research has shown that rapid increases in stress, controlling behaviors (often a means of coping with trauma), sudden shifts in daily routines, the lack of available community resources, the loss of income and economic instability, and limited access to social support systems are all factors that increase risks of domestic violence (Campbell, 2020)—and all of these factors have occurred during the current pandemic. In fact, a recent study from Xue and colleagues (2020), which examined over one million tweets about family violence and the COVID-19 pandemic, found that women and children have been disproportionately affected by domestic violence during the pandemic, while many victims of domestic violence are also from the LGBTQ community. Xue et al.'s (2020) study further shed light on this phenomenon, as they found that factors such as alcohol abuse, financial constraints, and stay-at-home measures have contributed to incidents of domestic violence during the pandemic.

The stress and associated risk factors of domestic violence, such as reduced or lost income, limited or lost employment, limited access to social support, and inadequate resources are also likely to compound as the pandemic continues. Moreover, alcohol abuse, which has been identified as a factor that intensifies domestic violence, is increasing—and with restaurants and bars closed or limited to takeout only, perpetrators who consume alcohol are more likely do so at home, which further increases the risk of domestic violence (Campbell, 2020). While some countries are loosening restrictions and permitting venues such as bar and restaurants to open, alcohol consumption will likely still contribute to increased rates of domestic violence. As we continue to deal with uncertainty about the future of the COVID-19 pandemic, it is unclear whether pandemic-related closures and restrictions will become common parts of our daily lives.

When critically examining stay-at-home measures imposed because of the pandemic, the home is not always a safe space. In fact, for children and adults living with a perpetrator of domestic violence, the home is often a space where physical, psychological, and sexual abuse occurs (Bradbury-Jones & Isham, 2020). This is because the home can be a place where power dynamics are distorted and practiced. Therefore, during the COVID-19 pandemic, stay-at-home measures can have major repercussions for children and adults who live in abusive and controlling households. This means that victims' avenues for escape and help are limited when lockdowns are implemented. Furthermore, the concept of "home" has changed during the pandemic. While the home has often been considered a space for pleasure, relaxation, and safety, the pandemic has transformed that comfortable space into a workplace (for those who are working from home), a school (for students), and/or a caretaking facility (for those who are supporting the elderly and children). Therefore, restrictions placed on people's homes have increased stress in households, which has further exacerbated domestic violence (Bradbury-Jones & Isham, 2020). The social isolation that people have been experiencing as they stay at home may also expose or aggravate mental health vulnerabilities, which is another major factor that perpetuates domestic violence (Bradbury-Jones & Isham, 2020).

Although women are predominantly victims of domestic violence, another group that is a common target is children (Sharma & Borah, 2020) since violent parent(s) can be violent toward their children (Browne & Finkelhor, 1986;

Finkelhor, 2010; Wood & Sommers, 2011). Increased violence among parents can negatively affect children and such interactions also impact their mental health. Moreover, due to the pandemic, it is not only challenging for parents to access support from family and the community but losing childcare can create more stress and responsibility for parents, which can further exacerbate domestic abuse (Sharma & Borah, 2020). Losing childcare services can also further increase the stress levels of both children and parents, due to limited access to food and education, and a lack of support for children's overall development (Sharma & Borah, 2020).

COVID-19 AND DOMESTIC VIOLENCE AROUND THE WORLD

Campbell's (2020) review of literature and research found that there is often a significant increase in domestic violence after catastrophic events. For example, alcohol abuse and domestic violence reports increased by 46 % in Othello, Washington after the eruption of Mount St Helens in 1980, and after Hurricane Katrina in 2005, reports of psychological abuse among women by their partner increased 35 % (Campbell, 2020). Similarly, substantial increases in domestic violence cases have been reported following tsunamis, earthquakes, hurricanes, and many other catastrophic events around the world, including the 2009 "Black Saturday" bushfires in Australia and the 2010 earthquake in Haiti (Campbell, 2020). It should also be noted that while there are similarities, the COVID-19 pandemic may result in longer closures of key organizations compared to the aftermath of natural disasters (Campbell, 2020), which means that increased domestic violence cases related to the current pandemic may have even greater consequences than previous catastrophic events. In addition, increased rates of domestic violence after a natural disaster often extends for several months after the tragedy occurs. In fact, Campbell (2020) found that in the aftermath of natural disasters in the United States and Canada, victim requests for domestic violence services increased for a full year following a major crisis.

Although it is difficult to estimate an exact percentage in the surge of domestic violence at this time, countries' preliminary reports show an alarming increase in rates of domestic violence. For example, the number of cases that were reported to the police in Jingzhou, a city in Hubei province at the epicenter of the COVID-19 outbreak, tripled in February 2020 compared to the number of cases the year before (Allen-Ebrahimian, 2020). In fact, domestic violence in China is estimated to have tripled during the government-imposed lockdown (Campbell, 2020). In France in March 2020, the Minister of Interior reported a 30 % increase in the cases of domestic violence across the country (Ertan et al., 2020). In Paris, officials reported a 36 % increase in the number of domestic violence cases from one week to the next in March 2020 (Ertan et al., 2020; Rauhaus et al., 2020). Brazil estimated that rates of domestic violence rose by 40–50 % (Ertan et al., 2020), and Italy and Germany similarly indicated that domestic violence reports were on the rise (Graham-Harrison et al., 2020).

High rates of domestic violence are common elsewhere in the world. In Iraq, reports have shown an increase in domestic violence due to a lack of knowledge on how to access assistance (Mahmood et al., 2021). The prevalence of domestic violence pre-lockdown and post-lockdown increased dramatically in Iraq, with reports of emotional abuse increasing from 29.5 % to 35 %, physical violence increasing from 12.7 % to 17.6 %, and sexual violence increasing from 10.4 % to 11.3 % (Mahmood et al., 2021). In India, the National Commission for Women (NCW) found a 45 % increase in reports of domestic violence in the first three weeks of March 2020, and the total number increased from 116 to 257 during the final week of March (Kundu & Bhowmik, 2020). However, the actual rates of domestic violence in these countries and elsewhere are likely to be higher as many women, especially those from rural areas, may be afraid to report incidents of abuse and may not be able to file a report during lockdown (Kundu & Bhowmik, 2020).

Several other countries also witnessed increased rates of reported cases of domestic violence during lockdown. The number of calls to emergency helplines to report domestic violence increased by 25 % in the UK, 20 % in Spain, and 30 % in Cyprus within the first few days of the lockdown (Graham-Harrison et al., 2020). In Argentina, domestic violence calls have increased by 25 % since their lockdown on March 20, 2020, and by 33 % in Singapore (Boserup et al., 2020). A national helpline for children in Norway reported a significant increase in the number of calls from worried children when the lockdown started, with many expressing concerns about conflicts and tension at home (Øverlien, 2020). Moreover, there has been an increase in needs for emergency shelters in Canada, Germany, and the United States (Ertan et al., 2020). Along with the surge in the number of calls for assistance, the number of people visiting websites and conducting Google searches about domestic violence and family-related help also increased (Stubbs-Richardson & Sinclair, 2020). Refuge, a UK-based charity supporting victims of domestic abuse, reported a 150 % increase in visits to their website for information about domestic violence support after the UK government imposed a lockdown (Bradbury-Jones & Isham, 2020).

Domestic violence is on the rise in Canada and the United States. A survey by Statistics Canada conducted between March 29 and April 3, 2020, reported that one in 10 women were concerned about the increase in domestic violence (Statistic Canada, 2020). Canada's Assaulted Women's Helpline reported 20,334 calls between September 1 and December 31, 2020, compared to 12,352 calls during the same period in the previous year (Thompson, 2021). Data from the United

States suggests a similar spike in cases. For example, when comparing March 2020 to March 2019, there was a 22 % increase in arrests related to domestic violence in Portland, Oregon (Sharma & Borah, 2020). Similarly, Jefferson County, Alabama experienced a 27 % increase in domestic violence calls, and New York City experienced a 10 % increase in domestic violence calls during March 2020, compared to March 2019 (Sharma & Borah, 2020).

There are growing concerns around the globe about increasing risks of domestic violence-related homicide. Campbell (2020) reported concern of increases in gun and ammunition sales in the United States during the crisis, given the link between firearm access and casualties of domestic violence. Similarly, Spain saw an increase in domestic violence-related homicide (Campbell, 2020). Unfortunately, the trend of increased homicide is expected to continue around the world as stress continues to build while shelter-in-place measurements are extended (Campbell, 2020).

Thus, data suggest that rates of domestic violence increased around the world during the COVID-19 pandemic, especially at the beginning of the pandemic. This surge in domestic violence cases may continue as the status of the COVID-19 pandemic remains uncertain, and mental health issues caused by social isolation and domestic violence may increase as well. Moreover, it is important to keep in mind that the data presented here likely only represent the "tip of the iceberg," as many victims may still be trapped with their perpetrators and unable to report abuse. Rates of domestic violence may be worse than what we know.

ADDRESSING DOMESTIC VIOLENCE DURING COVID-19

Since the beginning of the COVID-19 pandemic, many factors have prevented victims of domestic violence from seeking help and receiving protection from their abusers. Although emergency departments and shelters are often a haven for victims of domestic violence, victims may not have full access to these resources because of pandemic-related issues, such as concerns about COVID-19 transmission. Moreover, as the number of domestic violence victims increases, emergency departments and shelters may not have the capacity to support them (Evans et al., 2020). To deal with these challenges, government agencies and non-government organizations have been working to address domestic violence and assist victims (Ertan et al., 2020).

Ertan et al. (2020) noted that some countries have used a digital system for reporting, monitoring, and accessing help online during the pandemic, and text message services and online calls have been promoted as a medium to support those in need. For example, in Canada, the Canadian Women's Foundation launched the "Signal for Help" campaign[2] to support victims to report domestic violence without being conspicuous or leaving a digital footprint (Canadian Women's Foundation, 2020).

Some governments asked community organizations and businesses for help in making it easier for victims of domestic violence to report an incident. For example, programs in Europe and South America allow victims of domestic violence to report abuse at pharmacies. In Spain, victims can use the code word "mask 19" to report domestic violence anonymously (Rauhaus et al., 2020). Similarly, the governments of France, Italy, and Germany adopted a code word system for reporting domestic violence cases without alerting perpetuators (Rauhaus et al., 2020). In Argentina, women who have experienced domestic violence are encouraged to request a red face mask in pharmacies as a coded request for help (Eisner & Nivette, 2020).

The governments of Italy and France arranged access to hotel rooms for women who leave violent homes and seek safety from abuse, as admission to domestic violence shelters may violate social distancing requirements during lockdown measures (Eisner & Nivette, 2020). Similarly, in the United States, Los Angeles County established a program called "Behind Closed Doors" to assist victims who are afraid of filing claims of abuse and reporting violence (Rauhaus et al., 2020). This campaign called on delivery drivers, landscapers, postal workers, and others in Los Angeles County to contact police if they witnessed signs of abuse in residential homes (Stone et al., 2020). The Los Angeles mayor, Eric Garcetti, also announced the provision of hotel rooms as a shelter for victims of domestic violence during the COVID-19 pandemic (Rauhaus et al., 2020). The mayor credited the advocacy of this work to the celebrity Rihanna and Twitter CEO Jack Dorsey, who had provided financial support for victims, including housing, food, and counseling services (Rauhaus et al., 2020).

Other countries worked to mitigate domestic violence by limiting factors that could exacerbate the problem. For example, the Philippines, South Africa, Greenland, and India aimed to curb rates of domestic violence by banning alcohol sales during lockdown due to concerns of potential increases of domestic violence (Eisner & Nivette, 2020).

Shortcomings of These Programs

There are many factors that have negatively impacted programs designed to support victims of domestic violence during the COVID-19 pandemic, such as an increased focus on public health and economic aspects of the pandemic. Moreover, despite calls from the United Nations for worldwide action to fight the surge of domestic violence by focusing on women's safety as governments respond to the pandemic (Taub, 2020), the discussion surrounding the pandemic in most countries remained focused on the global health perspective of the pandemic and uncertain economies, rather than building a support system for domestic violence victims (Rauhaus et al., 2020). Therefore, there is an urgent need for addressing this issue to minimize the long-term impact of domestic violence during and post-pandemic periods.

Research shows that, unlike other forms of violence, domestic violence is mostly reported by victims after the alleged perpetrator has left the scene (Campbell et al., 2017). This issue is particularly problematic during the pandemic, as many victims are stuck at home with their perpetrators and may not get a chance to leave and report the abuse. Therefore, cases may never get reported, and victims may continue to suffer without access to help and support. During lockdown measures, some countries allowed access to shelters to support those who seek help and leave the violent home (Ertan et al., 2020). However, due to social distancing requirements, these shelters may not have the capacity to accommodate many people. Moreover, many shelters only have the capacity to provide short-term support to women (and often, their children), which increases the risk of victims returning home to an abusive partner when alternatives are not available (Bradbury-Jones, & Isham, 2020).

Social distancing further impacts the communication between victims and the healthcare professionals, as victims who are in the vicinity of their perpetrators do not necessarily have the privacy to openly communicate with their counselors or access help during a telemedicine appointment (Matoori et al., 2020). Moreover, some programs available at pharmacies and other institutions may be difficult for victims of domestic violence to access, as their perpetrators often attempt to limit their contact with the outside world. If reporting is the first step toward addressing domestic violence, then the speed at which law enforcement may act against offenders or abusers is the second step. However, studies show that although suspect identification is more likely when the suspect and the victim are related, arrests are more likely when victims and suspects are strangers (Tasca et al., 2013). Additionally, it is quite common that a victim's prior history (e.g., drug abuse) may also delay the arrest process; and potential delays in arrest are more problematic during a pandemic, as a delay means that the victim and the perpetrator continue to occupy the same space, which may perpetuate further violence (Sharma & Borah, 2020). Overall, these programs do not offer all of the support that victims may require. There is a need for more comprehensive and accessible programs to address domestic violence during and after the COVID-19 pandemic.

POLICY IMPLICATIONS AND RECOMMENDATIONS

Today, policy reforms to address domestic violence and issues related to domestic violence are paramount, especially in times of crises like the current COVID-19 pandemic. The pandemic caught the world by surprise, but it also underlined gaps in existing programs offered for domestic violence victims. This context can provide lessons that policymakers can apply to address gaps and establish more inclusive policies and comprehensive programs. Furthermore, many policies such as alcohol sales and consumption and challenges in accessing support and reporting can negatively impact domestic violence victims. Therefore, policies should be informed by feminist critical theory to ensure that victims' experiences, gap in the existing programs, cultural practices, and patriarchal privileges are not undermined during planning and implementation to avoid any negative effects on policies concerning domestic violence.

Programs and Services

Domestic violence response services require proper knowledge and tools to support victims with different profiles and address increased incidents of physical and emotional violence (Perez-Vincent et al., 2020). In addition, there is a need for a prevention strategy/program, which is not possible until this issue is addressed from the root and the causes that stimulate the vulnerability of people to abuse are highlighted. For instance, a great majority of domestic violence such as physical, sexual, and/or emotional abuse is perpetrated by a victim's intimate partner. Therefore, understanding the causes of this issue must prioritize various policy and academic debates (Perez-Vincent et al., 2020). Some factors of intimate partner violence are deeply rooted in social norms of violence, persistent gender inequality, chronic poverty and alcohol consumption. As such, policymakers should have better tools to control the situation and tackle these issues from the root cause. Therefore, there is a need for policymakers to address these issues and to ensure that other policies and programs do not exacerbate domestic violence during and after the pandemic.

Alcohol Consumption

A rise in alcohol consumption may lead to increased outbursts of domestic violence. Moreover, the data during the COVID-19 pandemic highlighted a clear association between alcohol intake and violence. Therefore, in some countries, alcohol bans were used as one of the strategies to control rates of domestic violence during the pandemic. However, this strategy could also exacerbate the issue of domestic violence, as perpetrators who are struggling with alcohol addiction may be more prone to more violence if they are not able to access alcohol. Moreover, as some countries are easing restrictions, caution is required to prevent a subsequent surge in post-quarantine drinking (Matzopoulos et al., 2020). By examining alcohol consumption as a factor of increased domestic violence, policymakers should ensure that alcohol-related policies do not add to this surge.

Reporting

Improving processes for reporting incidents of domestic violence also requires heightened attention. Policymakers and governments must establish rules and regulations for flexible reporting to allow victims to come forward and seek help more easily. Victims often fear coming forward due to extensive paperwork and long waiting periods for reporting (Sharma & Borah, 2020). Shortening this process or setting a specific timeline in which victims receive support could also encourage more reporting. This system would assure victims that legal support will be available to them, despite constraints on other resources. This is significant because some victims may not want to take legal action or involve police due to fear of status loss and embarrassment, protection of the perpetrator, fear of retaliation, opportunity costs, or victims' own criminal past (Sharma & Borah, 2020).

Policy Implications

The discussion above highlights policy implications of domestic violence during the pandemic and presents a call for action to address these issues not only during pandemic but also beyond. How domestic violence cases are handled by authorities also has immediate policy implications (Bright et al., 2020). Domestic violence victims must know that their needs are prioritized and that there are support systems available for them. This can encourage victims to trust the system, come forward and report incidents of domestic violence. Although the COVID-19 pandemic challenged service provisions to domestic violence victims, it is important for victims to learn and understand which services are available to them. Bright et al. (2020) suggest that to ensure that victims' needs are prioritized during times of crisis, there is a need for domestic violence awareness training for all stakeholders who are involved in service provisions and are in contact with the domestic violence victims. Moreover, the allocation of funding and resources to increase the number of available shelters and other social and economic support systems for victims who leave home is fundamental. It is important to note that different policies concerning domestic violence must be informed by a feminist critical framework to ensure that these policies are gender conscious and that victims' experiences, and cultural practices are not undermined in policy development.

CONCLUSION AND CALL FOR ACTION

The reality is that we were hardly "winning" the fight to end domestic violence even before the COVID-19 pandemic. Many organizations around the globe were already experiencing pressures of increased workloads and diminishing resources. Now, many find themselves facing even greater barriers and challenges during the pandemic. Therefore, it is important more than ever to establish different strategies to address this global concern and develop long-term and comprehensive policies to address domestic violence and overcome economic, psychological, and physical vulnerabilities that the pandemic has exacerbated. These policies can be designed through different programs that impact domestic violence as discussed above. It is also important to note that one size won't fit all, and that policy and programs should thus be tailored based on the needs identified in each country, as circumstances can be unique to each region.

The multifaceted challenges associated with domestic violence require collaboration, cooperation, and partnerships among different actors and agencies in the public, private, and non-profit sectors such as healthcare professionals, civil society organization and advocates, researchers, law enforcement, local and international level responders and protective networks and social services (Rauhaus et al., 2020). Furthermore, there is a need for community partnerships such as faith-based organizations, youth clubs, libraries, sports clubs, postal workers, garbage collectors, food delivery staff, and everyone in community networks to come together and address this problem (Campbell, 2020).

Moreover, improving community collaborations and partnerships can help incorporate values of compassion, ethics of care, and empathy into the emergency context and promote individual agencies as key stakeholders to ensure public safety during a pandemic (Rauhaus et al., 2020). When and if victims cannot report domestic violence, the roles of community members, neighbors, and other bystanders become more vital. Therefore, it is important for governments to educate the public about domestic violence and encourage citizens to help one another and report incidents of violence when they notice it.

Studies also suggest that a major reason for domestic violence includes a lack of psychological capital (e.g., hope, resilience, optimism, self-efficacy) and creating this capital is a crucial step for creating a positive future (Sharma & Borah, 2020). Therefore, it is important to take this proactive approach and invest in psychological capital (e.g., accessible counseling programs, self-care trainings and more), rather than cultivating a reactive approach (i.e., acting after violence). This strategy might be more useful to combat domestic violence during the pandemic, as many stressors can exacerbate the situation. Guaranteeing a victim's economic safety and strengthening social supports are also necessary and can enhance this process.

If we allow domestic violence to remain in the shadows, it will continue to increase and become more challenging. Therefore, it is important to take this issue seriously and fight the pandemic within homes as much as outside. Stressors such as unemployment, child and elderly care, financial instability, fear of virus, illness or death combined with the mental health toll of social distancing measures are all factors that exacerbate domestic violence during the pandemic. Therefore, there is a need for significant attention from policymakers, government and non-profit agencies to address domestic violence during the post-pandemic period. This study provided an in-depth analysis on the increment of domestic violence during the pandemic and the policy implications of this issue. Therefore, this chapter can serve as a foundation and a first step toward addressing domestic violence issues during the pandemic and beyond.

NOTES

1 Department of Integrated Studies in Education, McGill University.
2 Signal for Help is a simple single-hand gesture that can be visually and silently displayed during video calls to alert family, friends, or colleagues that an individual needs help and that they would like someone to check in safely with them. For more information, visit the Canadian Women's Foundation website.

REFERENCES

Allen-Ebrahimian, B. (2020, March 7). *China's domestic violence epidemic*. Axios. https://www.axios.com/2020/03/07/china-domestic-violence-coronavirus-quarantine

Bidin, A., & Yusoff, J. (2015). Abuse of the Malaysian Elderly: An analysis on the adequacy and suitability of the Domestic Violence Act 1994 (Act 521) to protect the elderly victim. *Journal of Management Research, 7*(2), 71.

Boserup, B., McKenney, M., & Elkbuli, A. (2020). Alarming trends in US domestic violence during the COVID-19 pandemic. *The American Journal of Emergency Medicine, 38*(12), 2753–2755.

Bouillon-Minois, J., Clinchamps, M., & Dutheil, F. (2020). Coronavirus and quarantine: Catalysts of domestic violence. *Violence Against Women*. https://doi.org/10.1177/1077801220935194

Bradbury-Jones, C., & Isham, L. (2020). The pandemic paradox: The consequences of COVID-19 on domestic violence. *Journal of Clinical Nursing, 29*(13–14), 2047–2049.

Bright, C., Burton, C., & Kosky, M. (2020). Considerations of the impacts of COVID-19 on domestic violence in the United States. *Social Sciences & Humanities Open, 2*(1).

Browne, A., & Finkelhor, D. (1986). Impact of child sexual abuse: A review of the research. *Psychological Bulletin, 99*(1), 66–77.

Bullinger, L., Carr, J., & Packham, A. (2021). COVID-19 and crime. *American Journal of Health Economics, 7*(3), 249–280.

Buzawa, E. S., & Buzawa, C. G. (2017). Introduction: The evolution of efforts to combat domestic violence. In *Global responses to domestic violence* (pp. 1–19). Springer.

Campbell, A. (2020). An increasing risk of family violence during the COVID-19 pandemic: Strengthening community collaborations to save lives. *Forensic Science International: Reports, 2*.

Campbell, A., Hicks, R., Thompson, S., & Wiehe, S. (2017). Characteristics of intimate partner violence incidents and the environments in which they occur: Victim reports to responding law enforcement officers. *Journal of Interpersonal Violence, 35*(13–14), 2583–2606.

Canadian Women's Foundation. (2020, April 14). *Signal for Help campaign launches to help people experiencing gender-based violence during home isolation.* https://canadianwomen.org/signal-for-help-campaign-launches-to-help-people-experiencing-gender-based-violence-during-home-isolation/

Chan, J., Yuan, S., Kok, K., To, K., Chu, H., & Yang, J., Xing, F., Liu, J., Yip, C. C., Poon, R. W., Tsoi, H. W., Lo, S. K., Chan, K. H., Poon, V. K., Chan, W. M., Ip, J. D., Cai, J. P., Cheng, V. C., Chen, H., Hui, C. K., ... Yuen, K. Y. (2020). A familial cluster of pneumonia associated with the 2019 novel coronavirus indicating person-to-person transmission: A study of a family cluster. *The Lancet, 395*(10223), 514–523.

Creedon, P. (1993). Acknowledging the infrasystem: A critical feminist analysis of systems theory. *Public Relations Review, 19*(2), 157–166.

Eisner, M., & Nivette, A. (2020). *Violence and the pandemic.* Urgent questions for research (HFG Research and Policy in Brief). HFG.

Ertan, D., El-Hage, W., Thierrée, S., Javelot, H., & Hingray, C. (2020). COVID-19: Urgency for distancing from domestic violence. *European Journal of Psychotraumatology, 11*(1), 1800245.

Evans, M., Lindauer, M., & Farrell, M. (2020). A pandemic within a pandemic: Intimate partner violence during COVID-19. *New England Journal of Medicine, 383*(24), 2302–2304.

Finkelhor, D. (2010). *Sexually victimized children.* Free Press.

Graham-Harrison, E., Giuffrida, A., Smith, H., & Ford, L. (2020, March 28). Lockdowns around the world bring rise in domestic violence. *The Guardian.* https://www.theguardian.com/society/2020/mar/28/lockdowns-world-rise-domestic-violence

Kundu, B., & Bhowmik, D. (2020). Societal impact of novel corona virus (COVID-19) pandemic in India. *SocArXiv.* https://doi.org/10.31219/osf.io/vm5rz

Lawrence, C. R., III, Matsuda, M. J., Delgado, R., & Crenshaw, K. W. (1993). Introduction. In M. J. Matsuda, C. R. Lawrence III, R. Delgado, & K. Crenshaw (Eds.), *Words that wound: Critical Race Theory, assaultive speech, and the first amendment* (pp. 1–16). Westview Press.

Mahmood, K., Shabu, S., M-Amen, K., Hussain, S., Kako, D., Hinchliff, S., & Shabila, N. (2021). The impact of COVID-19 related lockdown on the prevalence of spousal violence against women in Kurdistan region of Iraq. *Journal of Interpersonal Violence, 37*(13–14), NP11811–NP11835.

Matoori, S., Khurana, B., Balcom, M., Koh, D., Froehlich, J., & Janssen, S., Kolokythas, O., & Gutzeit, A. (2020). Intimate partner violence crisis in the COVID-19 pandemic: How can radiologists make a difference? *European Radiology, 30*(12), 6933–6936.

Matzopoulos, R., Walls, H., Cook, S., & London, L. (2020). South Africa's COVID-19 alcohol sales ban: The potential for better policy-making. *International Journal of Health Policy and Management, 9*(11), 486.

Øverlien, C. (2020). The COVID-19 pandemic and its impact on children in domestic violence refuges. *Child Abuse Review, 29*(4), 379–386.

Perez-Vincent, S. M., Carreras, E., Gibbons, M. A., Murphy, T. E., & Rossi, M. A. (2020). *COVID-19 lockdowns and domestic violence*. Inter-American Development Bank.

Rauhaus, B., Sibila, D., & Johnson, A. (2020). Addressing the increase of domestic violence and abuse during the COVID-19 pandemic: A need for empathy, care, and social equity in collaborative planning and responses. *The American Review of Public Administration, 50*(6–7), 668–674.

Rhode, D. L. (2018). *Feminist Critical Theories [1990]* (pp. 333–350). Routledge.

Sharma, A., & Borah, S. (2020). COVID-19 and domestic violence: An indirect path to social and economic crisis. *Journal of Family Violence, 37*, 759–765.

Statistic Canada. (2020, May 8). Canadian Perspectives Survey Series 1: Impacts of COVID-19. https://www150.statcan.gc.ca/n1/daily-quotidien/200408/dq200408c-eng.htm

Stone, A., Mallin, A., & Gutman, M. (2020, April 25). *Fewer domestic violence calls during COVID-19 outbreak has California officials concerned*. ABC News. https://abcnews.go.com/US/fewer-domestic-violence-calls-COVID-19-outbreak-california/story?id=70336388

Stubbs-Richardson, M., & Sinclair, C. H. (2020, December 4). *Intimate partner violence has increased during pandemic, emerging evidence suggests*. The Conversation. https://theconversation.com/intimate-partner-violence-has-increased-during-pandemic-emerging-evidence-suggests-148326

Tasca, M., Rodriguez, N., Spohn, C., & Koss, M. P. (2013). Police decision making in sexual assault cases: Predictors of suspect identification and arrest. *Journal of Interpersonal Violence, 28*(6), 1157–1177.

Taub, A. (2020, April 6). A new COVID-19 crisis: Domestic abuse rises worldwide. *The New York Times*. https://www.nytimes.com/2020/04/06/world/coronavirus-domestic-violence.html

Thompson, N. (2021, February 15). *Reports of domestic, intimate partner violence continue to rise during pandemic*. CTV News. https://www.ctvnews.ca/health/coronavirus/reports-of-domestic-intimate-partner-violence-continue-to-rise-during-pandemic-1.5309118

Tracy, S. (2007). Patriarchy and domestic violence: Challenging common misconceptions. *Journal of the Evangelical Theological Society, 50*(3), 573–594.

Whelehan, I., & Pilcher, J. (2004). *Fifty key concepts in gender studies*. Sage.

Wood, S., & Sommers, M. (2011). Consequences of intimate partner violence on child witnesses: A systematic review of the literature. *Journal of Child and Adolescent Psychiatric Nursing, 24*(4), 223–236.

World Health Organization. (2013, October 20). *Global and regional estimates of violence against women: Prevalence and health effects of intimate partner violence and non-partner sexual violence*. https://www.who.int/publications/i/item/9789241564625

Xue, J., Chen, J., Chen, C., Hu, R., & Zhu, T. (2020). The hidden pandemic of family violence during COVID-19: Unsupervised learning of tweets. *Journal of Medical Internet Research, 22*(11), e24361.

PART II

Education

Education

CHAPTER FOUR

Making Sense of Zoombombing in the Context of COVID-19 and Mandatory Online Learning: An Exploratory Study

AMANDA COUTURE-CARRON, MICHELE PICH, AND NAWAL AMMAR[1]

Abstract: To slow the spread of the highly contagious COVID-19 virus, universities across the United States closed their doors to students and transitioned to online learning, including the use of video-conferencing platforms. One unanticipated problem of this transition was the phenomenon of "zoombombing" in which unwanted individuals join virtual meetings and verbally shout or graphically show pornography, and make racist statements and/or sexual remarks. Given the novelty of zoombombing, our understanding of it and its consequences are limited. This chapter considers whether zoombombing can be understood as harassment, cyberbullying, or something else, in which case it would be rendered as a distinct phenomenon worthy of its own focus and analysis. The chapter provides an overview of these two types of attacks (i.e., harassment and cyberbullying), how they compare to zoombombing in the university classroom context, and their potential impacts on students. We conclude that there are important distinctions between zoombombing and these types of attacks, which in turn limit their ability to account for the complexities of zoombombing. There are, however, aspects of harassment and cyberbullying that offer insight into elements of zoombombing, which together shed light on this novel phenomenon.

Keywords: zoombombing, COVID-19 pandemic, online learning, harassment, cyberbullying, universities

INTRODUCTION

In March 2020, the World Health Organization declared COVID-19 a global pandemic (Viner et al., 2020). To slow the spread of this highly contagious (and sometimes fatal) virus, universities across the United States closed their doors to students, faculty, and staff (Murphy, 2020). In response, universities also rapidly transitioned to online learning models (Murphy, 2020), including the use of video-conferencing platforms to replace face-to-face (in-vivo) interactions (see Chapter Six). Overall, universities expected several technological and social issues to emerge with this transition. One unanticipated problem, however, was the phenomenon of "zoombombing" on various video-conferencing platforms.

With its name derived from the online video-conferencing platform, Zoom, combined with the term "photo-bombing," the novel phenomenon of zoombombing refers to unwelcomed and uninvited individuals joining a virtual meeting, often verbally shouting or graphically showing pornography, making racist statements, and/or sexual remarks assailing audience members (Elmer et al., 2020). A recent study on zoombombing found that almost 87 % of YouTube compilations of zoombombing incidents involved racist, misogynistic, homophobic, sexual, and other offensive content (Elmer et al., 2020). Approximately 72 % of the videos that the researchers studied involved "mob-like interruptions, with multiple voices, screams, profanities and other sounds occurring at the same time" (Elmer et al., 2020).

The media documents numerous incidents of zoombombing within various institutions and organizations, including Alcoholic Anonymous (Bindley, 2020), churches (Molina, 2020) and universities (Redden, 2020). In March 2020, the FBI issued a statement documenting nationwide reports of zoombombing, declaring it a cybercrime that should be reported to the FBI (Setera, 2020). The frequency of zoombombing during online university events and activities is currently unknown. However, numerous articles from educational media sources (e.g., The Chronicle of Higher Education, Inside Higher Ed, University Business) suggest that zoombombing across U.S. universities intensified during the pandemic lockdown.

The focus of this chapter is on occurrences of zoombombing in university-level classroom settings as it relates to students, with faculty members being part of this setting. We focus on zoombombing attacks of a sexual nature, including those that intersect with racist attacks. Since this chapter focuses on zoombombing at universities, here are a few examples reported in newspapers and personal communication with one of the authors:

> Early on in the lockdown at a public university in the mid-Atlantic region of the U.S., a "women's studies" second year (sophomore) course was zoombombed by a person who

targeted the professor (who is female presenting), using anti-Semitic and sexist attacks and also attacked a few women students by using sexual profanities (personal communication).

At another public university in the western region of the U.S., an astronomy class was zoombombed within five minutes of its start. According to the student, "[The professor] gave them the space to ask their questions, then the professor was bombarded by someone repeatedly referring to him in the n-word" (personal communication).

The March 26, 2020, Inside Higher Education edition reports on a 150-student "introduction to storytelling" course at Arizona State University. One of the participants used a Zoom feature that lets a user display an image or a video in the background to show a pornographic video. The professor did not notice it until one student drew his attention to the video. The professor noted that participants were using fake screen names, some of which he said were very offensive. The chatroom was very active with comments outside the lecture's topic, which used "vulgar, racist, and misogynistic" language. (Redden, 2020)

Despite the increased attention on zoombombing, our understanding of it and its consequences are limited. As such, various stakeholders have referred to zoombombing incidents in several ways, including cyberbullying, harassment, and racist/hate talk. The FBI has called these attacks cyber harassment (Andone, 2020), and the Anti-Defamation League has identified zoombombing as perpetuating hate (Associated Press, 2021). The purpose of this chapter is to consider where zoombombing falls vis-à-vis the various types of attacks by which it has been described. In particular, we consider whether zoombombing can be understood as traditional harassment, or cyberbullying, or something else, rendering it a distinct phenomenon worthy of its own focus and analysis. We provide an overview of these two types of attacks and how they compare to zoombombing in the university classroom context and its potential impact on students. We conclude that there are important distinctions between zoombombing and the aforementioned types of attacks, which in turn limit their ability to account for the complexities of zoombombing. There are, however, aspects of harassment and cyberbullying that offer insight into elements of zoombombing, which together shed light on this novel phenomenon.

ZOOMBOMBING AND HARASSMENT

In this section of the chapter, we examine the similarities and differences of harassment and zoombombing as forms of unwanted sexual behavior (i.e., attacks). The objective of this comparison is to answer the question of whether zoombombing is a distinct phenomenon of unwanted behavior, including those of a sexual nature, worthy of its own focus and analysis.

Harassment is pervasive on U.S. university campuses. For example, the 2019 Association of American Universities' (AAU) Campus Climate Survey of 33 universities on sexual assault and misconduct indicated that 41.8 % of students reported experiencing at least one sexual harassment incident, while 18.9 % of students reported experiencing sexually harassing behavior that interfered with their overall university experience. Klein and Martin (2019) noted that findings indicated that being a woman, White, or a sexual minority increased a student's likelihood of experiencing sexual harassment while at a college/university. Researchers also found that trans students nationwide report greater levels of harassment and discrimination (Dugan et al., 2012; Garvey & Rankin, 2015; James et al., 2016). In contrast, research on LGBTQ+ students' experiences with harassment is limited. According to the AAU, about three in four LGBT students report experiencing sexual harassment (Cantor et al., 2015). The incidence of sexual misconduct among those who identify as trans, gay, queer, or nonconforming was 39.1 %, the highest rate among all demographics of students (Cantor et al., 2015).

Title IX

Title IX, which is part of the U.S. Education Amendments of 1972, is the statute that protects against sexual harassment and encourages equal treatment regardless of sex in educational institutions. Title IX defines sexual harassment as "unwanted and unwelcome sexual behaviour which interferes with your life" (American Association of University Women, 2020). The U.S. Department of Education's Office for Civil Rights (OCR) monitors and delegates sexual discrimination cases that fall under Title IX (Puluse, 2020). Title IX states: "no person in the United States shall, on the basis of sex, be excluded from participation in, be denied the benefits of, or be subjected to discrimination under any education program or activity receiving Federal financial assistance" (U.S. Department of Education Office for Civil Rights, 2015).

In addition to its enforcement activities, OCR provides technical assistance, information and guidance to schools, universities, and other agencies to assist them in voluntarily complying with the law (U.S. Department of Education Office for Civil Rights, 2015).

Title IX initially focused on what happens in the classroom (FindLaw's Team, 2017). That focus soon shifted to sports spaces (e.g., playing field), personal spaces (e.g., bedrooms), and public spaces (e.g., bathrooms). Over the past five decades, the understanding of non-discrimination underlying Title IX has steadily drifted from eliminating institutional barriers to educational opportunity for women and girls, and toward the aim of changing the way we think about sex differences, gender roles, and sexuality in general (Green, 2018). One of the changes in Title IX took place in 2010 to include sex-based cyberbullying as a type of harassment that is prohibited by law. The OCR issued a guidance document in October 2010, specifying that Title IX prohibits sex-based bullying and harassment that interferes with a student's education, whether it is conducted in person or electronically (Beavers & Halabi, 2017). Between 2011 and 2016, OCR offered a reinterpretation and expansion of Title IX of the Education Amendment of 1972 (Beavers & Halabi, 2017). In what has become known as the "Dear Colleague Letter" (DCL) during the Obama administration (Melnick, 2018), the definition of "discrimination" under Title IX became broad and covered: "Sexual harassment of students, which includes acts of sexual violence ... [s]exual violence, as the term is used in this letter, refers to physical sexual acts perpetrated against a person's will or where a person is incapable of giving consent due to the victim's use of drugs or alcohol" (Beavers & Halabi, 2017, p. X). The DCL also clarified that Title IX's prohibition against sex-based discrimination extends to claims of discrimination based on gender identity (FindLawa's Team, 2017). The DCL told schools to "take immediate action to eliminate the harassment, prevent its recurrence, and address its effects" (FindLawa's Team, 2017). One clear instruction of the DCL was that the level of proof the plaintiff must provide is based on the "preponderance of the evidence" standard (i.e., a greater than 50 % chance that a claim is true) rather than a higher standard, such as "clear and convincing evidence," to determine whether an incident of sexual harassment or assault occurred (FindLawa's Team, 2017).

The DCL Title IX guidelines drew harsh bi-partisan criticisms, because they threatened "due process" and "freedom of speech" (Melnick, 2018). In November 2018, the Trump administration's Department of Education proposed major changes to Title IX enforcement (Gersen, 2020). The Trump administration's Title IX regulations limited the definition of sexual harassment to "severe" and "pervasive," or else the charge would be dismissed (Gersen, 2020). The new regulations allow schools to choose between the preponderance standard or the higher "clear and convincing evidence" standard, which would demand heavier proof to find that an accused is responsible (Gersen, 2020). Colleges and universities were required to hold live hearings with the option of a cross-examination of the accuser and the accused, in which each party picks an adviser (Gersen, 2020). In early March 2021, President Biden ordered education officials to start considering how to rollback Trump administration rules that bolster the rights of the accused and limit the cases schools must handle. The campaign promise he made was to reinstate Obama-era Title IX guidelines (Murakmi, 2021).

Zoombombing and Title IX

Zoombombing is an attack that many colleges and universities in the United States have identified as harassment—racial and sexual—not only because it involves unwanted attention or actions by a perpetrator against one or multiple victims, but also because of the 2010 changes in Title IX. In both types of attacks (sexual harassment and sexual zoombombing attacks), perpetrators often target victims who are members of a specific demographic based on race, gender, ethnicity, sexual orientation, religion, or another minority category (Wolff et al., 2017). Zoombombing incidents in most U.S. universities have been included under the auspices of Title IX for students, unless there is an egregious racial attack (Wolff et al., 2017). The question we are posing in this section relates to whether sexual zoombombing attacks[2] are similar or different from sexual harassment, and whether they require a different kind of response and university services than those available through Title IX.

Similarities Between Zoombombing and Harassment

There are several similarities between in vivo sexual harassment and zoombombing. Perpetrators of both forms target their victims based on gendered characteristics. In both cases, there are often witnesses who may or may not wish to be active bystanders. Similarly, although sexual zoombombing occurs via video-conferencing platforms (i.e., virtually), it still occurs in a public space or forum—albeit digital—where a group has gathered (e.g., a course lecture). As such, like in-vivo sexual harassment, sexual zoombombing is often witnessed by others in public spaces. Both zoombombing and sexual harassment also occur in real time. Sexual harassment attacks have an impact on the victim and empirical research shows that in-vivo sexual harassment impacts health and may cause depression, anxiety, eating disorders, post-traumatic stress disorder, and suicidal ideation, as well as the inability to study or pay attention in class, skipping class, or transferring altogether from the institution (Fedina et al., 2016). While little research on the precise impact of zoombombing sexual attacks (ZSAs) has been conducted, one can extrapolate that the impact could be similar with some variation. ZSAs are often a one-time occurrence; however, they may lead to ongoing fear that it could happen again. In this way, it is similar to in-vivo sexual harassment (Wolff et al., 2017). Additionally, at this point in time, under Title IX, U.S. universities are responsible for reporting both zoombombing and sexual harassment incidents and referring students to available services. One other similarity between ZSAs and in-vivo sexual harassment is that in both cases, there has been very little research on the characteristics of the perpetrator.

Differences Between Zoombombing and Harassment

There are some characteristics of ZSAs that are distinct from traditional, in-vivo sexual harassment situations. These include legal recourse, clarity of targets, persistence/recurrence, and location. ZSAs do not have a distinct legal recourse and universities in the United States. have been dealing with them under Title IX,[3] Title VI,[4] and VII[5] (for students),[6] more for expediency and not as a deliberate response. As a result, and unlike in-vivo sexual harassment, the legal recourse is not clearly articulated, nor are guidelines that account for the discrepancies between the experiences of in-vivo and virtual sexual harassment provided. Another distinction between ZSAs and in-vivo sexual harassment is the precision of the target. Oftentimes, it is unclear who the perpetrator is specifically targeting during a zoombombing attack. Sometimes the perpetrator is using racial and sexual slurs targeting the entire group, while sometimes individuals are targeted by name and subjected to sexual and racial insults. Additionally, the zoombomber may only decide on the target once they enter the virtual room. Moreover, the nature of how Zoom (and other video-conferencing platforms) displays participants on the screen during large public forums makes it difficult to ascertain who and how many people are targeted. ZSAs are also distinct from sexual harassment because the latter is a recurring and unremitting attempt to badger a victim (Hinduja & Patchin, 2020). On the other hand, ZSAs are often a single incident, in that the perpetrator does not repeatedly target the same individuals (Hinduja & Patchin, 2020). Sexual zoombombers—unlike traditional sexual harassers—may be difficult to identify, hold accountable, or stop. As such, this may exacerbate the fear of zoombombing, which may be further intensified given that virtual meetings and classrooms will likely continue even beyond the current pandemic. Another difference between ZSAs and traditional sexual harassment includes its location. Although both occur in public spaces, ZSAs simultaneously occur in private physical and social spaces (albeit online) often perceived as safe, such as in one's home or a classroom. Since many students and faculty members log into video-conferencing platforms from their homes, and even from their own bedrooms, ZSAs invade the sanctity of these spaces, as they have become the scene of these attacks (Redden, 2020).

ZOOMBOMBING AND CYBERBULLYING

Cyberbullying is another existing type of attack that zoombombing may fall within. Cyberbullying refers to the use of information and communication technology to create disturbances that are intentional and often repeated, and they target a specific group or individual (Akbulut & Eristi, 2011; Faucher et al., 2015). Specifically, Faucher et al. (2014, p. 3) note that "cyberbullying uses language that can defame, threaten, harass, bully, exclude, discriminate, demean, humiliate, stalk, disclose personal information, or contain offensive, vulgar or derogatory comments ... intended to harm or hurt the recipient." Cyberbullying takes a variety of forms, including creating and sharing embarrassing images or videos; sending homophobic, racist, or sexist material; creating fake accounts; hijacking; and/or stealing online identities to embarrass someone or cause trouble using their name (Faucher et al., 2014; Myers & Cowie, 2017). Cyberbullying refers to several different online bullying activities, with varying perspectives on what to include (Shariff, 2015). As such, various scholars suggest that not every case of sexting[7] might be uniformly harmful or considered as an attack (Shariff, 2015; Jewkes & Wykes, 2012).[8] Perasso and colleagues (2020) noted that there are two distinct forms of cyberbullying victimization: visual and written. Female-presenting students are associated more often with written cyberbullying victimization.

There is a common misconception that cyberbullying happens during early teenage years and that it does not happen at the university level (Myers & Cowie, 2017). This idea has been challenged by several empirical researchers who show that young adults appear to be vulnerable to this type of cyberbullying online attack. A 2017 Pew Research Center study showed that 67 % of young adults aged 18–29 had been harassed online, and 41 % had experienced severe online harassment. Research on university students shows that one-quarter report being victims of cyberbullying (Chisholm, 2014; MacDonald & Roberts-Pittman, 2010). Moreover, Schenk and Fremouw (2012) noted the rates of cyberbullying among adults range from 8 % to 21 %, with a worrisome impact on students' mental health and academic performance.

Example Cases

Given its prevalence among university students and the emphasis of this chapter, we focus on sexual cyberbullying at the university level. For illustration, we consider its manifestation in public cases, such as the senior thesis sex joke perpetrated by student Karen Owen of Duke University on 13 student members of a university's lacrosse, baseball, and tennis teams in 2010, and the case of Tyler Clementi of Rutgers University in 2010 (Washington, 2015). We summarize Karen Owen's case below but emphasize Tyler Clementi's story because the cyberbullying cost him his life and resulted in ongoing advocacy to pass the *Tyler Clementi Higher Education Anti-Harassment Act* (TCHEAHC). These two cases illustrate forms of cyberbullying that can take place on university campuses, as well as the traumatizing consequences of cyberbullying.

Karen Owen

Karen Owen, the cyberbullying perpetrator, prepared a mock senior thesis and summarized it in a PowerPoint with pictures where she evaluated her sexual liaisons with 13 student athletes during her years at the school and posted it on "horizontal academics" (Seelye & Robbins 2010; Washington, 2015). One of her friends shared the thesis online, which went viral. The thesis went out on listservs, was published by Jezebel (for women) and Deadspin (for sports addicts), and eventually spread on Twitter (Hill, 2010). The widespread dissemination of the thesis instigated discussions about the internet and privacy (Hill, 2020).

Tyler Clementi

In his last year of high school, Clementi began the journey of coming out to close family and friends. In August 2010, Clementi entered his freshman year as a student at Rutgers University, New Jersey. Clementi's roommate, Dharun Ravi, had conducted background research prior to the start of the academic year and discovered that Tylor was gay. Ravi tweeted, "found out my roommate is gay." With the help of a friend, Ravi secretly filmed Clementi's sexual encounters in the dorm room on two separate occasions. First, Ravi and his friend Wei privately watched the stream together then turned it on for others in the room to watch. Ravi then streamed the video live broadcasting it to his 150 Twitter followers, outing Clementi in the process. Ravi tweeted, "roommate asked for the room till midnight. I went into Ravi Molly's room and turned on my webcam. I saw him making out with a dude. Yay" (Pilkington, 2010; Washington, 2015). On the second occasion, Ravi tweeted that it is "happening again," but Clementi eventually noticed the camera and unplugged it to prevent further video streaming during his date. Before the camera was unplugged, Ravi and his friend watched and streamed it on Twitter (Washington, 2015). Ravi, alerted by his dorm resident adviser that Clementi was aware of his spying and wanted a room change, sent Clementi a text and an email apologizing. No one is sure whether Clementi ever received the apology, because the text was sent at approximately the same time that Clementi jumped off a bridge (Miller, 2017; Parker, 2020).

Similarities Between Zoombombing and Cyberbullying

Cyberbullying and zoombombing have several features in common. One such similarity is their legal status. It took several years for cyberbullying to be recognized as distinct from traditional bullying, while zoombombing is still an emerging phenomenon under the umbrella of sexual and racial attacks that happen online. However, cyberbullying (like zoombombing) continues to be an issue addressed by laws that are not specifically tailored to it (e.g., related to harassment, discrimination, defamation, internet obscenity, fraud, or school policies). The lack of federal laws regulating cyberbullying, which has been a much more persistent problem on the public scene than zoombombing, may foreshadow what to expect from zoombombing attacks, if post-COVID-19 modes of instruction at universities continue to use video-conferencing platforms.

Zoombombing and cyberbullying are both attacks of liminal legal status in the sense that they oscillate between being identified within other forms of harassment. Moreover, it seems that in their progression, they have been subsumed under subsets of physical space attacks—cyberbullying as a subclass of bullying and zoombombing as a subclass of harassment (sexual and racial). It is worth analyzing the current laws covering cyberbullying in the United States, because they demonstrate the potential progression of zoombombing attacks in the legal system in the coming years.

Differences Between Zoombombing and Cyberbullying

Although cyberbullying and zoombombing share common characteristics, there are many aspects that differentiate them. In cyberbullying, the relationship between the victim and the perpetrator is often different from traditional bullying. Victims often do not know the perpetrator well or even at all, and hence are unable to react appropriately (Raskauskas, 2010).[9] Perpetrators of cyberbullying are more aggressive and less understanding of the effects of their actions on the victim than perpetrators of traditional bullying, since they cannot see victims or do not know them well or even at all (Eristi & Akbulut, 2019). Unlike traditional bullying, where physical power and peer status are sources of social power (Patchin & Hinduja, 2015), in cyberbullying, greater technological expertise could provide a power imbalance (Slonje et al., 2013; Vandebosch & Van Cleemput, 2008).[10]

In cyberbullying, a provocative post by a perpetrator could be reposted by those who are not the initial perpetrator. Unlike conventional in vivo harassment where victims may get some reprieve whenever separated from the physical presence of their aggressor, cyberbullying is a persistent asynchronous form of attack, which continues even after the initial interaction has ended (Nathan, 2021). Studies report a range of reactions to cyberbullying, including anger, sadness, crying vulnerability, fear, frustration, self-blame, suicidal ideations and, as in the case of Clementi, suicide (Eristi & Akbulut, 2019; Schenk & Fremouw, 2012).

Reactions to cyberbullying differ between high school and undergraduate students. University students are more likely to react with countermeasures relative to high school students, who predominantly react by avoidance (Eristi & Akbulut, 2019). There is also a difference between female- and male-presenting students' reactions to cyberbullying, where male-presenting students more frequently choose revenge and female-presenting students are more prone to choose countermeasures (Eristi & Akbulut, 2019).

While both types of attacks occur online, attackers use different platforms to target their victims. Cyberbullies often use a variety of social media and other online communication platforms, such as Ask.fm, Facebook, Instagram, Snapchat, Twitter, Yolo, YouTube, and WhatsApp (Securly, 2019), while zoombombers exclusively use video-conferencing platforms, including Zoom, WebEx, Google Meet, Microsoft Teams, Facebook Messenger Rooms, and Skype. (For a comprehensive list, see stopbullying.gov in the references.) Using video-conferencing platforms means that zoombombing attacks can take two forms: audio and/or visual. Both of those potential forms occur in real time and during regular university/event hours. Cyberbullying, on the other hand, can occur asynchronously, which makes it possible for these attacks to occur at all hours. Zoombombing attacks are often one-time incidents (not repeated), sudden, and temporally brief (i.e., can be ended relatively quickly and have no permanent record beyond those present if the session were recorded). On the other hand, cyberbullying is often more persistent (not necessarily repetitive), lasts longer, and the content of the attacks can remain on the internet in the long term.

In the context of higher education, zoombombers often attack formal/professional lectures, events, or meetings. As such, zoombombing happens in more formal gatherings and educational settings (Joia & Lorenzo, 2021), whereas cyberbullying (in educational settings) often occurs on social media platforms (Securly, 2019) that are arguably a more informal setting (Patchin & Hinduja, 2006). Zoombombing differs from cybercrime because it is a one-time harassment that—wittingly or unwittingly—targets both individuals and a group simultaneously. The consequences of this simultaneous intimidation of zoombombing are experienced by individuals and the entire group of students and faculty member(s) attending the Zoom session. Since the intimidation takes form in a group's formal setting, the norms and behaviors existing in this group require resetting through tailored support.

Cyberbullying and zoombombing both contribute to cybervictimization (Raskauskas, 2010). Several researchers using victimology's lifestyle-routine activities perspective, which derives from Cohen and Felson's routine activities theory, have noted that this type of victimization is related to time spent using communication technologies (Bossler & Holt, 2009; Finn, 2004). Cohen and Felson's (1979) routine activities theory framed victimization relative to time spent in at-risk situations without a capable guardian and a motivated offender (Bossler & Holt, 2009; Raskauskas, 2010). In the case of cyberbullying, cybervictimization can be understood within such a lifestyle-routine activity perspective because of the increasing number of individuals using electronics (more time in the at-risk situation), and several motivated savvy techies (i.e., offenders) waiting for an innocent user (i.e., victim), with often neither having a capable guardian.

However, in the case of zoombombing at the university level, the lifestyle-routine theory lacks one of its necessary variables: the non-existence of capable guardianship. While COVID-19 has increased the time in the at-risk situation (moving classes to virtual video conferencing) and there are a number of motivated savvy potential offenders waiting for the innocent user, there has almost always been a capable guardian (e.g., professor, student leader) present in zoombombing incidences. Moreover, post-pandemic, as university teaching returns to the classroom, or a blended model of in-person and virtual activities, the variable of at-risk situations will greatly diminish.

The Legal Progression of Cyberbullying

Until the mid-2000s, there were no specific cyberbullying laws at either the federal or state levels in the United States (King, 2010). State laws have been enacted in response and all 50 states have laws that address cyberbullying. Some 45 states have laws that clearly criminalize it, while the other five states and the District of Columbia only require school or district policies to address it (Zapal, 2020).[11]

Despite the lack of federal laws addressing cyberbullying, all federally funded universities must respond if students experience cyberbullying as a civil right violation. However, cyberbullying state laws mostly focus on the occurrence of cyberbullying on K-12 school property and not outside. Hence, universities do not have much legal guidance and often resort to laws aimed at related offenses and investigate extreme cases of cyberbullying using Title IV and Title VI of the *Civil Rights Act* of 1964, Title IX of the *Education Amendments* of 1972, Section 504 of the *Rehabilitation Act* of 1973, Titles II and III of the *Americans with Disabilities Act*, *Individuals with Disabilities Education Act* (IDEA) and federal anti-stalking law (18 U.S.C. § 2261A) (King, 2010; Nathan, 2021).

There are other federal laws that permit law enforcement to investigate and prosecute cyberbullying, including (1) the *Computer Fraud and Abuse Act* of 1986 (CFAA) (Title 18 U.S.C. Section 1030), which is a cyber security law protecting computers connected to the internet from being used as instruments of fraud (King, 2010; Miller, 2017); (2) the *Electronic Communication Privacy Act* of 1986 (ECPA), which addresses the use of wiretaps while investigating a crime, and prohibits "any person," including a law enforcement officer, from making an illegal interception, disclosing or using the illegally intercepted material (King 2010; Miller, 2017); (3) the *National Information Infrastructure Protection Act* of 1996 (NIIPA), which was created to further expand the protections granted by the *Computer Fraud and Abuse Act* of 1986; (4) the *Controlling the Assault of Non-Solicited Pornography and Marketing Act* of 2003 (CAN-SP AM), which was established to prevent the fraudulent use of commercial email, also known as spam; (5) Cyber stalking statute, 18 U.S. Code section 2261A, which prohibits the crime of stalking and was amended to impose penalties for someone who "uses the mail, any interactive computer service or electronic communication service or electronic communication system" with the intent to injure, intimidate, kill, harass, or survey someone; and (6) the *Communications Decency Act* (CDA), which seeks to prevent obscenity on the internet while promoting constitutionally protected forms of speech (King 2010; Miller, 2017). Despite all of these laws, the perpetrators of cyberbullying seem to elude being held accountable by the criminal justice system. In 2009, a proposed law, the *Megan Meier Cyberbullying Prevention Act* aimed to establish legal measures against the commitment of cyberbullying crimes (Govtrack, 2014S. 2164 113th Congress, 2014). Similarly, the *Tyler Clementi Higher Education Anti-Harassment Act* (TCHEAHA) was introduced in 2010 and reintroduced in 2014 and 2019 (Congress. Gov., 2015, 2019). TCHEAHA would require colleges and universities to include a harassment policy in their annual security report. It would also grant funds to schools that improve anti-harassment programs, counseling services, and harassment education programs (Congress.Gov, S. 1492 116th Congress, 2019–2020). These bills have yet to be denied or approved, due to pandemic delays. However, Vines (2015) noted that the bills' ambiguous language, their references to LGBTQ groups and sexual orientation, as well as the ongoing debate about restrictions on freedom of speech have kept the two proposed statutes from moving through the legislative process.

DISCUSSION AND CONCLUSION

Christensen and Horn's (2008) prediction of great disruptions in education from online learning came in response to a larger disrupter of society: the COVID-19 pandemic. The cancellation of in-person classes across universities in the United States and the transition to remote learning instruction introduced several challenges at the forefront. Some of these challenges include the clear technological divide between financially secure students and less affluent students, keeping students engaged, the pricing of virtual teaching tuition, and zoombombing. In this chapter, we explored zoombombing in comparison with harassment (sexual and racial) and cyberbullying to understand where it is placed among those various forms of existing attacks. We examined the existing concepts of harassment and cyberbullying to determine whether these concepts can be used to understand a novel form of attack, zoombombing. The comparison reveals important distinctions that limit the ability of existing concepts to individually account for the complexities of zoombombing. Some of these differences include legal issues, means/tools of assault, clarity of targets, real-time occurrence, invisibility of the perpetrator, persistence/recurrence, impact on the victim, and location. As such, we argue that zoombombing cannot be subsumed within any *one* of the assaults discussed in this chapter, because such a conceptualization overlooks key distinctions that make zoombombing and its impact unique.

These existing concepts, however, do share some similarities with zoombombing. Consistent with traditional harassment, zoombombing victims are often (although not always) members of protected classes targeted based on that membership. As news of zoombombing circulates, it has the potential to affect the larger community by creating fear and making the university environment less welcoming. Zoombombing is particularly insidious because, similar to cyberbullying, it invades and contaminates victims' private spaces virtually, rendering them unsafe. Furthermore, like cyberbullying, perpetrators use technology for their assaults and to remain invisible, making it difficult for authorities to stop and hold them accountable, which may exacerbate victims' trauma.

Knowing that existing concepts used to describe other types of attacks cannot independently account for zoombombing is significant, because it demonstrates that institutions cannot respond to zoombombing using the same reliefs, laws, statutes, and services that they use to respond to traditional instances of harassment, and cyberbullying. Instead, institutions and policymakers must develop novel responses that account for the unique features and impacts of zoombombing. Responses, however, may be informed by a combination of aspects of existing responses to harassment and cyberbullying, given that there are some meaningful similarities between zoombombing and these types of attacks. This is particularly important because, as in the case of cyberbullying, if specific harmonious and intentional reliefs, policies, laws, and statutes are not developed, victims at universities will spend decades dealing with the impacts of zoombombing.

Online instruction has become a feature of the educational landscape and it will likely not disappear with the end of the COVID-19 pandemic. With the rapid shift to online learning without time to fully prepare for this change and its unintended consequences (such as zoombombing), the variation in responses among universities will lead to several fault lines in virtual online modalities that should be explored further. In this chapter, we offered a preliminary insight into zoombombing.

While it may appear that we can make several recommendations on how universities should deal with zoombombing differently from the other two forms of attacks discussed in this chapter, we prefer to do so once we complete empirical research. Perhaps the single most important recommendation we can offer at this point is that Title IX officers at universities should ensure that zoombombing is not treated as if it were straightforward harassment. It should be understood as a hybrid, carrying with it some of the impacts of traditional harassment and cyberbullying. Our other recommendation is that universities should advocate for further support and services over and above the Title IX resources in addressing victims of zoombombing.

The validity of the assertions made in this chapter would benefit from empirical research. Hence, based on other existing types of attacks, throughout this chapter we have opined the motivation for some zoombombing incidents as well as its possible impact on victims. Future research, however, is needed to empirically confirm these speculations. Future research exploring universities' policies and responses to zoombombing, as well as their transparency and disclosure of incidents will expand the discussion and provide a basis for potential regulations and policies. While some responses to traditional harassment and cyberbullying, may be a suitable baseline to start building university responses, the uniqueness of zoombombing and the consequences discussed above may indicate that responses based on existing assaults are not sufficient to fully address zoombombing.

NOTES

1. Law and Justice Studies, Rowan University.
2. We are using the term sexual zoombombing attacks, knowing fully well that such attacks often have an intersectional component of racial and religious attacks.
3. Title IX specifically forbids "discrimination based on sex in education programs or activities that receive Federal financial assistance" (U.S. Department of Education, 2020a).
4. Title VI (for faculty/staff) of the Civil Rights Act of 1964 "prohibits discrimination based on race, color or national origin in programs or activities which receive federal financial assistance" (U.S. Department of Education, 2020b).
5. Title VII (for faculty/staff and students employed by the university) of the Civil Rights Act of 1964 similarly forbids discrimination in places of employment.
6. Due to limited space this chapter addresses legal context for students in the context of zoombombing.
7. Sexting as the sending and receiving of sexually explicit images or texts (or "sexts") (Ringrose et al. 2013).
8. Shariff's (2015) book, *Sexting and Cyberbullying: Defining the Line for Digitally Empowered Kids*, noted the problem with framing sexting as a "bullying" or "deviant" behavior in all situations. Specifically, she stated: "Many of these activities of sexual exploration… have moved from the back of a car, to playing itself over social media" (p. xiii).
9. In the case of Clementi, his roommate did not know him well. They had been roommates for almost 3 weeks.
10. In the case of Tylor Clementi, his roommate had sophisticated technological skills and apparatuses.
11. For state-by-state cyberbullying laws, see Cyberbullying Research Center (n.d.) Cyberbullying Research Center (n.d.), Cyberbullying Laws Across America. This information is accessible via this website: https://cyberbullying.org/bullying-laws.

REFERENCES

Akbulut, Y., & Eristi, B. (2011). Cyberbullying and victimisation among Turkish university students. *Australasian Journal of Educational Technology, 27*(7), 1155–1170.

American Association of University Women. (2020). *Quick facts, Title IX.* https://www.aauw.org/app/uploads/2022/12/Title-IX-Quick-Facts-Nov-2022.pdf

Andone, D. (2020, April 3). *FBI warns video calls are getting hijacked. It's called "zoombombing."* CNN. https://www.nbcconnecticut.com/news/local/attorney-general-says-his-call-was-zoombombed urges-safe-video-conferencing/2249848/

Associated Press. (2021, April 27). Pandemic gives rise to anti-Semitic "Zoom bombing." *New York Times.* https://nypost.com/2021/04/27/pandemic-gives-rise-to-antisemitic-zoom-bombing

Beavers, J. M., & Halabi, S. F. (2017). Stigma and the structure of Title IX compliance. *The Journal of Law, Medicine & Ethics, 45,* 558–568.

Bindley, K. (2020, April 4). Zoombombing harms the Alcoholics Anonymous community. *Wall Street Journal.* https://www.wsj.com/articles/zoombombing-harms-the-alcoholics-anonymous-community-11586091602

Bossler, A. M., & Holt, T. J. (2009). On-line activities, guardianship, and malware infection: An examination of routine activities theory. *International Journal of Cyber Criminology, 3,* 400–420.

Cantor, D., Fisher, B., Chibnall, S., Townsend, R., Lee, H., Bruce, C., & Thomas, G. (2015). *Report on the AAU Campus Climate Survey on Sexual Assault and Sexual Misconduct.* The Association of American Universities. https://www.aau.edu/sites/default/files/%40%20Files/Climate%20Survey/AAU_Campus_Climate_Survey_12_14_15.pdf

Chisholm, J. F. (2014). Review of the status of cyberbullying and cyberbullying prevention. *Journal of Information Systems Education, 25,* 77–87.

Christensen, C. M., & Horn, M. (2008). *Disrupting class: How disruptive innovation will change the way the world learns.* McGraw-Hill.

Cohen, L. E., & Felson, M. (1979). Social change and crime rate trends: A routine activity approach. *American Sociological Review, 44,* 588–608.

Congress.Gov. (2015). *H.R.1421—Tyler Clementi Higher Education Anti-Harassment Act of 2015.* 114th Congress (2015–2016). https://www.congress.gov/bill/114th-congress/house-bill/1421

Congress.Gov. (2019). *S.1492—Tyler Clementi Higher Education Anti-Harassment Act of 2019* 116th Congress (2019–2020). https://www.congress.gov/bill/116th-congress/senate-bill/1492/text

Cyberbullying Research Center. (n.d.). *Bullying laws across America.* https://cyberbullying.org/bullying-laws

Dugan, J. P., Kusel, M. L., & Simounet, D. M. (2012). Transgender college students: An exploratory study of perceptions, engagement, and educational outcomes. *Journal of College Student Development, 53,* 719–736.

Elmer, G., Burton, A. G., & Neville, S. J. (2020, June 9). *Zoom-bombings disrupt online events with racist and misogynist attacks.* The Conversation. https://theconversation.com/zoom-bombings-disrupt-online-events-with-racist-and-misogynist-attacks-138389

Eristi, B., & Akbulut, Y. (2019). Reactions to cyberbullying among high school and university students, *The Social Science Journal, 56,* 10–20.

Faucher, C., Jackson, M., & Cassidy, W. (2014). Cyberbullying among university students: Gendered experiences, impacts, and perspectives. *Education Research International, 2014,* 1–10.

Faucher, C., Jackson, M., & Cassidy, W. (2015). When online exchanges byte: An examination of the policy environment governing cyberbullying at the university level. *Canadian Journal of Higher Education, 45*, 102–121.

Fedina, L., Holmes, J. L., & Backes, B. (2016). How prevalent is campus sexual assault in the United States? *National Institute of Justice, 277*, 26–30.

Feinberg, T., & Robey, N. (2008). Cyberbullying. *Principal Leadership, 9*, 10–14.

Findlawa's Team. (2017). *Title IX protections for transgender students.* https://www.findlaw.com/education/discrimination-harassment-at-school/title-ix-protections-for-transgender-students.html

Finn, J. (2004). A survey of online harassment at a university campus. *Journal of Interpersonal Violence, 19*, 468–483.

Garvey, J. C., & Rankin, S. R. (2015). Making the grade? Classroom climate for LGBTQ students across gender conformity. *Journal of Student Affairs Research and Practice, 52*, 190–203.

Green, E. L. (2018, August 29). New US sexual misconduct rules bolster rights of accused and protect colleges. *The New York Times.* https://www.nytimes.com/2018/08/29/us/politics/devos-campus-sexual-assault.html

Gersen, J. S. (2020, May 16). How concerning are the Trump administration's new Title IX regulations? *The New Yorker.* https://www.newyorker.com/news/our-columnists/how-concerning-are-the-trump-administrations-new-title-ix-regulations

Govtrack, 2014S. 2164 (113th). *Tyler Clementi Higher Education Anti-Harassment Act* (2014). https://www.govtrack.us/congress/bills/113/s2164

Hill, K. (2010, September 30). The privacy landmine that is Duke graduate Karen Owen's "Senior Thesis." *Forbes.* https://www.forbes.com/sites/kashmirhill/2010/09/30/the-privacy-landmine-that-is-duke-graduate-karen-owens-senior-thesis/?sh=56424b0169bc

Hinduja, S., & Patchin, J. W. (2020). *Cyberbullying identification, prevention, and response.* Cyberbullying Research Center.

James, S., Herman, J., Rankin, S., Keisling, M., Mottet, L., & Anaf, M. (2016). *The report of the 2015 US Transgender Survey.* National Center for Transgender Equality.

Jewkes, Y., & Wykes, M. (2012). Reconstructing the sexual abuse of children: "cyber-paeds", panic and power. *Sexualities, 15*, 934–952.

Joia, L. A., & Lorenzo, M. (2021). Zoom in, zoom out: The impact of the COVID-19 pandemic in the classroom. *Sustainability, 13*, 1531.

King, A. V. (2010). Constitutionality of cyberbullying laws: Keeping the online playground safe for both teens and free of speech. *Vanderbilt Law Review, 63*, 846–884.

Klein, L. B., & Martin, S. L. (2019). Sexual harassment of college and university students: A systematic review. *Trauma Violence Abuse, 22*(4), 777–792. https://pubmed.ncbi.nlm.nih.gov/31635552/

MacDonald, C. D., & Roberts-Pittman, B. (2010). Cyberbullying among college students: Prevalence and demographic differences. *Procedia Social and Behavioral Sciences, 9*, 2003–2009.

Melnick, R. S. (2018). *The transformation of Title IX regulating gender equality in education.* Brookings Institution Press.

Miller, K. (2017). *Cyberbullying and its consequences: How cyberbullying is contorting the minds of victims and bullies alike, and the law's limited available redress.* USC Gould School of Law. https://gould.usc.edu/why/students/orgs/ilj/assets/docs/26-2-Miller.pdf

Murakami, K. (2021, March 9). *Rethinking Title IX*. Inside Higher Education. https://www.insidehighered.com/news/2021/03/09/president-biden-tells-education-department-examine-title-ix-rules

Murphy, M. P. A. (2020). COVID-19 and emergency e-learning: Consequences of the securitization of higher education for post-pandemic pedagogy. *Contemporary Security Policy, 41*, 492–505.

Myers, C., & Cowie, H. (2017). Cyberbullying across the lifespan of education: Issues and interventions from school to university. *International Journal of Environmental Research and Public Health, 16*, 1217–1231.

Nathan, G. (2021). *Cyberbullying laws, charges & statute of limitations*. National Federal Defense Lawyer Group. https://www.federalcharges.com/cyberbullying-laws-charges

Parker, I. (2020, February 6). *The story of a suicide: Two college roommates, a webcam, and a tragedy*. Satya Blog. http://www.satyablog.org/2012/04/24/new-yorker-the-story-of-suicide-on-dharun-ravi-and-tyler-clementi-case

Patchin, J. W., & Hinduja, S. (2006). Bullies move beyond the schoolyard: A preliminary look at cyberbullying. *Youth Violence and Juvenile Justice, 4*(2), 148–169.

Patchin, J. W., & Hinduja, S. (2015). Measuring cyberbullying: İmplications for research. *Aggression and Violent Behavior, 23*, 69–74.

Perasso, G., Carone, N., & Barone, L. (2020). Written and visual cyberbullying victimization in adolescence: Shared and unique associated factors. *European Journal of Developmental Psychology, 5*, 1–20.

Pew Research Center. (2017, July 11). *Online harassment*. Pew Internet. https://www.pewinternet.org/2017/07/11/

Pilkington, E. (2010). Tyler Clementi, student outed as gay on internet, jumps to his death. *The Guardian*. https://www.theguardian.com/world/2010/sep/30/tyler-clementi-gay-student-suicide

Puluse, T. (2020). Sexual harassment on college campuses: The insufficiency of Title IX. *Rampo Journal of Law and Society, 5*, 121–127.

Raskauskas, J. (2010). Text-bullying: Associations with traditional bullying and depression among New Zealand adolescents. *Journal of School Violence, 9*, 74–97.

Redden, E. (2020, March 26). *"Zoombombing" attacks disrupt classes*. Inside Higher Education. https://www.insidehighered.com/news/2020/03/26/zoombombers-disrupt-online-classes-racist-pornographic-content

Ringrose, J., Harvey, L., Gill, R., & Livingstone, S. (2013). Teen girls, sexual double standards and "texting": Gendered value in digital image exchange. *Feminist Theory, 14*, 305–323.

Schenk, A. M., & Fremouw, W. J. (2012). Prevalence, psychological impact, and coping of cyberbully victims among college students. *Journal of School Violence, 11*, 21–37.

Securly. (2019, October 19). *8 Cyberbullying apps parents should know about*. Securely. https://blog.securly.com/2019/10/14/8-anonymous-cyberbullying-apps-you-should-know-about

Seelye, K. Q., & Robbins, L. (2010, October 7). Duke winces as a private joke slips out of control. *The New York Times*. https://www.nytimes.com/2010/10/08/us/08duke.html

Setera, K. (2020). *FBI warns of teleconferencing and online classroom hijacking during COVID-19 pandemic*. FBI.

Shariff, S. (2015). *Sexting and cyberbullying. Defining the line for digitally empowered kids*. Cambridge University Press.

Slonje, R., Smith, P. K., & Frisén, A. (2013). The nature of cyberbullying, and strategies for prevention. *Computers in Human Behavior, 29*, 26–32.

U.S. Department of Education. (2020a). *Title IX and sex discrimination.* https://www2.ed.gov/about/offices/list/ocr/docs/tix_dis.html

U.S. Department of Education. (2020b). *Education and Title VI.* https://www2.ed.gov/about/offices/list/ocr/docs/hq43e4.html

U.S. Department of Education Office for Civil Rights. (2015). *Title IX and sex discrimination.* https://www2.ed.gov/about/offices/list/ocr/docs/tix_dis.html

Vandebosch, H., & Van Cleemput, K. (2008). Defining cyberbullying: A qualitative research into the perceptions of youngsters. *CyberPsychology & Behavior, 11*, 499–503.

Viner, R. M., Russell, S. J., Croker, H., Packer, J., Ward, J., Stansfield, C., Mytton, O., Bonnell, C., & Booy, R. (2020). School closure and management practices during coronavirus outbreaks including COVID-19: A rapid systematic review. *Lancet Child & Adolescent Health, 4*, 397–404.

Vines, J. (2015). *An embedded case study of the proposed Mega Meier Cyberbullying Prevention Statute & the proposed Tyler Clementi Higher Education Anti-Harassment Statute* [Doctoral dissertation, Clemson University].

Washington, E.T. (2015). An overview of cyberbullying in higher education. *Adult Learning, 26*, 21–27.

Wolff, J. M., Rospenda, K. M., & Colaneri, A. S. (2017). Sexual harassment, psychological distress, and problematic drinking behavior among college students: An examination of reciprocal causal relations. *The Journal of Sex Research, 54*, 362–373.

Zapal, H. (2020, October 6). *A state-by-state guide to cyberbullying laws.* The Bark Blog. https://www.bark.us/blog/cyberbullying-laws

CHAPTER FIVE

"What Will Happen to Us?": Policy Barriers and International Student Marginalization in Canada During the COVID-19 Pandemic

SHANNON HUTCHESON[1]

Abstract: Valued in billions of dollars, international education is a lucrative enterprise in Canada. In recent years, the country has prioritized international student recruitment to compensate for decreasing public funding for universities. At first glance, this seems like an ideal solution—universities benefit from the cultural exchange, international students enjoy a more "worldly" education, and universities can compensate for less funding. Upon closer inspection, however, international students face inequities, particularly around non-citizen/resident rights, access to social protections like healthcare, and financial burdens. Not only did the COVID-19 pandemic expose some of these inequities, but it also exacerbated them. Using policy as a lens for analysis, this chapter investigates the inequities and unique challenges international students face as COVID-19 changes the landscape of international higher education. Specifically, this chapter examines four major themes: (a) the monetization of higher education and the pitfalls of the international student as a "cash cow" mentality, (b) inequities around access to financial resources and social protections, (c) discrimination, and (d) immigration flows, borders, and barriers. Thus, this chapter employs a critical analysis to pinpoint the vulnerabilities of international students in a neoliberal market that often prioritizes profit over well-being.

Keywords: international students, international education, inequity, immigration, critical policy analysis, discrimination, COVID-19 pandemic

INTRODUCTION

While the COVID-19 pandemic has forced individuals, institutions, and governments around the globe to adjust to an unprecedented reality, one sector that continues to struggle is international education. In Canada, March 2020 was marked by sudden campus closures and international students in visa limbo. In an effort to secure campuses, university dorms closed without adequate notice, leaving many international students in precarious situations without housing (Geary, 2020; McKenna, 2020). In the United States, international students were left reeling after Immigration and Customs Enforcement (ICE) announced that if an institution was not holding in-person classes, they would have to leave the country (ICE, 2020).

While both examples show the precarity of non-citizenship status for students studying outside of their home countries, before the pandemic, there were already demonstrable policy-related flaws in international education, particularly regarding equity (e.g., Karram, 2013; Tannock, 2018). Healthcare inaccessibility, skyrocketing tuition costs, discrimination, and the commodification of international students have been a focal point for several scholars (Hutcheson, 2020; Karram, 2013, Lomer, 2014; Tannock, 2018). These pre-pandemic issues quickly worsened during the pandemic, thereby exacerbating existing inequities for international students.

It is important to note that international education is a significant industry for many countries. Canada, the United States, Australia, and the United Kingdom rely heavily on international student fees. In 2019, there were nearly 640,000 international students studying in Canada, contributing roughly $22 billion to its economy each year (Government of Canada, 2019). Canada is the third leading destination for international students, after the United States and Australia (Canadian Bureau for International Education [CBIE], 2019). With decreased public funding for education and an aggressive internationalization strategy from the government, international student tuition has become a financial "lifeboat" for many Canadian institutions (Basen, 2016). However, since it is uncertain how the pandemic will continue to impact the number of international students—and consequently, the Canadian economy—Canadian stakeholders in international education are closely observing policies regarding who can come to Canada, and under what conditions. Moreover, international students worldwide who are already in their host country of study or those hoping to come to their host countries may wonder "what will happen to us?" as they look for support and answers in public forums (Tabnawr, 2020).

This chapter examines how international students have been marginalized by policies in international education before and during the COVID-19 pandemic. I present a policy-forward review that exposes neoliberalism as a major force affecting international students' lives and, in doing so, unpack how international education relevant policy impacts international students. Much of this chapter will focus on policies in Canada, with an emphasis on Quebec. When appropriate, I also incorporate a comparative perspective, calling attention to relevant policies from outside Canada. This comparative lens between nations is beneficial due to the connectedness of systems in international education—the global, national, and local are inextricably linked (e.g., Marginson & Rhoades, 2002; Webster, 2019). Canada, the United States, Australia, and the UK are direct competitors in international education, and events in one country create ripples in the others. For example, the "Trump effect" is believed to have increased international student enrollment in Canada (Potok, 2017). Given the interconnected, global context of international higher education, employing a critical international lens is advantageous.

This chapter surveys the pandemic context of international higher education through policies and actions of the Canadian and U.S. governments, as well as academic institutions that have impacted international students. Moreover, this chapter identifies some of the most pressing issues in higher international education as they pertain to international students' experiences by analyzing social commentary, media articles, and relevant literature. Recognizing the novelty of the pandemic, as well as the numerous policy issues that have emerged and have been exacerbated by the pandemic, a wide survey of the current landscape is warranted.

This chapter is structured as a literature and policy review, guided by critical analysis (e.g., Lawless & Chen, 2019; Nixon et al., 2017), critical discourse analysis (Mullet, 2018; Rogers, 2011), and critical policy analysis (e.g., Diem et al. 2014; Young & Diem, 2018). I employ critical methods to evaluate "the distribution of power, resources, and knowledge" and "the role of inequality and privilege" (Diem et al., 2014) and examine differences in resource distribution between international students and Canadian students. Applying this critical lens, I also consider how neoliberalism plays a mediating role in international students' experiences. The holistic approach offered by critical methods is useful to the analysis of policies and practices in international education, as it provides a framework that demonstrates how the pandemic and the four themes around international education (i.e., the monetization of higher education, access to resources, discrimination, and immigration) are not only related, but also mutually constitutive.

THE MONETIZATION OF INTERNATIONAL HIGHER EDUCATION

International students, who contribute roughly 22 billion dollars to the Canadian economy each year and who are routinely characterized as "cash cows" are relied on to compensate for decreased public funding for education (e.g., Crawley, 2017; Study International, 2017). While the number of international students in Canada has risen dramatically in recent years, support services are not necessarily proportionate to this growing number (e.g., Basen, 2016; Guo & Guo, 2017; Scott et al., 2015). As higher education continues to shift toward a neoliberal business model, greater emphasis has been placed on generating income rather than ensuring the well-being of students (De Wit, 2016; Forbes-Mewett & Nyland, 2013; Karram, 2013). Karram identified this tension, pinpointing how "one sees international students as an economic market to be engaged with, while the other seeks to understand and support their day-to-day lived experience" (2013, p. 5).

To illustrate how critical the financial contributions of international students are to universities where international education is a key component of the economic strategy, particularly during a pandemic, consider this example from the United States: The University of Illinois at Urbana-Champaign, which feared losses in international student revenue, took out an insurance policy for protection against the anticipated drop in Chinese students (Bothwell, 2018). This drop in students would have had a detrimental, if not catastrophic impact on the University's budget. Sylvie Lomer believed this could signal a trend of similar precautions worldwide (Bothwell, 2018). As universities will inevitably seek new ways to weather the pandemic with less of the international student income that many universities in Canada and the United States have become dependent on, other universities may seek similar insurance strategies. This is one of the ways in which the pandemic has revealed the fragility of international higher education and the repercussions of over-reliance on international students as a revenue stream, particularly as international student enrollment quotas fall short (e.g., Deuel, 2020). Overall, this emphasis on revenue and quotas is indicative of a neoliberal ideology.

Neoliberalism in International Education

Pervasive in the current context, McChesney (1999) called neoliberalism the "defining political economic paradigm of our time" (para. 1). Neoliberalism, as defined by Harvey (2007), is the "deregulation, privatization, and withdrawal of the state from many areas of social provision" (p. 3). In practice, neoliberalism becomes an economic ideology where monetary gain is paramount and takes precedence over social issues. Giroux (2002) contextualized the implications of neoliberalism by explaining that higher education has been commercialized and viewed as a commodity such that students are framed as consumers and the university as a business. Concerning international students, neoliberalism is a ubiquitous philosophy that impacts their experience in unique ways. In Quebec, tuition fees have been deregulated, which means that universities are allowed to determine "fair" tuition prices for international students, thereby raising tuition at their discretion (Latulipe Loiselle & Jouhari, 2018). This preceded a roughly 7 % increase in tuition for international students in Canada for the 2020–2021 academic year (Statistics Canada, 2021). The decision to raise fees during a pandemic surprised and frustrated many students, especially since classes were online and students could not access on-campus amenities. As educational systems across Canada struggled to adapt to virtual learning and diminished classroom capacity, students asked why they were paying more for less (Amin et al., 2020; Keung, 2020; see Chapter Six).

In Canada, international students pay tuition rates that are on average three times more—and at times, four times more—than their Canadian peers (Canadian Federation of Students, 2020). The higher tuition rate has contributed to several stereotypes about international students, one being that all international students have disposable wealth. This stereotype is pervasive and presents itself in memes. To illustrate, one meme depicts a Chinese takeout container with a Coco Chanel emblem, golden chopsticks, and gold necklaces for noodles with a caption that reads, "What international students have for lunch" (Nagesh, 2018). While there are affluent international students, this stereotype does not reflect the wealth of the general population of international students. Such stereotypes are harmful and obfuscate the reality that many international students struggle financially (CBIE, 2018; Charles & Overlid, 2020; Etem, 2012; Nagesh, 2018; World Education Services, 2020).

Scholars have critiqued using international students as "a blank check" (Deuel, 2020). Adding to the perception of international students as a form of revenue is the fact that the government categorizes international education as an export (Government of Canada, 2019). Lomer (2014) asserted that this kind of objectifying discourse positions international students as "economic objects." This narrative has been particularly evident during the pandemic, as universities are concerned about the impact of international student enrollment and subsequent income losses, perhaps more than the students themselves.

The Commodity of Education

Education is commodified in neoliberal societies (Giroux, 2002) and universities are globally marketed as goods/services to the international student consumer. To sell itself to prospective students, Canada has become a brand—one that promotes itself as a leading study destination. Canada's internationalization strategy entitled *Harnessing Our Knowledge Advantage to Drive Innovation and Prosperity* emphasizes this imagery by presenting Canada as safe, reliable, multicultural, and immigration friendly (Global Affairs Canada, 2014). Since branding also implies competition, which is a major tenet of neoliberalism (Giroux, 2002; Johnstone & Lee, 2017), Canada not only sells that it is safe and welcoming, but that it is also safe(r) and (more) welcoming compared to competitor countries and thereby more appealing to their international student-consumers. In Canada's pandemic economic recovery agenda, the priority is to "leverage and promote the 'Canada' brand domestically and internationally, emphasizing value addition and innovation" (Canada Industry Strategy Council, 2020, p. 23). By reframing the imagery of safety during the pandemic, the government's agenda now includes the "launch of public health messaging campaigns abroad to instill confidence in potential international students" (Canada Industry Strategy Council, 2020, p. 23).

Competition reinforces and perpetuates the notion that education is a commodity and that universities are businesses with all students as consumers and international students as exports. Since international students are positioned as "consumers," it is important to consider what students-consumers want. Marginson (2020) suggested that moving forward, students will prioritize institutions that offer better "health security." Commenting on the Australian context, Lehmann and Sriram (2020) predicted that the treatment of current international students will have consequences on a country's image such that international students "could help shape our country's reputation as a safe and welcoming destination in the post-pandemic world—but only if we look after them" (para. 1).

As consumers in a neoliberal market, students are closely observing the policy choices made by institutions of higher education. Marginson (2020) predicted that as higher education recovers from the impacts of the pandemic, competition for recruiting international students will become even fiercer. It will be valuable for research in this field to investigate the (re)branding of universities and countries post-pandemic and the impacts of such efforts on the experiences of international students. Headlines such as "International Recruitment—Is Canada Facing a Big Squeeze?" (Nicol, 2020) and "Can Canada's Universities Survive COVID?" (Ansari, 2020) displayed the urgency of the financial crisis in higher education. Challenging these financial concerns, this chapter implores universities to look beyond depictions of international students as "lifeboats," "cash cows," and "blank checks" and, instead, attend to them as human beings by supporting their health, safety, and education and reducing the inequities they experience.

SOCIAL PROTECTIONS: FINANCIAL AID, FINANCIAL SECURITY, AND HEALTH

Critiquing the commercialization of higher international education, Tannock (2018) focused on international students as exports, identifying that:

> flesh and blood individual human beings are reframed to become just another income generating market commodity, that is no different from an automobile or pharmaceutical

product that has been packed into a shipping container and sent overseas for distribution and purchase. (p. 41)

The objectifying language around international students may result in overlooked rights. Exports and economic *objects* do not require healthcare and supports, but flesh and blood *people* do.

At times when the cultural contributions of international students are commended, there is often a caveat to their financial contributions. On September 22, 2020, the Minster of Immigration, Refugees and Citizenship Canada, Marco Mendecino (2020), tweeted, "International students enrich our culture & communities, and contribute $22B to Canada's economy." International students make large financial contributions to Canada, but this relationship should not be unilateral. It is therefore essential to inquire what international students *need*?

In this section, I discuss access to resources, particularly around healthcare and financial supports, since international students have struggled with access to healthcare (Redden, 2020) and a lack of financial support from both universities and the government (e.g., Firang, 2020). This lack of access has become more apparent during the pandemic. Specifically, Bilecen (2020) identified the necessary support that international students have required during the pandemic as "social protection," which refers to a set of resources that bolster and protect against various risks, such as discrimination and poverty. These social protections are both tangible and intangible resources that can be mobilized against risks and may include government initiatives or more local organizations, such as student committees (Bilecen, 2020). My review of pandemic-related policies and practices in Canada highlights how international students' access to social protections is often precarious.

Although international students are stereotyped as affluent, economic prosperity is not a reality for many of them. With large tuition bills, less access to financial aid, and precarious job prospects, many international students struggle not only to pay for tuition, but also necessities such as groceries and rent (CBIE, 2018; Charles & Overlid, 2020; World Education Services, 2020). This financial vulnerability opens international students to exploitation, particularly as they must navigate the 20-hour cap on work hours (Government of Canada, 2022).

In response to the financial difficulties that arose during the pandemic, such as job losses and decreased work opportunities, the Government of Canada created the Canada Emergency Response Benefit (CERB) to mitigate financial losses (Government of Canada, 2021b). Students, including international students, could access the CERB by demonstrating that they earned more than $5,000 in the past year. However, this $5,000 cap presented numerous barriers. First, many students had not earned enough money in the past year to reach the $5,000 threshold (Kamil, 2020; World Education Services, 2020).

Second, due to study permit restrictions, some international students have worked "under the table" to supplement their finances (Tomlinson, 2019). This created a problem for them, since income from undocumented work does not count toward the CERB's $5,000 requisite. Another barrier to the CERB is that a Social Insurance Number is required, which some international students simply do not have for a number or reasons including gaps between visas and processing delays for renewals (Matassa-Fung, 2020). The CERB also did not protect from losses of *potential* income, meaning students were expecting jobs that were no longer available due to the pandemic.

Furthermore, the initial campaigns used to inform the public about the CERB and other financial relief programs did not mention international students, leaving many international students confused as to whether or not they were eligible for the CERB. Interestingly, many Canadian students were also unable to access the benefits associated with the CERB, so Canada launched the Canada Emergency Student Benefit (CESB), which was created to fill the gaps and support the need of students (Government of Canada, 2021d). Unfortunately, however, international students were entirely excluded from the CESB (Kamil, 2020). Overall, even though Canada acknowledged the dire financial situation of many of its citizens and students, the country's provision of financial aid to international students was conspicuous: Canada relies on international students for its economic survival, but international students cannot count on Canada for their economic survival, even in the time of a crisis.

These omissions have also been prevalent as international students have tried to access healthcare, both before and during the pandemic. The *Canadian Health Act* (1985) stated that all Canadians have access to healthcare, but this legislation does not apply to international students who study, work, and pay taxes in Canada (Reitmanova, 2008). International students are often required to pay out of pocket for costly private healthcare in addition to their inflated tuition fees. Additionally, private healthcare is not always accessible. For instance, Quebec's RAMQ program grants Quebec residents access to a large network of healthcare providers, but international students residing in Quebec do not qualify (Quebec Regie de l'Assurance Maladie, n.d.). At the beginning of the pandemic, student clinics at institutions such as McGill University in Montreal closed, leaving many international and out-of-province students without access to affordable healthcare, since insurance coverage is limited once students leave their university networks.

In addition to the omission from services and supports, students also encountered rapidly changing policies. Wong (2020) noted that university administrators were "mercurial" in their responses to the pandemic, since they consistently and quickly changed policies as well as enforcement measures. One heavily critiqued pandemic response was the sudden closure of student residences, which was implemented to help slow the spread of COVID-19 since students live together in close quarters. However, this measure left many international students in precarious and stressful circumstances. In one instance, Concordia University in Montreal only gave students living in dorms four days to vacate the premises (McKenna, 2020). Students were told that if they did not leave the residences, they could be accommodated following a review and subsequent confirmation by the university (McKenna, 2020). Many Canadian students could return to their family homes in Canada, but with closing borders, exorbitant travel costs, and scarce time to strategize, many international students lacked viable options (Morin, 2020). International students therefore had to immediately find secure, new housing that was safe and affordable—even though they were already navigating the challenges of the pandemic and, for many, inadequate finances. Thus, although pandemic-related policies, like the closing of student residences, were intended to protect the health and safety of students, they inadvertently created many more problems for international students (McKenna, 2020).

DISCRIMINATION, XENOPHOBIA, AND RACISM

Access to social protections like financial aid, healthcare, and housing are crucial to support international students. However, students must also feel *safe*. The emphasis on safety has been part of Canada's internationalization strategy to recruit more international students by promoting the country as safe and welcoming. However, before the pandemic, many racialized international students experienced discrimination and racism in countries like the United States and Canada (e.g., Lee & Rice, 2007; Houshmand et al., 2014; Smith & Khawaja, 2011; Rutherford, 2019; Verghis, 2009). Furthermore, the pandemic has shifted what notions of safety look like for international students, particularly racialized students from Asia who have been targets of discrimination and harm, as they have been blamed for the spread of COVID-19 (Kong et al. 2021). Such incidents have increased since the onset of the pandemic and contradict the image that Canada aims to promote, namely that the country is safe and immigration friendly (Global Affairs Canada, 2014).

As indicated on Canada's website for newcomers, international students in Canada are protected by the *Canadian Charter of Rights and Freedoms* (1982), a bill of rights entrenched in the Constitution. Section 15 of the statute outlines equality rights and protections against discrimination. Although *all* individuals living in Canada are protected by the *Charter* (Government of Canada, 2017), the active discrimination against Asian and other racialized students do not align with the non-discriminatory grounds outlined in the *Charter*.

The pandemic has exacerbated discrimination against certain groups of racialized international students. In March 2020, former U.S. President Donald

Trump referred to COVID-19 as the "Chinese virus" and introduced the term "Kung Flu" in July 2020 (BBC, 2020). This language was intentionally used to perpetuate the racist and xenophobic view that Chinese people are to blame for the proliferation of COVID-19. The framing of COVID-19 as the "Asian" virus increased anti-Asian sentiments worldwide, including toward Asian international students, who represent a large proportion of international students in Canada and have experienced higher rates of discrimination and hate crimes since the beginning of the pandemic (Kong et al., 2021; Litam, 2020; Ziems et al., 2020).

In Canada, from March 2020 to February 2021, there were 1,150 reported instances of racism across the country (Kong et al., 2020). Of these cases, 84 % of victims self-identified as or were identified as East Asian (Kong et al., 2020). These manifestations of racism and xenophobia are also present online. Mittelmeier and Cockayne (2020), who analyzed tweets portraying international students, uncovered perpetuation of many negative stereotypes, such as Twitter users claiming to distance themselves from groups of Asian international students on public transit, and professors making discriminatory jokes about COVID-19 when Asian international students coughed during their lecture.

Since the beginning of the pandemic, visible minorities have reported feeling less safe than non-visible minorities (Statistics Canada, 2020). However, feelings of unsafety were more pronounced among Asian populations (Statistics Canada, 2020). Cognizant of the mounting racism against international students, the Canadian government created a guide for international students arriving in Canada, specifically stating that international students should be protected from racism and discrimination in Canada (Government of Canada, 2021a). The guideline urges designated learning institutions (DLIs), which are schools pre-approved provincially to host international students to "ensure that local communities and campuses are safe and welcome places for international students, free of any biases or racism that may be associated with COVID" (section 5, para. 2).

Universities have a responsibility to keep international students safe, but some universities dismissed xenophobic rhetoric against Asian students during the pandemic and appeared unconcerned about how such rhetoric would contribute to Asian students feeling, or being, unsafe. One Instagram post from the University of California, Berkeley stated that xenophobia against Asian students was a "normal" reaction to the COVID-19 pandemic (Asmelash, 2020). The post attempted to sympathize with non-Asian students struggling with the pandemic and listed a number of "typical" reactions, notably, "xenophobia: fears about interacting with those who might be from Asia and guilt about these feelings" (Asmelash, 2020). Wong (2020) retorted that this widely critiqued post "shows that the administration, at best, is failing to tackle head-on an insidiously propagated belief that hostility towards a racial 'other'—for so long somewhat concealed—could be permitted in times of crisis" (para. 11). Much of the racism directed at

Asian students, including international students from Asia comes from a place of xenophobia, but also a view that students with Asian backgrounds are potentially dangerous as carriers of COVID-19.

IMMIGRATION FLOWS: BORDERS AND BARRIERS

It is important to note that, in addition to the vulnerabilities listed above, including those specific to the pandemic, the very status of being an international student can render students vulnerable since their status is conditional and contingent on several factors, such as not exceeding work hour limits, providing up-to-date paperwork, and maintaining enrollment criteria (Government of Canada, 2021c). International students are welcome in Canada, but only under a specific set of conditions dictated by immigration authorities (Government of Canada, 2021c). Being an international student is fraught with administrative and bureaucratic hurdles, such as providing extensive documentation to ensure that their study permits are valid for the duration of their studies. However, these processes are further complicated during the pandemic. For example, students experienced large delays in visa processing times (Matassa-Fung, 2020). In another case, due to conflicting COVID-specific information, students were fearful about unintentionally violating the terms of their students visas due to uncertainties, such as the number of hours students with essential jobs could work (Rukavina, 2020).

In addition to the bureaucratic hurdles, immigration is not always a steadfast practice, as seen with the swift regulatory changes following the onset of the COVID-19 pandemic. Several factors can impact immigration, such as economic stimulation, workforce shortages, humanitarian immigration, education, and geopolitics (e.g., Government of Canada, 2019; Lee et al., 2006; OECD, 2011; Webster, 2019). The insecurity of immigrant status during the pandemic was demonstrated when ICE announced on July 24, 2020, that international students at universities with online-only instruction would need to depart or be deported from the United States (ICE, 2020).

At the time of writing, Canada's borders are open to international students whose universities appear on the approved list of DLIs assessed to be student ready (Government of Canada, 2021e). This may be a relief to some students who have been eager to come to Canada due to difficult learning conditions such as unstable internet connections and taking synchronous classes with significant time differences. While pandemic-related restrictions that currently allow international students to come to Canada may change as COVID-19 persists, they offer some hope for students wishing to be physically located in Canada. Ultimately, government responses to COVID-19 and the treatment of international students may impact the decision of prospective students wishing to attend DLIs on the approved "student-ready" list.

RECOMMENDATIONS

By revisiting the impact of the pandemic on international higher education and international students, this chapter identifies emergent themes on inequity that international students have experienced before and during the COVID-19 pandemic. Through a critical lens, I examined salient policies, practices, and social media posts that related to issues of international education during the pandemic and highlighted the work of scholars, social commentators, and news media to provide further context of these issues. Though these issues warrant further exploration, I propose some recommendations to better serve international students during and after the pandemic.

Confronting (and Challenging) the Contradictions

Perhaps the most important is an ideological shift in the perception of international students' role in Canadian international higher education. Currently, the institution of international higher education is a contradiction. Naming this contradiction, Patel (2020) lamented, "why is it that today those societies which demonstrate stereotypical, prejudicial and discriminatory behaviours about international student communities are those who embrace the international student dollar with open arms?" (para. 15). The current unilateral approach in which international students are primarily perceived as sources of income creates an inequitable situation, which can lead to exploitation. Throughout history, there have been numerous motivations for promoting international education including global cooperation, innovation, and humanitarianism (de Wit & Merkx, 2012). Emphasis on the economic potential of international students is a relatively new phenomenon not seen until the second half of the twentieth century (de Wit & Merkx, 2012). International higher education must reconcile how neoliberalism has rapidly changed the educational landscape and re-examine both its purpose and its relationship with students, without whom international education would not exist. Stakeholders must harmonize imagery against execution; it is irresponsible institutions to spend money and project the image that Canada is safe and welcoming with world class services to international students without investing the same amount of money—or more—to ensure that image is a reality.

Another important step to promote reconciliation and equity for international students is to make international higher education more human-centered. Institutions should prioritize the needs of their international students and provide tailored financial, emotional, and administrative support. Echoing this sentiment even before the pandemic, Choudaha (2017) suggested that, in the future, universities need to find balance between recruitment and "corresponding support services that advance student success" (p. 831). Karram (2013) similarly suggested focusing on the holistic international student experience. Universities should work to ensure that international students feel safe and supported and thrive in their host countries, especially during crises such as the ongoing pandemic. Given the disproportionate financial contributions international students put into institutions, these students should not be disproportionately omitted from being the beneficiaries of student supports and funding opportunities because of citizenship criteria.

Another step for recentering international students and their needs is language. Treating students as "cash cows," "exports," "economic objects," and "blank checks" is inherently dehumanizing, and it detracts from the inherently beneficial virtue of a diverse campus body. Institutions should revisit their policy briefs, internationalization strategies, and other similar documents to ensure that the language does not project an objectifying view of international students and, importantly, that it remains human-centered.

Advocacy, Policy, and Action

While an ideology shift is important, this needs to be accompanied by tangible action—and institutional change cannot happen alone. Change requires collaboration from universities, governments, and community organizations. Community groups like Migrant Students United (MSU) have advocated for the rights of international students studying at Canadian institutions. MSU puts a lot of emphasis on *fairness*, speaking out against immigration injustice as well as work exploitation. For example, MSU (2020) send a letter to Canadian PMs and asked for better healthcare access, federal income support for international students who lost income during the pandemic, support coping with mounting tuition fees and costs associated with mandatory quarantine, and permanent residency reform. MSU has other ongoing policy recommendations, such as creating easier immigration pathways and abolishing the 20-hour work limit so students can better support themselves financially during their studies.[2]

Labor from groups like MSU is particularly important, as many countries with large international student populations do not have specific legislation or policies that protect the rights of international students, and instead embed those protections within broader policies and legislation (Ramia, 2017). Australia and New Zealand are some of the only countries that have legal frameworks explicitly for international students, centered around rights. Canada would benefit from similar frameworks of care and policy tailored toward the dignity and non-exploitation of international students. The CBIE created a Code of Ethical Practice (2013), which asserts that institutions must "ensure that international students have access to support services that promote their adjustment to life and study in Canada, and to assist in areas that could affect their programs, including physical and mental health services" and "promote understanding among staff and faculty of the special academic, social and cultural needs of international students, with emphasis on the needs of vulnerable groups." This accountability should be enforced and extend beyond CBIE and include all stakeholders in international higher education.

Lastly, in addition to fortified supports, revision of exclusionary policies, and models for best practices, action must be taken to support students who are further marginalized by race. While anti-Asian rhetoric was highlighted during the pandemic, it is just the cusp of a more pervasive problem. Thus, there is an urgent need for educational interventions and research in this area.

Clear, Timely, and Compassionate Communication

International students are often omitted from policy, and when information is tailored to this demographic, it can be confusing, contradictory, or lacking in compassion (Asmelash, 2020; McKenna, 2020). Often when information is disseminated to students, the onus is on the international student to decipher whether the information includes their population or not. With the case of CERB, it was not immediately clear whether international students were eligible as language did not specifically name them. When releasing statements, care must be taken to explicitly indicate whether it is applicable to *all* students, or *some* students to alleviate the additional burden of deciphering when international students are included or excluded. If universities and governments consider the policy-related vulnerability of international students, they can make better decisions and effectively communicate with all their students.

CONCLUSION

Making sense of competing policies, practices, and social commentary, social media posts is no small feat. Even more challenging, the many policies shaping the pandemic and consequently international student experiences, are not static documents—they are subject to change, and COVID-19 is a rapidly evolving landscape. Since the onset of the pandemic, the academic milieu has also changed dramatically, and this article was written in the midst of the pandemic as I experienced it. Writing while enduring a life-defining world event is challenging, but also insightful. It can be difficult to get a clear focus when experiencing something from up close, much like understanding the impact of a storm while you're still in it. With time and perspective, I anticipate that research in this field will be enriched further.

On that note, it is important to recognize that this chapter is not comprehensive in its analysis of the policy barriers and marginalization that international students have experienced during the pandemic, nor was it intended to be. However, in analyzing what I believe are the most salient topics, this chapter pushes the field forward and explores some of the most influential and pressing matters in the contexts of Canada and international education.

The pandemic has perpetuated many inequities that international students experience, such as access to healthcare, job security, and cross-border mobility. Through critical analysis, this chapter exposed issues of inequity in higher education, particularly related to neoliberal ideologies, and examined how the pandemic exacerbated existing issues, including financial hardship, limited support services, discrimination, and policy omissions. Listening to student voices like those from MSU will bring some more humanity to the neoliberal-driven franchise of international higher education. Despite the outlined concerns, there is hope that international education can be honest and non-exploitative. For equitable education and general best practices, students need "resources, respect, recognition, love, care, and solidarity" (Lynch, 2014, p. 132). Centering policies and practices around this philosophy will help ensure that international students receive the support they deserve, during the pandemic and beyond.

NOTES

1 Department of Integrated Studies in Education, McGill University.
2 On October 7, 2022, Canadian Immigration Minister Sean Fraser announced that the 20-hour limit on work hours was temporarily suspended, effective November 15, 2022, and ending December 31, 2023.

REFERENCES

Amin, F., Yawar, M., & Bignell, Q. (2020, October 19). *International post-secondary students call for lower tuition fees as classes move online due to the pandemic.* CityNews. https://toronto.citynews.ca/2020/10/19/international-post-secondary-students-tuition-fees-canadian-universities/

Ansari, S. (2020, September 18). Can Canada's universities survive COVID? *Macleans.* https://www.macleans.ca/education/can-canadas-universities-survive-covid/

Asmelash, L. (2020, February 1). *UC Berkeley faces backlash after stating "xenophobia" is "common" or "normal" reaction to coronavirus.* https://www.cnn.com/2020/02/01/us/uc-berkeley-coronavirus-xenophobia-trnd/index.html

Basen, I. (2016). *Foreign exchange* [Documentary]. CBC. http://www.cbc.ca/player/play/2697845102

BBC News. (2020, June 24). *President Trump calls coronavirus "Kung Flu."* BBC News: US & Canada. https://www.bbc.com/news/av/world-us-canada-53173436

Bilecen, B. (2020). Commentary: COVID-19 pandemic and higher education: International mobility and students' social protection. *International Migration, 58*(4), 263–266. https://doi.org/10.1111/imig.12749

Bothwell, E. (2018). *Insuring against drop in Chinese students*. Inside Higher Ed. https://www.insidehighered.com/news/2018/11/29/university-illinois-insures-itself-against-possible-drop-chinese-enrollments

Canada Industry Strategy Council. (2020). Restart, recover, and reimagine prosperity for all Canadians. https://www.ic.gc.ca/eic/site/062.nsf/vwapj/00118a_en.pdf/$file/00118a_en.pdf

Canadian Bureau for International Education. (2013). *Code of ethical practice*. https://cbie.ca/member-community/our-network/code-of-ethical-practice/

Canadian Bureau for International Education. (2018). *The student's voice: National results of the 2018 CBIE international student survey*. https://cbie.ca/wp-content/uploads/2018/08/Student_Voice_Report-ENG.pdf

Canadian Bureau for International Education. (2019). https://cbie.ca/infographic/

Canadian Charter of Rights and Freedoms, Part 1 of the *Constitution Act, 1982*, being Schedule B to the *Canada Act 1982* (UK), 1982, c 11.

Canadian Federation of Students. (2020). *Fight the fees*. https://cfs-fcee.ca/campaigns/fight-the-fees/

Canadian Health Act. (1985, c. C-6). https://www.canlii.org/en/ca/laws/stat/rsc-1985-c-c-6/latest/rsc-1985-c-c-6.html

Charles, C. H., & Overlid, V. (2020, July 3). *Tuition hikes exacerbating existing challenges for international students*. Institute for Research on Public Policy. https://policyoptions.irpp.org/magazines/july-2020/tuition-hikes-exacerbating-existing-challenges-for-international-students/

Choudaha, R. (2017). Three waves of international student mobility (1999–2020). *Studies in Higher Education, 42*(5), 825–832. https://doi.org/10.1080/03075079.2017.1293872

Crawley, M. (2017, July 12). *Universities growing more reliant on foreign student fees*. CBC News. https://www.cbc.ca/news/canada/toronto/international-students-universities-ontario-tuition-1.4199489

De Wit, H. (2016). The institutional race for international student tuition dollars: Are the costs acceptable? *WENR*. https://wenr.wes.org/2016/05/placing-international-student-mobility-in-a-quality-and-ethical-perspective

De Wit, H., & Merkx, G. (2012). The history of internationalization of higher education. In D. K. Deardorff, H. De Wit, D. Heyl, & T. Adams (Eds.), *The SAGE handbook of international higher education* (pp. 43–60). SAGE Publications.

Deuel, R. P. (2020, June 16). *Not a blank check*. Inside Higher Ed. https://www.insidehighered.com/views/2020/06/16/colleges-must-change-how-they-view-international-students-opinion

Diem, S., Young, M. D., Welton A. D., Mansfield, K. C., & Lee, P.-L. (2014). The intellectual landscape of critical policy analysis. *International Journal of Qualitative Studies in Education, 27*(9), 1068–1090.

Etem, J. (2012). *Will work for words* [Documentary].

Firang, D. (2020). The impact of COVID-19 pandemic on international students in Canada. *International Social Work, 63*(6), 820–824. https://doi.org/10.1177/0020872820940030

Forbes-Mewett, H., & Nyland, C. (2013). Funding international student support services: Tension and power in the university. *Higher Education, 65*(2), 181–192. https://doi.org/10.1007/s10734-012-9537-0

Geary, A. (2020, April 15). *Housing uncertainty adds to pandemic stress for international students in Manitoba*. CBC. https://www.cbc.ca/news/canada/manitoba/manitoba-international-students-housing-uncertainty-1.5533553

Giroux, H. (2002). Neoliberalism, corporate culture, and the promise of higher education: The university as a democratic public sphere. *Harvard Educational Review, 72*(4), 425–463.

Global Affairs Canada. (2014). *Canada's international education strategy: Harnessing our knowledge advantage to drive innovation and prosperity.* https://international.gc.ca/global-markets-marches-mondiaux/assets/pdfs/overview-apercu-eng.pdf

Government of Canada. (2017, December 7). *Human rights.* https://www.canada.ca/en/immigration-refugees-citizenship/services/new-immigrants/learn-about-canada/human-rights.html

Government of Canada. (2019). *Building on success: International education strategy 2019–2024.* https://www.international.gc.ca/education/strategy-2019-2024-strategie.aspx?lang=eng

Government of Canada. (2021a, February 19). *Covid-19: A guide for international students in Canada arriving from abroad.* https://www.canada.ca/en/immigration-refugees-citizenship/corporate/publications-manuals/guide-international-students-arriving-abroad.html

Government of Canada. (2021b, March 23). *Canada emergency response benefit.* https://www.canada.ca/en/revenue-agency/services/benefits/emergency-student-benefit.html

Government of Canada. (2021c, April 27). *Study in Canada as an international student.* https://www.canada.ca/en/immigration-refugees-citizenship/services/study-canada.html

Government of Canada. (2021d, April 30). *Canada emergency student benefit.* https://www.canada.ca/en/services/benefits/ei/cerb-application.html

Government of Canada. (2021e, May 6). *Coronavirus (COVID-19): Designated learning institutions reopening to international students.* https://www.canada.ca/en/immigration-refugees-citizenship/services/coronavirus-covid19/students/approved-dli.html

Government of Canada. (2022, October 24). *Work off campus as an international student.* https://www.canada.ca/en/immigration-refugees-citizenship/services/study-canada/work/work-off-campus.html

Guo, Y., & Guo, S. (2017). Internationalization of Canadian higher education: Discrepancies between policies and international student experiences. *Studies in Higher Education, 42*(5), 851–868. https://doi.org/10.1080/03075079.2017.1293874

Harvey, D. (2007). *A brief history of neoliberalism.* Oxford University Press.

Houshmand, S., Spanierman, L. B., & Tafarodi, R. W. (2014). Excluded and avoided: Racial microaggressions targeting Asian international students in Canada. *Cultural Diversity & Ethnic Minority Psychology, 20*(3), 377–388. https://doi.org/10.1037/a0035404

Hutcheson, S. (2020). Sexual violence, representation, and racialized identities: Implications for International Students. *Education & Law Journal, 29*(2), 191–221.

Johnstone, M., & Lee, E. (2017). Canada and the global rush for international students: Reifying a neoliberal imperial order of western dominance in the knowledge economy era. *Critical Sociology, 43*(7–8), 1063–1078.

Kamil, Y. A. (2020, May 6). "Not actually Canadian": Left out of CERB, many international students in Canada ask what's next. *Study International.* https://www.studyinternational.com/news/cerb-for-students/

Karram, G. L. (2013). International students as lucrative markets or vulnerable populations: A critical discourse analysis on national and institutional events in four nations. *Canadian and International Education, 42*(1), 1–14. https://doi.org/10.5206/cie-eci.v42i1.9223

Keung, N. (2020). What's a Canadian education worth—without the "Canada" part? Universities, colleges try to keep lucrative international students amid COVID-19. *The Star.* https://www.thestar.com/news/gta/2020/09/07/whats-a-canadian-education-worth-without-the-canada-part-universities-colleges-try-to-keep-lucrative-international-students-amid-covid-19.html

Kong, J., Ip, J., Huang, C., & Lin, K. (2021). A year of racist attacks: Anti-Asian racism across Canada one year into the COVID-19 Pandemic. *Chinese Canadian National Council Toronto Chapter.* https://mcusercontent.com/9fbfd2cf7b2a8256f770fc35c/files/35c9d aca-3fd4-46f4-a883-c09b8c12bbca/covidracism_final_report.pdf

Latulipe Loiselle, A., & Jouhari, Y. (2018). *Brief on the deregulation of tuition fees for international students.* https://unionetudiante.ca

Lawless, B., & Chen, Y. W. (2019). Developing a method of critical thematic analysis for qualitative communication inquiry. *Howard Journal of Communications, 30*(1), 92–106.

Lee, J., & Rice, C. (2007). Welcome to America? International student perceptions of discrimination. *Higher Education, 53*(3), 381–409.

Lee, J. J., Maldonado-Maldonado, A., & Rhoades, G. (2006). The political economy of international student flows: Patterns, ideas, and propositions. In Smart, J. C. (Ed.), *Higher education handbook of theory and research* (Vol. 21). Springer.

Lehmann, A. Sriram, A. (2020, September 1). International students can make or break Australia's international reputation. *The National Interest.* https://nationalinterest.org/blog/reboot/international-students-can-make-or-break-australias-international-reputation-168111

Litam, S. (2020). "Take your kung-flu back to Wuhan": Counseling Asians, Asian Americans, and Pacific Islanders with race-based trauma related to COVID-19. *The Professional Counselor, 10*(2), 144–156.

Lomer, S. (2014). Economic objects: How policy discourse in the United Kingdom represents international students. *Policy Futures in Education, 12*(2), 273–285.

Lynch, K. (2014). Why love, care, and solidarity are political matters: Affective equality and Fraser's model of justice. In A. G. Jonasdottir & A Ferguson (Eds.), *Love: A question for feminism in the twenty-first century* (pp. 173–189). Routledge.

Marginson, S. (2020, March 26). Global HE as we know it has forever changed. *Times Higher Education.* https://www.timeshighereducation.com/blog/global-he-we-know-it-has-forever-changed

Marginson, S., & Rhoades, G. (2002). Beyond national states, markets, and systems of higher education: A glonacal agency heuristic. *Higher Education, 43*(3), 281–309. https://doi.org/10.1023/A:1014699605875

Matassa-Fung, D. (2020, April 16). *Coronavirus: Migrant workers, foreign students across Canada calling for aid.* Global News. https://globalnews.ca/news/6830196/coronavirus-migrant-workers-foreign-students-assistance/

McChesney, R. W. (1999). Noam Chomsky and the struggle against neoliberalism. *Monthly Review, 50*(11), 40–40.

McKenna, K. (2020, March 19). *Concordia University kicking students out of residence with only 4 days' notice.* CBC. https://www.cbc.ca/news/canada/montreal/concordia-evicting-students-1.5502455

Mendecino, M. [@marcomendecino]. (2020, September 22). *International students enrich our culture and communities and contribute $22B to Canada's economy* [Tweet]. Twitter. https://twitter.com/marcomendicino/status/1308523015823646721?ref_src=twsrc%5Etfw

Migrant Students United. (2020, April 2). *International students need specific COVID-19 supports* [Letter]. https://migrantworkersalliance.org/wp-content/uploads/2021/05/Migrant-Students-United-Covid19-Supports-Letter.pdf

Mittelmeier, J., & Cockayne, H. (2020). Global depictions of international students in a time of crisis: A thematic analysis of Twitter data during COVID-19. *SSRN.* http://dx.doi.org/10.2139/ssrn.3703604

Morin, S. (2020, March 23). *Some international students left in Canada as borders close around the world.* CBC. https://www.cbc.ca/news/canada/new-brunswick/international-students-stuck-canada-covid19-1.5506606

Mullet, D. R. (2018). A general critical discourse analysis framework for educational research. *Journal of Advanced Academics, 29*(2), 116–142.

Nagesh, A. (2018, April 5). *What are the facts behind the "rich international student" meme.* BBC. https://www.bbc.co.uk/bbcthree/article/390db907-eb87-43bf-b7ca-d5b8293f4fb0

Nicol, L. (2020, October 31). *International student recruitment–is Canada facing a big squeeze?* University World News. https://www.universityworldnews.com/post.php?story=20201028145737147

Nixon, S. A., Yeung, E., Shaw, J. A., Kuper, A., & Gibson, B. E. (2017). Seven-step framework for critical analysis and its application in the field of physical therapy. *Physical Therapy, 97*(2), 249–257.

OECD. (2011). *Who studies abroad and where?* https://www.oecd.org/education/skills-beyond-school/48631079.pdf

Patel, F. (2020, September 5). *Humanising international higher education.* University World News. https://www.universityworldnews.com/post.php?story=20200831081906379

Potok, M. (2017). *The Trump effect.* Southern Poverty Law Center. https://www.splcenter.org/fighting-hate/intelligence-report/2017/trump-effect

Quebec Regie de l'Assurance Maladie. (n.d.) https://www.ramq.gouv.qc.ca/fr

Ramia, G. (2017). Higher education institutions and the administration of international student rights: A low and policy analysis. *Studies in Higher Education, 42*(5), 911–924.

Redden, E. (2020, June 30). *International students' worries during the pandemic.* https://www.insidehighered.com/news/2020/07/01/survey-international-students-main-concerns-center-issues-health-safety-and

Reitmanova, S. (2008). Health insurance for international students: Taxation without representation. *Policy Options, 29*(3), 71–74. http://www.irpp.org/po/archive/mar08/reitmanova.pdf

Rogers, R. (2011). *An introduction to critical discourse analysis in education* (2nd ed.). Routledge. https://doi.org/10.4324/9780203836149

Rukavina, S. (2020, July 21). *International students misinformed about pandemic-related changes to work rules.* CBC. https://www.cbc.ca/news/canada/montreal/international-students-work-covid-19-essential-services-1.5656075

Rutherford, K. (2019, September 11). *International students describe threats, intolerance while in Sudbury.* CBC. https://www.cbc.ca/news/canada/sudbury/diversity-discrimination-international-students-cambrian-laurentian-1.5256577

Scott, C., Safdar, S., Trilokekar, R., & El Masri, A. (2015). International students as "ideal immigrants" in Canada: A disconnect between policy makers' assumptions and the lived experiences of international students. *Canadian and International Education, 43*(3).

Smith, R. A., & Khawaja, N. G. (2011). A review of the acculturation experiences of international students. *International Journal of Intercultural Relations, 35*(6), 699–713.

Statistics Canada. (2020). *Perceptions of personal safety among population groups designated as visible minorities in Canada during the COVID-19 pandemic.* https://www150.statcan.gc.ca/n1/pub/45-28-0001/2020001/article/00046-eng.htm

Statistics Canada. (2021). *Tuition fees for degree programs increase in 2020/2021.* https://www150.statcan.gc.ca/n1/daily-quotidien/200921/dq200921b-eng.htm

Study International. (2017, July 13). *Foreign students are cash cows for Canadian universities.* https://www.studyinternational.com/news/foreign-students-cash-cows-canadian-universities/

Tabnawr/International Student. (2020, August 6). [Comment on the post "Australia student visa applications drop by a third"]. The PIE News. https://thepienews.com/news/student-visa-australian-drop/

Tannock, S. (2018). *Educational equality and international students: Justice across borders?* Palgrave Macmillan. https://doi.org/10.1007/978-3-319-76381-1

Tomlinson. (2019, April 5). False promises: Foreign workers are falling prey to a sprawling web of labour trafficking in Canada. *The Globe and Mail.* https://www.theglobeandmail.com/canada/article-false-promises-how-foreign-workers-fall-prey-to-bait-and-switch/

U.S. Immigration and Customs Enforcement. (2020). https://www.ice.gov/news/releases/sevp-modifies-temporary-exemptions-nonimmigrant-students-taking-online-courses-during

Verghis, S. (2009, September 10). Australia: Attacks on Indian students raise racism cries. *TIME.* http://content.time.com/time/world/article/0,8599,1921482,00.html

Webster, S. (2019, October 18). How geopolitics impacts the world of international education. *New Business.* https://www.newbusiness.co.uk/articles/trainingeducation/how-geopolitics-impacts-world-international-education

Wong, B. (2020, March 25). Universities are failing their students during the coronavirus outbreak. *Times Higher Education.* https://www.timeshighereducation.com/blog/universities-are-failing-their-students-during-coronavirus-outbreak

World Education Services. (2020). *Impact of COVID-19 on the economic well-being of recent migrants to Canada.* https://knowledge.wes.org/canada-report-impact-of-COVID-19-on-the-economic-well-being-of-recent-migrants-to-canada.html

Young, M. D., & Diem, S. (2018). Doing critical policy analysis in education research: An emerging paradigm. In C. R. Lochmiller (Ed.), *Complementary research methods for educational leadership and policy studies* (pp. 79–98). Springer International.

Ziems, C., He, B., Soni, S., & Kumar, S. (2020). Racism is a virus: Anti-Asian hate and counter-hate in social media during the COVID-19 crisis. *arXiv.* https://arxiv.org/pdf/2005.12423.pdf

CHAPTER SIX

Exploring Educational Issues During the COVID-19 Pandemic: A Focus on Students, Teachers, and Families in Ontario, Canada

LAURIE HIGGINS AND WILLIAM T. SMALE[1]

Abstract: The sudden closure of schools in Ontario, Canada during the start of the COVID-19 pandemic in March 2020 impacted educators, children, and families, and it created barriers for disadvantaged populations. As such, this chapter examines the disparities related to pivoting to a digital format of instruction and the disregard for equity in the classroom. We argue that educators' pedagogical practices have been questioned as they navigate their responsibilities, namely, teaching the mandated curriculum to students while keeping everyone safe. In addition, we investigate how educators have been directed to return to in-person instruction while the world continues to deal with the pandemic, and how such efforts have impacted educators. The chapter also considers the government's role in education and how this may or may not rebut what families and educators are requesting in terms of needs and support. We contend that further research is needed to understand the impacts of the COVID-19 pandemic on learners and educators as we continue to uncover and deal with the challenges this pandemic has generated. Overall, we conclude that COVID-19 has greatly influenced how educators approach teaching, including as we move forward, and that members of educational communities must collectively adjust their best practices to support all in a post-pandemic world.

Keywords: education, COVID-19 pandemic, inclusion, safety, pedagogy, mental health, government

INTRODUCTION

At a news conference on March 13, 2020, the Ontario Minister of Education, Stephen Lecce, announced that Ontario schools would be closed for two weeks following the March break, due to an increase of people infected with the novel coronavirus, COVID-19. This sudden closure began weeks of uncertainty for many families and educators. Ontario schools were shut down for two weeks following the March break to help fight the spread of COVID-19. The unprecedented move by the Ford government—believed to be a first for the province and country—began March 23 and impacted "the province's more than two million students" (Rushowy & Benzie, 2020, para. 2). Due to the school closure, discussions regarding a safe return to work for fall 2020 began. These discussions included months of planning to decide on options such as distance learning, learning at school, or a hybrid form of online/in-person learning. Regardless of the uncertainties, anxiety, and inability to escape the threat of COVID-19, families were looking for a way to get back to a "normal" life. For example, Subramanian (2020), the mother of two elementary school students, explained: "I know, I know, it's awful. There's going to be COVID in schools. But we've decided we're taking the risk. They [the students] need to go" (para. 6).

During the spring and summer of 2020, the news and social media provided updates on the virus. The province of Ontario discussed where it could support education and stated that Ontario would be "providing an extra $309 million for COVID-related expenses in schools in 2020, of which $30 million could be used for teachers and educators to reduce class sizes" (Miller, 2020b, para. 11). Regrettably, however, class sizes have not been reduced. The number of students in "bubbles" expanded, and they consist of a faux cohort, since smaller classrooms were not feasible. Subramanian (2020) stated that Public Health "tells us, still, to stay in our bubbles of 10 people; no overlapping bubbles. But kids in elementary school will spend their days with as many as 29 other kids" (para. 8).

Recommendations for working in school cohorts included wearing a facemask, physical distancing, and extensive handwashing. Some studies reported that children were less likely than adults to spread the COVID-19 virus; however, other research stated that transmission could occur and that a spike was inevitable. Some claimed that the numbers of infected patients in Ontario were low and unlikely to spike, but other countries made the same claims and had a different result. For example, numbers were also "low in Germany," but they "spiked in schools in the two weeks after those schools reopened" (Subramanian, 2020, para. 11). Educators in Ontario were anxious to know if their back-to-school plan would be beneficial or detrimental to children. This uncertainty posed many questions for educators who were anxious about returning to work, such as: Will I be responsible for making my family sick? Will I be able to implement my teaching philosophies and best practices with all the restrictions enforced? And, how can I possibly support all my students while I am wearing a mask and a shield and practicing physical distancing?

One of the many challenges has been the uncertainty about how COVID-19 affects the human body and how the virus mutates. At this point in the pandemic (the fall of 2021), we are working to flatten the curve and keep infection numbers down, and we are constantly bombarded with changes to safety protocols and best practices for schools. One concern involves whether children will be up-to-date with their COVID-19 vaccinations or if schools will require a new vaccine that has not yet been completely tested. Another concern is the need for a culturally responsive approach to examining families' choices regarding their children's care and respecting families' decisions. As Modan (2020) reported, "The percentage of children starting kindergarten with exemptions from vaccination requirements has been slightly increasing over the past few years" (para. 5).

Educators are being asked to adapt to a new form of teaching which includes many facets that may be familiar and others that are foreign. Some teachers have taken a synchronous approach and used video platforms such as Zoom, Skype Meet Now, or Google Meet to teach in real time on a regularly occurring date, an approach that comes with its own set of challenges (see Chapter Four). In contrast, other teachers have taken an asynchronous approach, preferring to apply methods that do not require real-time interaction and provide content that is available online for students to access whenever. Whatever approach they take, these twenty-first century educators are now required to manage and prevent the spread of the COVID-19 virus in addition to implementing good pedagogy—all while wearing a mask and shield.

These requirements and challenges raise the following question: How has COVID-19 impacted children's, educators', and families' social interactions, learning experiences, and overall mental health? This chapter examines the impacts of the current pandemic on education, with a particular focus on the province of Ontario. We examine issues of equity and inclusion, particularly those related to students with special needs. We also explore safety procedures and public health issues that educators and families deal with as they engage with different types of teaching and learning. As well, we focus on pedagogical challenges and the many responsibilities that educators are being required to take on. Overall, this chapter discusses and considers the ongoing challenges in education that various stakeholders must adapt to and overcome with the ongoing COVID-19 pandemic.

EQUITY AND INCLUSION

Families with children are struggling with distance learning, working from home, and insufficient (or no) childcare. These problems are particularly challenging for families with special needs children and families who were receiving services and support at home before the pandemic. According to Phoenix (2020), "[T]he lack of support and resources, paired with extra care responsibilities during COVID-19, may compound the physical and mental health challenges already experienced by many parents of children with disabilities" (para. 8). Online learning is not necessarily an option for all children, as accessibility can be a problem, and some families may be challenged by technology. Kadvany (2020) noted that attempting distance learning with children with disabilities is difficult because they tend to be "more hands-on, sensory (learners)," and distance learning can prevent sensory learning (p. 5) while "new research conducted during COVID-19 showed that approximately half of parents with children learning remotely had at least one child struggling with distance learning, which in turn was associated with higher parental stress" (Gallagher-Mackay et al., 2021) which in turn impacted social and family conditions. While children may generally opt to use FaceTime, Zoom, Skype, or a phone to talk to a peer, children with special needs may not have these same options. How do teachers promote and advance social inclusion for students with disabilities, including those who lack social media skills and literacy? When using online learning, some educators are not able to discover which technology will best meet their students' needs. As the changes to the delivery of learning shifted during the pandemic, students of all ages encountered frustrations while trying to study from home as education shifted. However, it is important to note that while the pandemic requires quick decision-making from educational institutions, such decisions should not result in a lack of care or unclear communication with students (see Chapter Five).

One issue that families with children who have disabilities have confronted during the pandemic is that the parents are not professionally trained educators. Families may be drained, burnt-out, stressed about finances, experiencing job loss, and/or be taking on the role of support workers. All these factors exacerbate already challenging living conditions which according to Amiry, "during the COVID-19 pandemic, stay-at-home measures can have major repercussions for children and adults who live in abusive and controlling households" (see Chapter Three, p. 79).

"From March 14, 2020, to May 15, 2021, Ontario schools have been closed for 20 weeks total, longer than any other Canadian province or territory" (Gallagher-Mackay et al., 2021). The challenge for educators and families is to continue with a program that satisfies their children's needs. This process includes finding ways in which accommodations and modifications in a regular classroom setting can continue in a virtual world. Most children with exceptionalities use some form of technology enhancement to assist them with reading, writing, or speaking. The issue for educators is to learn how to support students who may require tools that their homes may be neither equipped with nor comfortable with. For example, students "with visual impairments might use screen-reader software to have text read aloud, or a braille reader to read the text themselves, but many online platforms are not compatible with assistive technology—and even when they are, other problems frequently arise" (Hill, 2020, para. 5). Due to online learning, many families have difficulty supporting their children's educational needs and providing technology support. As Couture-Carron et al. argued in Chapter Four, online instruction quickly became a feature of education during the pandemic, and it will likely remain, even in a post-pandemic world. However, since there was little time to consider the impacts of online instruction, we may continue to uncover unintended consequences of this shift in the years to come (see Chapter Four).

According to the legal doctrine of "standard of care," families could argue that educators are liable for failing to provide the necessities clearly documented in their Individualized Education Plan (IEP). The educator's legal role is described as *in loco parentis* (Latin for "in place of a parent"), and best practices should provide a firm, kind, and respectful discipline for all students. Educators may be overwhelmed by their inability to fully exercise this role during the pandemic. Their once responsive, inquiry-based, and accommodating way of delivering instructions, lessons, and tasks has been altered to a more prescribed, monotonous way of interaction. Some people may argue that the pandemic created an opportunity for creative thinking and more accessible teaching methods for students with disabilities. According to Kahn (2021), "[W]hile many students are looking forward to a return to normality, a return to how things were pre-pandemic is not ideal for students with mobility disabilities." Kahn (2021) also noted, however, that providing online learning for all students has created a more equal playing field for able-bodied and non-able-bodied students to access their studies than was available previously.

Families are also considering different options for education. Some more affluent families have created their own "bubbles" within their community by hiring their own educators, using wealth and affluence to create learning pods for their children instead of exposing them to the petri dish of a public school classroom. *The Globe and Mail* (2020) stated:

> Westview has one of the largest Black student populations in the country and sits in the northwest corridor of Toronto, which has become the epicenter for COVID-19 infections. Many students live in cramped housing, have parents who are essential workers and rely on public transit to get around, all things that contribute to the high infection rate—which is 10 times that of the least-infected parts of the city. The average

annual income for residents in the area is $27,984—half of what it is for Toronto as a whole. (p. 3)

Families who are unable to afford privatized schooling, which supports smaller classroom sizes, are exposed to increased risk of infection. Some families in low-income neighborhoods are also opting out of face-to-face learning and using distance learning because they either live with elderly family members or are in high-risk areas in the city. Moreover, others "live in high-rises and don't want to endure waits of an hour or longer just to take the elevator while pandemic-related capacity limits are in place—and they worry about physical distancing in such a cramped space" (Bascaramurty & Alphonso, 2020, para. 13). Schooling in general has never been equitable, and the reality is that education is even more inequitable during this pandemic.

As the Toronto District School Board (TDSB) considered online learning a form of higher education, "the adoption of e-learning is not recommended because it risks contributing to and reinforcing inequitable education policies as it fails to acknowledge race and discrimination which are factors seldom measured and addressed" (Allen et al., 2020) for many students living in marginalized groups that were not able to have access to such technology/learning.

The modality of learning in the past has involved face-to-face interactions, assessments, hands-on activities, and paper handouts. Now faced with a pandemic, educators are examining how formative assessments can be relevant in a teaching space that is virtual for some and socially distanced for others. How can educators ensure that students are on track with their learning? How do we measure our ability as educators to deliver information and learning in an asynchronous or synchronous learning space? According to Liberman et al. (2020), the challenge is that "teachers usually implement summative assessments whereby specific educational content is reviewed to determine the extent to which students reached the expected learning goals and acquired critical knowledge and skills" (para. 2). The Ontario Ministry of Education (2013) suggests that teachers should "plan instruction and assessments that are differentiated and personalized to meet students' learning strengths, needs, interests, and learning preferences " (p. 28). However, doing so can be a challenge with students who lack participation, operational cameras, and assistance from parents.

This new change in practice and roles also includes safety measures for educators. Many parents wonder about the effectiveness of wearing a mask and worry that most masks will not be adequate to keep their children safe. Masks will also become one of the added supplies that families will need to purchase for students this year. Children are asked to practice wearing a mask at home, as they will be asked to wear one while attending school. The age of students required to wear masks continues to change, and families struggle with these changes. According to Weikle (2020), "[M]asks are an important piece of the picture, but infectious disease experts warn they're not enough on their own to manage outbreaks" (para. 8). Families may find it difficult to convince their children to wear something on their face while they are playing, learning, and exercising at school. Teachers realize that wearing a mask makes it harder for children to hear them, prevents children from reading lips or facial expressions, and affects interactions. Teachers want all students to come prepared with at least two masks per day. Weikle (2020), in an opinion piece for CBC News, stated: "[W]hen your mouth gets moist or wet, if [the mask] feels like it's getting damaged in any way so that the integrity of it is not maintained, or if you think you've been sprayed with something or someone sneezed and you were right there, and it did its job protecting you, at that point you should be changing your mask" (Weikle, 2020, para. 31). How are schools supporting families with multiple children, low income, and an extra cost? Parents are hoping that most "schools in areas with mask mandates will allow some room for interpretation based on individual needs" (Weikle, 2020, para. 24). We should ask if we are creating a space that meets all learners' needs by requiring them to play and learn independently, wear a mask, and deal with unwanted stresses. When thinking about conducive learning spaces, teachers know that students learn best if teachers support all learning styles, have the ability to see facial expressions, and are given extra time to navigate all the changing components in a classroom.

According to Maxwell and McDonough (2018), it "is the school's responsibility to maintain and pupils' right to enjoy an institutional environment favorable to learning" (p. 229). The pandemic has challenged educators' practices and beliefs, as their new learning spaces are not favorable to learning. According to a *Public Health of Ontario Checklist* (2021), students will have assigned washroom areas, eat lunch in their classroom, and be divided into cohorts. Signage will be "posted informing students, teachers, school-based staff, and visitors of the maximum occupancy" (p. 9) and will limit capacity at any one time to the extent that is practical/feasible to facilitate physical distancing.

Students will no longer be permitted to use some materials that they are familiar with, and the delivery of information will differ from previous practices. An article in The Washington Post stated, "[F]orget physical books, pencils or papers for quick-writes; all reading and writing will be done on laptops, even if students are in physical classrooms" (Strauss, 2020, para. 5). For primary grades, this change becomes problematic, as young learners need books, singing, and paper. These are all things that are now forbidden in the classroom and will not be permitted. CBC News provided insight into what a kindergarten classroom in Ontario would be like during the pandemic: "Spaced out desks, single squares of carpet, bagged up water fountains and check marks above bathroom stalls and urinals are just some of the new features schools will have for students as they reopen during the COVID-19 pandemic" (Hristova, 2020). These classrooms will include few toys, limited interactions with peers, and frequent handwashing throughout the day. These conditions do not provide a typical entry to the school environment, and for some students who are returning to school, will pose a challenge.

LIABILITY/SAFETY PROCEDURES

Doug Ford's government in Ontario has tried to be transparent in the decisions it has made during the pandemic, such as those involving safety protocols and social distancing in public places, but this government's messages about education are often inconsistent and unclear. More transparent is the government's lack of understanding of the importance of social interactions and mental health, as educators are being asked to psychologically accept that school will be a "safe" environment. According to Ludwig (2020), "[O]ne of the most important ways to support employees during reopening is to follow pandemic best practices regarding sanitation and social distancing" (para. 6). Ludwig (2020) further observed that "[e]mployers should think about how to utilize spaces differently" than they were used previously, by providing "at least six feet of space between employees and, if possible, installing physical barriers to help prevent the transmission of airborne germs" (para. 6).

Although families and educators are fearful about returning to school, planning to return has begun. The curriculum and teaching techniques have been revised, revisited, and amended multiple times, causing uneasiness and stress for educators. The guidelines have changed from requiring everyone to wear a mask while indoors, to not requiring children under Grade 3 to wear masks, to now requiring all students to wear masks. These guidelines and requirements also differ greatly across the country. In British Columbia, "students and staff will not be required to wear masks in schools," and the province stated that the decision to do so is a "personal choice that will always be respected" (*The National Post*, 2020, para. 7)—but in Ontario, "masks will be mandatory for students in Grades 4 through 12, and will be strongly encouraged for younger kids when they're in indoor common areas. Staff will be expected to wear masks" (The National Post, 2020, para. 12).

The *National Post* (2020) emphasized that proper ventilation in schools and personal protective equipment (PPE) for all educators were necessary requirements for a safe return to work. In Ontario, the various teachers' unions have pressured the Ministry of Education regarding safety for all, but Premier Ford does not appear to be listening. Rushowy (2020) noted, "It warns it will use 'all legal avenues' to challenge that reopening plan" (para. 24). Although the government is pushing for a return to the classroom, "the Ontario Secondary School Teachers' Federation, claimed his union members" had not been consulted or "given an advance look at the plan" (Taube, 2020), stating that teachers were being forced back to work regardless of the concerns and risks in a face-to-face school setting while student numbers continue to rise.

MacKay et al. (2020), in their book entitled *Teachers and the Law: Diverse Roles and New Challenges*, discussed the safety of students and educators alike and highlighted several factors that administrations should consider when deciding whether to return to school in person. According to the *Occupational and Health and Safety Act* (1990), educators in Ontario schools have rights which include "a safe working environment" (MacKay et al., 2020, p. 244). This chapter discussed educators and students with special needs, but the same legislation is provided for workplace safety in general. Many teachers worry that this legislation may not provide appropriate protection, proper protocols or even best practices for teaching. According to the Canadian Press (2020), "Ontario's four major teachers' unions alleged that the province's back-to-school plan violates its own occupational health and safety legislation" and that "the provincial plan failed to provide adequate health and safety protections such as smaller class sizes, minimal measurable standards for ventilation in schools, and mandatory masking for younger children" (para. 4). The problem is whether educators and support staff in schools will be able to manage all their professional responsibilities during the pandemic. Miller (2020a) argued that "teachers and students are not infection-control specialists ... we cannot maintain physical distance if we are cleaning our classroom together. Nor will we have much time, because we will have already spent 3 hours of our day washing our hands" (para. 18).

Another issue for families and educators involves protocols when a child is sick or falls ill during the school day. During this COVID-19 pandemic, it is hard to know whether the child has caught COVID or the common cold. Do parents and educators take the risk of letting the child attend classes in person? Additionally, the fall return to school becomes more problematic as the flu season is beginning and variant strains of the COVID-19 virus are circulating globally. According to King (2020), "Kulik, who is also the founder and director of the Toronto medical clinic Kidcrew, said parents should keep kids at home and isolated for 14 days if they feel unwell, and extend that to other family members" (para. 8).

Families might need to keep their children at home, as they will be exposed to different groups of people and germs of school. King (2020) pointed out, "With flu season just weeks away, children with a runny nose, cough or sore throat could have either COVID-19, influenza or just the common cold" (para. 2).

Educators are now taking on the role of physician, nurse, and public health practitioner as they assess students' health and monitor possible symptoms on a daily basis. The teachers' goal is to curb the spread of the virus, and doing so means wearing many hats to ensure that if families and children are able to return "to school, they will be safe" (Mitsui, 2020, para. 5).

With the above considerations in mind, an educator's role now differs from what it was before the pandemic. Today's educators must often take on the roles of parent, social worker, environment manager, coach, mentor, role model, resource specialist, tutor, instructional leader, as well as counselor. In addition, and especially during this pandemic, one of educators' most important roles is that of an advocate. Bascaramurty and Alphonso (2020) argued that the "issue of advocating for a safe and equitable return to school is not about advocating for one's own community or one's own child" (para. 49). They further declared that advocating works only if people are advocating for something that will support everyone (Bascaramurty & Alphonso, 2020, para. 50).

Educators have always advocated for children's educational needs, but now must also take on the role of advocate for health and safety. This role includes advocating for a safe and healthy environment, one that supports learning and is not a breeding ground for viral infections. MacKay et al. (2020) stated that the *Education Act* was amended to include "placing an obligation on the school boards to promote a climate of acceptance and inclusion, including the support of students who want to create school-centered organizations to promote equality" (p. 218). How can an organization provide a space that includes teachers who are supporting students and fostering acceptance while wearing a facemask and invoking social distancing? MacKay et al. (2020) also discussed the duties of educators. They must have a collective agreement to protect and support employees who are taking on roles and responsibilities that are not part of the job description. Doing so now includes taking on the role of nurse practitioner, by assessing students' health upon their arrival at school and even taking temperatures. MacKay et al. (2020) further stated, "There must be a clause in the legislation or collective agreement that contemplates the assignment of additional duties" (p. 225). What are the liabilities in assessing, caring for and perhaps even diagnosing a child with a serious health condition such as the COVID-19 virus? How do educators see their role in infection control? Miller (2020b) reported that trustees had "heard from representatives of unions representing staff who raised concerns ranging from not enough custodians to disinfect desks twice a day to occasional teachers and other staff who work at multiple schools or in multiple classrooms" (para. 20). The Ontario government, and other provincial governments, must examine all the risks when asking educators to take on additional roles and work in what may not be a safe environment.

Robert Smol suggested that educators are in fact the profession that undergoes "the most stress" (as cited in MacKay et al., 2020, p. 243) due to burnout from not balancing their workloads. Experiencing emotional exhaustion, teaching in larger classrooms, and taking on different roles are some of common factors that cause tension within this profession. Now with COVID-19 and the many challenges that have come about during the pandemic, we anticipate that educators' stress and anxiety will be multiplied when we add more duties to their already full timetable.

PEDAGOGY

One of the many issues that educators are experiencing in the pandemic involves being able to provide a learning environment that complements their pedagogy. This issue looks very different in the wake of COVID-19, as teachers must navigate social distancing, handwashing, as well as wearing PPE. Bouffard (2020) stated, "my biggest concern is teachers needing to balance the importance of safety procedures with creating a welcoming and loving environment for our student" (para. 1). Kindergarten, for example, already includes many components, and due to COVID-19, the introduction to school will look very different. There will be no gathering times, no cozy corners, no small grouping, no assemblies (unless virtually), no sharing of materials and manipulatives, no book bins, no sharing of snacks, no helping each other get dressed for recess, no holding hands, and no playing closely together at recess. As children begin their first year of their education, the goal for educators is to provide an experience that is similar to children's experiences at home. This year, the worry is that the beginning of the school year could be a traumatic start rather than a positive one. The method of teaching for this year should be more fluid, flexible, and authentic than previous teaching methods. Children may be already struggling with reading facial expressions and mouths, as masks are hindering sound and articulation. Bouffard (2020) declared, "facial expressions are an important way of communicating and building relationships" (para. 6).

Early childhood educators have standards of practice to help guide and support them in facilitating learning for their students, such as the *Code of Ethics and Standards of Practice* (2017) from the College of Early Childhood Educators (CECE). According to CECE, as part of teachers' pedagogical practice, "it is important to critically reflect on child development and learning theories to consider what is missing when children and their families are viewed through linear, fixed stages that may not account for race, gender, socio-economic status or religion" (College of Early Childhood Educators, 2020, p. 4). Educators must think of methods that will support students, their families, and themselves during this time. In some spaces, pedagogy is referred to as "curriculum," which is the mandated teaching that the Ministry of Education requires of educators and includes the learning environment, invitations to play, as well as interactions with students. As CECE explained, "With a purposeful approach to pedagogy, the curriculum is meaningful for children" (College of Early Childhood Educators, 2020, p. 5). Implementing a pedagogy that supports and develops a responsive and reflective approach is the goal for educators. Achieving this goal will be a challenge when enforcing social distancing and other public health guidelines throughout the day. A guarantee of smaller class sizes to minimize learning interruptions would be optimal and support educators, who are trying to navigate new regulations and to follow best practices for all. Unfortunately, the Ontario provincial government does not see the need to provide these spaces. This government defended its "back-to-school plan as the most well-funded and comprehensive in the country but did not back down on elementary class sizes" (Modan, 2020). The government's intransigence may become taxing on educators, whose role has changed to include providing infection-control measures in their classrooms.

One of the benefits of teaching during a pandemic is that educators are making history. While working during unprecedented times, they are framing their teaching to meet the needs of the ongoing lived experiences of their students and themselves. They must create a balance for their classroom community, which should consist of spaces for everyone to discuss how they are feeling, the lack of a "normal" school day, and, perhaps, the lack of simple experiences such as sharing a pencil. Educators can utilize the pandemic conditions to teach lessons about empathy, compassion, and caring for others. Now more than ever, students' work should be individualized based on needs, interests, and overall health and well-being. Modifying the workload, changing the due dates, and making accommodations for those who may need them will ensure that students are able to learn. Educators' pedagogical approaches must evolve with the pandemic. Lee-Heart (2020) argued that it is "time to be more intentional than ever before about our pedagogy. Our survival depends on it" (p. 10). This awareness involves knowing what learning objectives educators aim for their students to achieve and what children's current capabilities and knowledge are.

CONCLUSION

The return to school in the fall of 2020 and spring of 2021 was not as simple as school returns in the past. Entering a space of uncertainties is not an ideal situation. The Ontario government is pushing for full-service education as our economy is in disarray from a months-long shutdown. Teachers now have evolving plans, gray-area protocols, and no guidelines for a safe return to work. CBC News (2020) reported that although about "two million Ontario students are heading back to school this month amid a global pandemic, the provincial government says there is no scenario in which a student will be required to take a COVID-19 test" (p. 1), so educators want answers for how they best can support children and families, keep themselves safe, and not overburden our healthcare system.

The needs for proper ventilation systems, maintaining social distancing, handwashing stations around schools, and multiple daily handwashing routines are just some of the many factors causing tension for educators during the pandemic, not to mention the responsibility of keeping children safe. Some experts believe that "children rarely develop severe symptoms, [but other] experts have cautioned that open schools might pose a much greater risk to teachers, family members, and the wider community than to students themselves" (Couzin-Frankel & Vogel, 2020). The government has spent over $25 million on internet and technology upgrades to improve the virtual delivery of teaching. Why not use this investment to continue to deliver remotely until the COVID-19 pandemic ends and is not looming as a third wave in our future?

If the 2020–2021 academic year was any indication of what is to come, the coming academic years that occur during this pandemic—or other pandemics—will pose many unforeseen challenges to students, educators, and parents. Specifically, we anticipate that academic years during a pandemic will present daunting learning curves to educators as they struggle to make their learning inviting, responsive, and equitable, and to create a sense of community in their classrooms despite the many public health restrictions and other safety concerns. According to Saavedra (2020), "what we need to avoid—or minimize as much as possible—is for those differences in opportunities to expand and cause the crisis to have an even larger negative effect on poor children's learning" (para. 3). Being creative, encouraging engagement, and staying connected with the children and their families will help overcome this learning crisis.

A study of secondary education students in Ontario who graduated in 2020, and had enrolled in a post-secondary program that fall showed "that the shift to online classrooms negatively affected academic experiences and mental and physical health—especially for those with disabilities or from low-income households" (Napierala et al., 2022). We recognize the impact that this global pandemic has set upon education, educators, children and their families. Collaborative efforts from all disciplines are necessary moving forward to uphold best practices as well as ways of adapting to a new norm of "schooling" that supports all.

NOTE

1 School of Education, Trent University.

REFERENCES

Allen, J., Mahamed, F., & Williams, K. (2020). Disparities in education: E-learning and COVID-19, who matters? *Child & Youth Services, 41*(3), 208–210.

Bascaramurty, D., & Alphonso, C. (2020, September 5). *How race, income and "opportunity hoarding" will shape Canada's back-to-school season*. The Globe and Mail. https://www.theglobeandmail.com/canada/article-how-race-income-and-opportunity-hoarding-will-shape-canadas-back/

Bouffard, S. (2020, August 4). *How to stay physically, but not emotionally, distant with kindergarten and pre-k students mind shift*. KQED. https://www.kqed.org/mindshift/56320/how-to-stay-physically-but-not-emotionally-distant-with-kindergarten-and-pre-k students

College of Early Childhood Educators (2017). *Code of ethics and standards of practice*. https://www.college-ece.ca/wp-content/uploads/2021/10/Code_and_Standards_2017-4.pdf

College of Early Childhood Educators (2020). *Practice guideline*. https://www.college-ece.ca/en/Documents/Practice_Guideline_Pedagogical_Practice.pdf

Couzin-Frankel, J., & Vogel, G. (2020, July 7). *Not open and shut: School openings across the globe suggest ways to keep the coronavirus at bay, despite outbreaks*. Science. https://www.science.org/doi/10.1126/science.369.6501.241/

Gallagher-Mackay, K., Srivastava, P., Underwood, K., Dhuey, E., McCready, L., Born, K. B., Maltsev, A., Perkhun, A., Steiner, R., Barrett, K., & Sander, B. (2021). *Covid-19 and education disruption in Ontario: Emerging evidence on impacts*. https://doi.org/10.47326/ocsat.2021.02.34.1.0

Hill, F. (2020, May 13). *The pandemic is a crisis for students with special needs*. The Atlantic. https://www.the atlantic.com/education/archive/2020/04/special-education-goes-remote-covid-19-pandemic/610231/

Hristova, B. (2020, August 26). *Here's what a Hamilton classroom will look like during COVID-19*. CBC News. https://www.cbc.ca/news/canada/hamilton /what-class-looks-like-covid-19-1.5699318

Kadvany, E. (2020, July 17). *What does special education look like during a pandemic?* Palo Alto Weekly. https://www.paloaltoonline.com/news/2020/07/17/what-does-special-education-look-like-during-a-pandemic

Kahn, G. (2021, March 3). *COVID-19 has made education more accessible for university students with mobility disabilities*. CBC News. https://www.cbc.ca/news/canada/montreal/disabilities-university-pandemic-access-distance-learning-1.5932146.

King, A. (2020, August 29). *Keep sick kids home from school even if they test negative for COVID-19, pediatricians warn parents*. CBC News. https://www.cbc.ca/amp/1.5704384

Lee-Heart, K., Dr. (2020, September 1). Pandemic pedagogy: A call to educators to bring their classrooms to reality. *Teaching Tolerance*. https://www.tolerance.org/magazine/pandemic-pedagogy-a-call-to-educators-to-bring-their-classrooms-to-reality

Liberman, J., Levin, V., & Luna-Bazaldua, D. (2020). *Are students still learning during COVID-19? Formative assessment can provide the answer*. World Bank Blogs. https://blogs.worldbank.org/education/are-students-still-learning-during-covid-19-formative-assessment-can-provide-answer

Ludwig, S. (2020, June 3). *How to support employees as they return to work post-coronavirus*. U.S. Chamber of Commerce. https://www.uschamber.com/co/run/human-resources/how-to-support-employees-as-they-return-to-work-post-coronavirus

MacKay, A. W., Sutherland, L. I., & Barnett, J. (2020). *Teachers and the law: Diverse roles and new challenges* (4th ed.). Emond Montgomery.

Maxwell, B., & McDonough, K. (2018). Reasonable limits on teachers' freedom of expression in the classroom. In W. T. Smale (Ed.), *Perspectives on Canadian educational law and policy* (pp. 221–244). Word & Deed Publishing.

Miller, M. (2020a, August 7). *Ontario teacher pens open letter expressing concerns about province's school plan.* BlogTO. https://www.blogto.com/city/2020/07/ontario-teacher-open-letter-school-plan/

Miller, J. (2020b, August 12). Lowering class sizes to 15 would require more than 1,000 teachers, says Ottawa school board. *Ottawa Citizen Newspaper.* https://ottawacitizen.com/news/local-news/lowering-class-sizes-to-15-would-require-more-than-1000-teachers-says-ottawa-school-board

https://files.ontario.ca/edu-learning-for-all-2013-en-2022-01-28.pdf

Mitsui, E. (2020, August 27). *Ontario reveals COVID-19 school outbreak plan, including rules for student dismissals and closures.* CBC News. https://www.cbc.ca/news/canada/toronto/covid-19-coronavirus-ontario-august-26-school-outbreaks-1.5700360

Modan, N. (2020, July 10). *Will schools mandate COVID-19 vaccine or face liability?* K-12 Drive. https://www.educationdive.com/news/will-schools-mandate-covid-19-vaccine-or-face-liability/580893/

Napierala, J., Pilla, N., Pichette, J., & Coylar, J. (2022, June 30). *Ontario learning during the COVID-19 pandemic: Experiences of Ontario first-year postsecondary students in 2020–21.* Higher Education Quality Council of Ontario. https://heqco.ca/pub/ontario-learning-during-the-covid-19-pandemic-experiences-of-ontario-first-year-postsecondary-students-in-2020-21/

National Post. (2020, August 12). I don't think anyone should be sending their kids back: Ontario teachers worried about return to school. *National Post Newspaper.* https://nationalpost.com/news/canada/covid-19-ontario-teachers-worried-about-return-to-school

Occupational and Health and Safety Act, R.S.O. 1990, c. O.1.

OHS Canada Magazine. (2020, August 14). *Teachers' unions Allege Ontario back-to-school plan breaks provincial law.* The Canadian Press. https://www.ohscanada.com/teachers-unions-allege-ontario-back-school-plan-breaks-provincial-law/

Ontario Ministry of Education. (2013). *Learning for ALL. A guide to effective assessment and instruction for all students, Kindergarten to Grade 12.*

Phoenix, M. (2020). *Children with disabilities face health risk, disruption and marginalization under coronavirus.* Brighter World. https://theconversation.com/children-with-disabilities-face-health-risks-disruption-and-marginalization-under-coronavirus-137115

Public Health Ontario. (2021, March 3). *CHECKLIST COVID-19 preparedness and prevention in elementary and secondary (K-12) schools.* https://www.publichealthontario.ca/-/media/documents/ncov/sch/2020/09/covid-19-checklist-preparedness-schools.pdf?la=en.

Rushowy, K. (2020, July 27). Opening Ontario schools safely amid COVID could require up to $3.2 billion funding for staff, cleaning supplies, say Liberals, staff union. *Toronto Star Newspaper.* https://www.thestar.com/politics/provincial/2020/07/27/opening-ontario-schools-safely-amid-covid-could-require-up-to-32-billion-funding-for-staff-cleaning-supplies-say-liberals-staff-union.html

Rushowy, K., & Benzie, K. (2020, March 13). Ontario schools to shut down for two weeks after March Break to fight the spread of COVID-19. *The Toronto Star*. https://www.thespec.co m/news/ontario/2020/03/13/ontario-schools-to-shut-down-for-two-weeks-after-march-break-to-fight-the-spread-of-covid-19.html

Saavedra, J. (2020, March 30). *Educational challenges and opportunities of THE Coronavirus (COVID-19) pandemic*. World Bank Blogs. https://blogs.worldbank.org/education/educational-challenges-and-opportunities-covid-19-pandemic

Strauss, V. (2020, May 8). Perspective | A teacher predicts what his classroom (and others) will look like in the fall. *The Washington Post*. https://www.washingtonpost.com/education/2020/05/08/teacher-predicts-what-his-classroom-others-will-look-like-fall/

Subramanian, S. (2020, August 24). Parents of Ontario, maybe it's time to call a strike. *Maclean's Magazine*. https://www.macleans.ca/opinion/parents-of-ontario-maybe-its-time-to-call-a-strike/

Taube, M. (2020, August 20). Opinion | DOUG FORD'S plan for education in Ontario TURNS political—thanks to the unions. *The Washington Post*. https://www.washingtonpost.com/opinions/2020/08/20/doug-fords-plan-education-ontario-turns-political-thanks-unions/

Weikle, B. (2020, August 21). *How many masks should my child take to school? Your back-to-school mask questions answered*. CBC News. https://www.cbc.ca/news/health/back-to-school-m ask-questions-covid-19-1.5693511

PART III

Health and Well-Being

CHAPTER SEVEN

Sex Work as Public Health: A Critical Discourse Analysis of Canada's COVID-19 Pandemic Response for Sex Workers

SARAH TOWLE[1] AND ALEXANDRA M. ZIDENBERG[2]

Abstract: During the first wave of the COVID-19 pandemic, public health messaging was a crucial method for managing the spread of SARS-CoV-2. Canada's initial response to the pandemic involved a lockdown and multiple restrictions, as well as occupational guidelines and social assistance for both the general population and specific communities. Despite this, sex workers were left out of many public health interventions, even though sex workers regularly come into close contact with other individuals. In our chapter, we present a case study and critical discourse analysis of how sex workers were represented in select public health communications across Canada during the first wave of the pandemic, and we juxtapose these publications with a community guide jointly released by two organizations that serve sex workers. Applying a public health ethics framework from the Public Health Agency of Canada and a legal framework built off the United Nations' Advisory Group on Sex Work (Overs & Loff, 2013), we demonstrate how governmental publications present a homogeneous view of sex work with limited attention to sex workers' health concerns, while the community guide provides a more intersectional and holistic approach. We conclude that further efforts are needed in Canada to better represent and meet the needs of sex workers during this pandemic and in future public health emergencies.

Keywords: sex work, sex workers, discourse analysis, policy analysis, COVID-19 pandemic, first wave, public health

INTRODUCTION

While the COVID-19 pandemic and its resulting public health crisis have affected many populations in Canada, recent data from news articles, personal narratives, and emerging research point to one group that has been particularly hard-hit: members of the sex work community. With most sex workers ineligible for social assistance programs (COVID-related or otherwise) due to the ambiguous legal status of their occupation, many of them are forced to continue to see clients in person to make an income. Although Canadian governments at regional, provincial, and federal levels have released countless operational protocols for workplaces, businesses, schools, community gatherings, and even places of worship, few guidelines exist for sex workers—despite the unique public health risks inherent to the intimate nature of sex work during a global pandemic.

The importance of accessible, inclusive, and consistent public health messaging—particularly during a pandemic—has been well-established in evidence-based practices and incorporated into regulatory guidelines (Public Health Agency of Canada [PHAC], 2020b; Kass, 2001). Though research on this topic remains limited, commentaries in journals such as *The Lancet* highlight that COVID-19 messages have focused too heavily on hygiene and social etiquette measures, while ignoring the needs of marginalized communities (Karamouzian et al., 2020, Platt et al., 2020). While there has been a relative explosion in the number of articles written about sex workers in later stages of the pandemic (e.g., Benoit & Unsworth, 2022; Cubides Kovascsics et al., 2022; Pearson et al., 2022; Shankar et al., 2022), at the time of writing, no one has explored public health messages aimed at sex workers during the first wave of the pandemic (i.e., the first wave of the pandemic has generally been defined as encompassing the time period between the first case reported and May 2020; Coccia, 2021; Kuniya, 2020), either in Canada or worldwide. Thus, given the importance in early messaging regarding the COVID-19 pandemic (Sauer et al., 2021; Zhang et al., 2021), this chapter focuses on public health messaging aimed at sex workers during the first wave of the pandemic.

Pre-pandemic findings point to stereotypical depictions of the community: sex workers are frequently represented as threats to public health and safety, substance users, "fallen women," and victims of violence (Benoit & Shumka, 2015; Benoit & Unsworth, 2022; Bruckert & Hannem, 2013; Parent, 2012; Shannon et al., 2007). Such framings can perpetuate a "discourse of disposal" and risk reinforcing or exacerbating inequalities that the sex work community already faces (Putnis & Burr, 2020).

In this chapter, we use the terms "sex work" and "sex workers." First, at a community level, these terms are preferred over morally charged alternatives, such as "prostitution" or "prostitute" (Bruckert et al., 2013). Second, the term "prostitution" is limiting, despite still being referenced in legal settings. In Canada's Bill C-36, "prostitution" refers to the purchase of a sexual service leading to sexual gratification of the purchaser (Parliament of Canada, 2014). However, this categorization ignores the broader sex work community, including those engaged in nude/exotic dancing, pornography, escort services, and/or other services. Further, the term "sex work"—in contrast to the term "prostitution"—acknowledges that the occupation and those engaged in it are worthy of protection, safety, and rights (Bruckert et al., 2013). Adopting the terms "sex work" and "sex worker" is therefore more inclusive of the community itself and the broad nature of the profession.

This chapter begins with an overview of the needs of sex workers in Canada, both generally and during the COVID-19 public health crisis, with a particular focus on the first wave. Next, we present a case study and critical discourse analysis of how sex workers are represented in select communications during the first wave of the pandemic. Three select provincial publications are juxtaposed with an analysis of a more comprehensive community guide jointly released by two organizations that serve sex workers. Drawing on both a public health ethics framework released by the PHAC during the pandemic and a legal framework built off the United Nations' Advisory Group on Sex Work (Overs & Loff, 2013), we demonstrate how representations in these two cases differ: the former presents a homogeneous view of the community with limited notions of their health concerns, while the latter takes a more intersectional and holistic approach. We conclude that further consideration is needed on behalf of regional, provincial, and federal governments to determine how to better represent and meet the established needs of sex workers during the ongoing pandemic.

COVID-19 AND THE CANADIAN PUBLIC RESPONSE

Though initially discovered in December 2019 during an outbreak in the Wuhan province of China, COVID-19—an infectious and potentially deadly upper-respiratory disease caused by the most recent strain of coronavirus—quickly spread worldwide, triggering a global pandemic. The first documented case of the virus was reported in Canada on January 27, 2020 (PHAC, 2020b), and by mid-March, the World Health Organization declared the disease a global pandemic. Consequently, federal and provincial governments imposed a complete lockdown of non-essential services. Businesses, schools, and other institutions have since reopened, with restrictive zones and guidelines varying based on provincial jurisdiction. There have been multiple waves of the pandemic in Canada (Mandel et al., 2022), with researchers generally agreeing that the first wave lasted from when the first case was reported to May 2020 (Coccia, 2021; Kuniya,

2020). Along with differences in symptomology and infection rates, there has been a notable difference in levels of knowledge related to COVID-19 among both lay people and medical professionals during the first and subsequent waves of the pandemic (Jain et al., 2021).

During the first wave, governmental responses to the pandemic were far-reaching, with many broad measures in place, such as border closures and restrictions on social gatherings due to the infectious nature of the virus (Government of Canada, 2020). With unemployment rates reaching record highs in these early days (Statistics Canada, 2020), the federal government released multiple financial programs for Canadians, totaling hundreds of billions of dollars (Government of Canada, 2020). The Canadian Emergency Response Benefit (CERB) provided monthly financial assistance to millions of Canadians dealing with loss of employment. Other forms of financial assistance have included subsidies for essential workers, holds on student-loan repayments, increases to child and senior tax benefits, improved assistance for persons with disabilities, and income and funding support to Indigenous communities (Government of Canada, 2020).

Additionally, non-financial federal responses have included the purchase of personal protective equipment (PPE) for essential workers, increased access to mental health services, a publicly available COVID-tracking app, as well as the release of public health guidelines for institutions, workplaces, faith leaders, and people experiencing homelessness or addiction (Government of Canada, 2020). Regional governments have also been implementing their own supports. While a review of all of these programs goes beyond the scope of this chapter, some notable measures include: the opening of temporary homeless and domestic violence shelters (see Chapter Three), the enforcement of masks and/or hand-sanitization before entering indoor public spaces, provincial guidelines for the reopening of elementary and secondary schools, and increased public restrooms and sanitation stations in areas known to deal with homelessness (City of Toronto, 2020; City of Vancouver, 2020; McElroy, 2020; Rukavina, 2020).

Canadian Sex Workers and the First Wave of COVID-19

Despite the Canadian governmental responses detailed above, no specific policies—beyond the few guidelines reviewed in this chapter—were developed with sex workers in mind, and sex workers continue to be excluded from the global conversation on COVID-19 (Banerjee & Burke, 2022). Information about how sex workers were coping with the first wave of the COVID-19 pandemic was mainly restricted to media reports and statements from advocacy groups. Multiple articles in mainstream media suggested that sex workers were being left out of Canada's response to the pandemic—most notably from accessing CERB, as many sex workers are either ineligible or too afraid to apply, due to the criminalized nature of their work (Pearson et al., 2022; Wright, 2020a).³ Personal narratives in the media suggested that these workers were in desperate need of financial support; some were experiencing homelessness, while others were returning to work in unsafe conditions in private or third-party establishments (Hensley & Bowden, 2020; Wright, 2020b). This concern was demonstrated in August 2020, when an exposure to COVID-19 was reported by staff and patrons in a reopened Toronto strip club (Toronto Public Health, 2020). While many sex workers have faced economic hardships, community organizations that serve sex workers have reported that those with dependents, disabilities, precarious housing, and precarious immigration status have reported the most adversity (Peterson, 2020). While some sex workers attempted to move their work online, the shifting legal status of online sex work made that a somewhat difficult option (Peterson, 2020). Moreover, transitioning to jobs outside of sex work can be quite difficult for these individuals because of the stigma associated with sex work (Peterson, 2020).

Advocates have called for sex work reform during the pandemic. Some proposals include the immediate decriminalization of the trade,⁴ extension of CERB or other financial assistance, access to PPE and improved healthcare services (Amnesty International, 2020; Fry, 2020). To date, the government's responses to calls for action have been underwhelming, and no federal return-to-work guidelines have been released for sex workers (Banerjee & Burke, 2022; Lewis, 2020). As one columnist noted in an online publication, "once again, people working in the sex industry are at the end of the list of government priorities" (Lewis, 2020).

Sex Work in Canada: Representations of Sex Workers, Ongoing Stigma, and Stereotypes

Independent of the COVID-19 pandemic, the sex work community in Canada faces multiple challenges which must be explored to contextualize the needs of the community and to recognize how such challenges may be exacerbated during a global pandemic. One such challenge includes the continued stigma and stereotyping of workers. Even in the wake of Bill C-36, notions that sex workers pose health risks to society, threaten family values, are substance users, and disrupt neighborhoods pervade media depictions, public and legal discourses, and even contemporary scientific studies (Benoit & Shumka, 2015; Bruckert & Hannem, 2013; Parent, 2012; Shannon et al., 2007). In addition, sex workers are stereotypically depicted as an "at-risk" population, one that is vulnerable to victimization by clients, pimps and traffickers (Bruckert & Hannem, 2013; Hallgrimsdottir et al., 2006).

There is no denying the existence of abusive situations in the sex work industry or the intersections of oppression that some sex workers face. Indigenous and trans women are overrepresented in sex worker communities, and street-based sex workers have been shown to be both more susceptible to violence and less likely to report violence to police (Benoit & Shumka, 2015; Bingham et al., 2014). Similar trends have been observed among victims of domestic violence (see Chapter Three). However, as Colette Parent (2012) noted, workers choose to sell sexual services for a variety of reasons, including extra income, unemployment, pleasure, and survival, and this plurality must be recognized in portrayals of the work. Moreover, mounting evidence suggests that much of what has been identified as harmful in sex work (e.g., sexual health risks, substance use, exposure to violence) results from the criminalized nature of the work and the lack of social and governmental support, rather than the sex work itself (Benoit & Shumka, 2015; Bruckert & Hannem, 2013; Krüsi et al., 2012).

Occupational Safety

Occupational safety has long been a concern for sex workers in Canada, despite community organizations and advocates aiming to improve work conditions. In our review of the literature, two main and overlapping occupational risks related to sex work emerged: sexual and/or physical violence and workers' health outcomes.

It is challenging to quantify incidents and risks of physical and/or sexual violence in sex work, due to a variety of compounding factors. First, sex work's recent (and still partial) illegality in Canada has been a barrier for workers reporting violence to police (Bruckert et al., 2013), and the aforementioned plurality of the trade and of workers themselves means that experiences with violence vary widely. Advocates maintain that the majority of transactions between sex workers and clients can and do occur safely (Benoit & Shumka, 2015), even though a global systematic review of the correlates of violence against sex workers found that incidents of workplace violence ranged from 32 % to 75 % (Deering et al., 2014). For street-based sex workers in Canada, a 2009 prospective cohort study based in Vancouver found that 57 % of 237 participants experienced gender-based violence over an 18-month period (Shannon et al., 2009).

A point supported by both advocates and evidence-based research is that the continued criminalization of sex work leads to increased risks of violence. Qualitative findings have demonstrated that workers' ability to practice safe sex is compromised by a lack of safe spaces to take clients and the adverse impacts of local policing (Shannon et al., 2008). These issues have not resolved with the adoption of Bill C-36; police enforcement toward clients impacts sex workers' safety by forcing them to rush screening of clients in public spaces and by displacing transactions to unpopulated areas (Krüsi et al., 2014). Indoor work environments have been shown to improve safety by promoting the capacity to refuse clients and to negotiate condom use. Researchers have concluded that indoor venues are a form of public health and violence prevention for sex workers (Krüsi et al., 2012).

The second identified occupational risk to sex workers, as mentioned above, relates to workers' overall health outcomes. Again, the sex worker experience implicates an intersection of identities that have individual bearings on the social determinants of health. Research findings on sex work suggest that there is no direct correlation between sex work and STIs (Spittal et al., 2003); rather, workers are at an increased risk of contracting STIs due to mitigating factors associated with street-level work, including intravenous drug use, engaging in unprotected sex with intimate partners, and being coerced into having unprotected sex (Benoit, 2015; Bingham et al., 2014). Sex workers who identify as visible minorities and/or as Indigenous also experience a higher level of sexual and physical health risks (Benoit, 2015; Bingham et al., 2014). Naturally, sex workers also have health needs beyond those associated with STIs and intravenous drug use, including concerns related to chronic pain, muscular-skeletal issues, and mental health (Benoit & Shumka, 2015).

As this section demonstrates, sex workers experience a wide range of occupational risks under non-pandemic conditions that affect their physical and sexual safety and overall health outcomes. It is also important to note that these risks may be exacerbated based on an intersection of the profession with individual identities that are historically and presently oppressed by society and/or with the type of sex work (indoor or outdoor) being undertaken.

Access to Healthcare and Social Services

Despite the complex health issues detailed above, sex workers continue to experience barriers in accessing health and social services (Lazarus et al., 2012; Phillips & Benoit, 2005; Socías et al., 2016). Often, these barriers stem from stigmatization of the profession. Findings demonstrate that sex workers feel uncomfortable disclosing their work status to healthcare professionals for fear of discrimination (Phillips & Benoit, 2005). This fear is heightened among sex workers who are pregnant or parenting, with this sub-population reporting a lack of financial governmental support (including maternity leave) and an avoidance of social services for fear of punitive measures regarding their children (Duff et al., 2015). Some community organizations have recognized the lack of support available to at-risk populations who face economic barriers and, during times of crisis, stepped in and offered valuable health resources (see Chapter Nine). Moreover, findings demonstrate that institutional barriers including hours of operation and requirements of provincial health cards also negatively impact sex workers' ability to access services (Socías et al., 2016). Implementation of peer health supports and community-led initiatives for sex workers have been shown to improve confidence in accessing services and increase knowledge about health issues (Benoit et al., 2017).

Sex Work and COVID-19

Research on the experiences of sex workers during the first wave of the pandemic emerged slowly due to the developing nature of the situation. Of the few empirical studies on the subject, results have found that male sex workers—in comparison to other sex workers—face considerable economic strain (Callander et al., 2020). Follow-up analyses have demonstrated that since May 2020, sex workers have begun to return to in-person work (Callander et al., 2020). Theoretical findings have highlighted multiple vulnerabilities facing the sex work community during the COVID era; workers might not seek or be eligible for healthcare social services and/or financial support and may also face increased police presence (and potential deportation for migrant populations) due to enforcement of pandemic regulations (Platt et al., 2020). It has also been suggested that sex workers with underlying health conditions may be more susceptible than the general population to contract a serious illness following a COVID-19 infection (Jozaghi & Bird, 2020). Moreover, those who continue to do in-person work may be putting themselves at an increased risk of contracting the virus (Platt et al., 2020).

Canadian scientific journals have raised concerns of the heightened risk of infection for sex workers and have urged federal and provincial governments to provide financial supports for the community (Jozaghi & Bird, 2020). To our knowledge, research has not yet explored any support or communication that Canadian governments have provided to sex workers during the pandemic's first wave and beyond, nor how sex workers are depicted in any such documents. Given the heightened vulnerabilities that this community faces during the pandemic, exploration of any official governmental supports or communication directed to sex workers represents a knowledge gap that we aim to fill.

METHODOLOGY

As noted above, research on sex work in Canada during the COVID-19 pandemic is lacking. At the time of writing, no one has yet explored existing supports nor analyzed the few published guides—both community and governmental—that exist for this population. Our chapter addresses this gap by considering the following research questions: How are sex workers represented in both official governmental and community-based publications that exist to provide support to this population during the COVID-19 pandemic? What supports and/or resources are being offered to sex workers during the COVID-19 pandemic in these publications?

To answer these questions, we adopted a multiple case study approach (Hesse-Biber & Leavy, 2011). We defined a "case" as a Canadian guide released during the first wave of the COVID-19 pandemic and targeted toward the sex work community. Case 1 represents those produced by official government sources, and Case 2 represents those produced by community-based organizations. The heterogeneity between cases provided a more comprehensive analysis, which allowed us to compare and contrast the representations of workers and depictions of their supports from distinct sources, and to identify areas of strengths and/or deficiencies in each sources' messaging.

We used purposive sampling strategies to collect government publications and community-based publications from July to September 2020. For Case 1, we collected all known publications at federal, provincial, and territorial levels of government. This led to the discovery of three documents from three distinct provincial governments (i.e., Alberta, British Columbia, and Newfoundland), which were included in the study. For Case 2, we examined a single community guide. We made this choice after a preliminary scan of multiple cross-Canada organizations that serve sex workers. Rather than produce their own guides, most organizations referenced and/or provided links to this particular guide, which was co-published by two Toronto-based organizations. It must be noted that the publications in both cases (four in total) are targeted toward multiple audiences. While the predominant audience is sex workers, it also includes clients (i.e., those who frequent sex workers), business owners where sex work takes place, and sex work allies (e.g., family members, friends, and harm-reduction workers). Sampling and subsequent analysis occurred in August and September 2020.

We adopted a critical discourse analysis for this study. Critical discourse analysis—based on Norman Fairclough's (1993) three-dimensional framework—allows for an awareness of the hegemonic power that discourse holds (Blommaert & Bulcaen, 2000). As evident in the literature, social stigma and stereotyping greatly impact sex workers, thereby hindering their abilities to feel safe and to access social services, and this may be exacerbated during the COVID-19 pandemic. As such, a critical discourse analysis of these publications acknowledges the importance of their linguistical choices, the situatedness of the texts, and the ideological effects these discourses may have for the sex work community during the pandemic (Blommaert & Bulcaen, 2000).

Our analysis was informed by two relevant frameworks: The PHAC's (2020a) *Public Health Ethics Framework*, released specifically to aid provincial governments, institutions, and organizations in decision-making on COVID-19, and Overs and Loff's (2013) legal framework for sex workers' health and human rights.

First, we chose Canada's *Public Health Ethics Framework* (2020) as it was intended to be a guide for public policy, communications, and decisions related to the pandemic. Of relevance, this framework highlights principles such as justice, intersectionality, minimizing harm, promoting well-being, and respect for individuals and communities (PHAC, 2020a). It also states that public health actions during the pandemic must promote the bio-psycho-social health of all communities, including those already marginalized, and must not "reproduce the biases and stereotypes that are further entrenching inequalities in this pandemic" (PHAC, 2020a, p. 6).

Second, we chose Overs and Loff's (2013) legal framework, *Toward a Legal Framework That Promotes and Protects Sex Workers' Health and Human Rights*, as it provides context on issues concerning sex workers. The following three principles in this framework were particularly noteworthy to our analysis: (1) a commitment to ensuring that commercial sex can take place under healthy and safe conditions; (2) guaranteed access for sex workers to health and social services; and (3) justice, including but not limited to, protection from violence, abuse, and discrimination (Overs & Loff, 2013). Together, these two analytic frameworks complement one another for our analysis, which lies at the intersection of both the pandemic and sex work.

FINDINGS FROM GOVERNMENT PUBLICATIONS: NARROW AND STEREOTYPICAL REPRESENTATIONS OF SEX WORKERS

The discourses in the three government publications generally depicted sex workers as a homogeneous group and perpetuated known stereotypes of this population. To our first point, beyond adopting gender-neutral language, only one publication made references to subsets of the sex work population. Non-binary and Indigenous sex workers were mentioned in links to external resources, and racial diversity was referenced once in a brief section geared toward clients (suggesting that they do not discriminate against Asian workers).[5] Aside from these indirect acknowledgments, the publications mainly depicted sex workers as a monolithic community with uniform needs. Moreover, the discourses suggested that sex workers worked indoors, were not entirely dependent on sex work income, had ample access to technology, and could easily implement COVID-19 sanitation measures.

Discourses in the government publications also perpetuated known stereotypes of sex workers through covert public health messages. Alongside mention of standard COVID-19 hygiene practices (e.g., frequent handwashing, isolating if symptomatic, disinfecting surfaces) were unrelated health messages. All publications highlighted at least one of the following: the importance of condom and birth control use; where to seek out STI screenings; harm-reduction approaches to substance use; and overdose awareness, including naloxone access. These messages were so heavily asserted that in one publication, the second sentence (in a section on COVID-19 and sex) stated that STIs are on the rise in the province and that "the safest sex partner is yourself," thereby recommending masturbation as an alternative to sex and/or sex work. While these messages may be relevant to sex workers depending on mitigating factors, their emphasis in publications meant to relay COVID-19 information should be questioned; they present sex workers as "at-risk" and may lead to further stigmatization of the population.

Our analysis further revealed that concrete resources and/or supports for sex workers were lacking. Discourses in the documents focused on individual behavioral changes sex workers could make to avoid COVID-19 exposure, such as ceasing in-person work, engaging in technology-based work, and screening clients for symptoms. The documents offered few external supports or resources that workers could potentially access. No mention was made of PPE or where to obtain it for those continuing in-person work. When COVID-19 testing was mentioned, it was unclear what kind of documents or finances one needed to obtain the test; existing COVID-19 mental health supports were not referenced; and only one document mentioned available economic assistance via a community organization. As such, the documents framed sex workers' health in relation to COVID-19 solely in physical terms (e.g., remaining COVID-negative) rather than taking a biopsychosocial—or more holistic—approach to health and well-being during the pandemic.

FINDINGS FROM THE COMMUNITY GUIDE: SEX WORKER COMMUNITY AS DIVERSE AND SELF-DETERMINING

Unlike the government publications, the community guide applied an intersectional lens to its depictions of sex workers. Discourses described the sex work community as diverse and called attention to the specific challenges that marginalized populations may face during the pandemic. For instance, the document acknowledged that queer, trans, low-income, and racialized sex workers—populations that are systemically disadvantaged in society and face disproportionately high rates of social insecurities and health challenges—may still need to work during the pandemic to address their basic needs for food, medicine, childcare, and rent.

Additionally, messages about COVID-19 in the community guide were not only relevant (i.e., they did not deviate into unrelated or stigmatizing topics) but also highlighted notions of self-determination and autonomy for sex workers. Content focused on detailed options for safer sex work during the pandemic, including sexual positions that avoid face-to-face contact and the use of condoms, dental damns, and gloves. As well, discourses directed toward sex workers were predominantly conditional rather than authoritative: "*if possible*, decline clients who have cold symptoms," "*whenever possible*, avoid kissing," and "*consider* offering services such as erotic massage or strip tease" [emphasis added]. This framing denoted a level of trust in sex workers to make individual decisions that balance the risks of COVID-19 with their potential dependency on sex work.

Overall, the community guide presented a broader depiction of sex workers. They were represented as a diverse group with the autonomy to make their own decisions according to their individual needs and/or barriers they came across during the pandemic. But beyond that, the self-determining discourse surrounding sex work and COVID-19 recognizes "the unique capacity of individuals and communities to make decisions about their own aims and actions" (Canada, Public Health Agency, 2020a, p. 7).

Our analysis also found that the community guide provided a more detailed list of supports and resources compared to the government publications. This was achieved in the discourse in two ways: (1) by highlighting the community effort required to support sex workers during the pandemic; and (2) by adopting a comprehensive, biopsychosocial approach to health and well-being.

First, the community guide included sections with information targeted toward clients, third parties (i.e., business owners), and sex worker allies (e.g., family, friends). Discourses drew attention to actions that this broader community could take, not only to stop the spread of COVID-19 but also to support workers. Clients were to respect workers' adjusted boundaries and tip generously; business owners were to implement public health signage and wave cancellation fees; and allies were to check in on workers to offer emotional and/or financial support.

Second, the community guide did not solely focus on hygienic practices but instead provided detailed resources on biopsychosocial approaches to well-being. The first sentence of the guide, for instance, referenced the "stress and panic" that the pandemic has caused the sex work community. A page was also dedicated to maintaining mental and physical well-being during the pandemic, with recommendations to avoid media overload, seek out trusted sources for COVID-19 updates, maintain a well-rounded diet, stay physically active, and reach out to friends and family online. Discursive framings constructed these broader concerns as equally essential to sex workers' health as remaining COVID-negative. Other sections provided lists of community and government financial resources and information on how to access COVID-testing freely and without documentation.

Two relevant points were absent from the guide: information on how to cope with COVID-19 after testing positive and how to deal with safety concerns during the pandemic, including increased police presence. As well, it must be noted that not all sex workers may have access to the stated community support or be eligible for the resources listed. Still, despite these omissions, the community guide provided a more comprehensive and holistic approach to support and resources than the government publications.

DISCUSSION

In this chapter, we aimed to analyze the differences and/or similarities between government publications and community-based publications targeted toward sex workers in Canada during the COVID-19 pandemic. Our findings clearly demonstrated how governments and community organizations differ in their representations of workers and in their framings of available supports and resources. Moreover, and as this discussion will examine, our analysis also indicated that while the government publications failed to meet certain ethical standards outlined in the frameworks of this study—the PHAC's *Public Health Ethics Framework* (2020a) and Overs and Loff's *Toward a Legal Framework That Promotes and Protects Sex Workers' Health and Human Rights* (2013)—the community guide more accurately attained them. Here, we argue that the latter provided better support to sex workers during the early pandemic and that future government publications need to be revised to be more inclusive and less stigmatizing of this often-marginalized population.

We turn first to the issue of representation of sex workers in these cases. Our findings demonstrated that, unlike the community guide, the government publications overlooked the known plurality (and plurality of needs) of the sex work population (Parent, 2012) and perpetuated "at-risk" stereotypes of workers. This aligns with previous research on sex worker depictions (Bruckert & Hannem, 2013; Hallgrimsdottir et al., 2006) and on the long-standing relationship between public health campaigns and the stigmatization of vulnerable populations (Guttman & Salmon, 2004). In this way, the government publications did not reflect the values of intersectionality and of respect for diverse communities outlined in frameworks of both Overs and Loff (2013) and the PHAC (2020a).

Moreover, we argue that these representations are harmful. Through their "at-risk" depictions of sex workers, the documents reproduced "the biases and stereotypes that are further entrenching inequalities in this pandemic" (PHAC, 2020a, p. 11). These stereotypes—that sex workers are substance users, susceptible to unwanted pregnancies, and/or STI-positive—may make workers feel stigmatized by the governing bodies producing these documents. As such, workers may be less likely to reach out for needed health and social services, which are more important during this global pandemic than ever before.

The question remains as to why this difference in representations of sex workers persisted between these two sources. At a surface level, the community-based publication clearly presented a peer-to-peer and self-empowering perspective in its messaging, one that a community organization would arguably be more attuned to due to its proximity to sex workers themselves. However, we believe the difference in messaging between these cases goes beyond the grassroots positioning of the community guide. Here, we point to the covert public health messages embedded throughout the government publications and their underlying purpose: to target sex workers against unrelated and presumptive health threats. To include these covert messages blatantly places public health interests (i.e., lowering STI and overdose rates) above the actual needs of sex workers during the pandemic. Rectifying this involves setting aside these public health interests (or including them in separate publications unrelated to sex work) and instead including information relevant to sex workers.

Turning to the second result that emerged from the findings—the framings of supports and resources—as demonstrated, the community guide provided a more comprehensive overview while also highlighting responsibilities that the broader community has in keeping sex workers safe from COVID-19. Whereas the government publications framed sex worker health solely in physical terms, the detailed content on support and resources in the community guide worked to better "promote and protect the physical, psychological and social health and well-being" of sex workers (PHAC, 2020a, p. 8). In this way, the community guide was more aligned with the values and principles of both analytical frameworks (PHAC, 2020a; Overs & Loff, 2013).

The incomplete information in the government publications surrounding PPE, the logistics of COVID-19 testing, and financial assistance is not only unethical but unacceptable given (1) the known barriers sex workers regularly face to accessing health and social services; and (2) the added disparities that this community faces during the pandemic. Effective and thorough health communication has been identified as a key factor in fighting the COVID-19 pandemic (Finset et al., 2020). Although the community guide was not without its deficiencies as established in the findings, it clearly supplants the government publications in providing meaningful, accurate, and empowering guidance to its target demographic.

While this chapter examines public health messaging during the pandemic, it is important to note that the issues identified in this chapter were not necessarily caused by the pandemic. The exclusion of sex workers and the relegation of their knowledge to "grey literature" predates COVID-19 and has been referred to as an epistemic injustice (Matos & Woods, 2022). Indeed, differences in content and focus have been noted between the issues presented in the academic literature and those presented by sex workers and their allies long before the pandemic (Matos & Haze., 2019). When examining research related to relationships and condom use, Matos and Haze (2019) observe a similar pattern of infantilization, denial of sex worker agency, and a hyper-focus on risk which is not always relevant to the situation at hand that we noted in our analysis of the government documents. While COVID-19 may have exasperated the issues inherent in public health messaging aimed at sex workers, as it did with many other public health issues (e.g., Barari et al., 2020; Nan et al., 2022), this seems to be an amplification of the issues observed prior to the pandemic rather than a novel phenomenon.

CONCLUSION

This chapter provided a case study of select publications from two distinct sources aimed at the sex work community in Canada during the first wave of the COVID-19 pandemic, applying relevant public health ethics and legal frameworks in a critical analysis. Findings outlined how the government publications are disconnected from sex workers and their needs during the pandemic and how the community-based publication was more firmly entrenched in the community it is meant to support. Homogeneous and ultimately stigmatizing representations of workers dominated the government documents, while the community guide applied an intersectional lens to its depictions. The latter also provided comprehensive support and resources that acknowledged a more holistic version of sex workers' health. The findings of Case 1 align with previous research on sex work stereotypes (Bruckert & Hannem, 2013; Hallgrimsdottir et al., 2006) and suggests that the representations in the government publications may be preventing sex workers from seeking important health and social services during the pandemic (Lazarus et al., 2012; Phillips & Benoit, 2005; Socías et al., 2016).

During this global health crisis, it is crucial that potentially vulnerable and marginalized populations such as sex workers have access to complete information that does not increase barriers to services. Peer health supports and community-led initiatives have been shown to improve sex workers' understanding of health issues and access to care (Benoit et al., 2017), and the community guide clearly reflects this in its approach. Further research is needed on how sex workers are responding to these COVID-related communications and what improvements they would propose. Still, moving forward, government communications targeted toward sex workers during the pandemic must work to diversify and destigmatize their approach. Only then can the disparities that already burden this population and that have been exacerbated during the pandemic begin to be addressed.

NOTES

1. Department of Family Medicine, McGill University.
2. Department of Psychology, King's University College.
3. There are many reasons why a sex worker may be ineligible for CERB. To qualify for benefits, workers must hold a valid social insurance number, have filed a 2018 or 2019 tax return, and have made at least $5,000 of taxable (reportable) income in the past 52 weeks. Advocates argue that barriers such as these disproportionately discriminate against sex workers who often may not report income and/or may be migrants.
4. *Bill C-36: Protection of Exploited Persons Act* was enacted as federal law in Canada in 2014 and effectively decriminalized solicitation by sex workers and bawdy houses (embracing what is commonly referred to as the "Nordic Model" of sex work regulation). However, the law still targets clients and outdoor transactions by criminalizing the purchase and advertisement of sex work in public spaces (PHAC, 2014; Parliament of Canada, 2014).
5. It has been noted that Asian sex workers in particular may be facing racism and discrimination during the pandemic, notably due to the virus having originated in China (Lam, 2020).

REFERENCES

Amnesty International. (2020, April 23). *The rights of sex workers are being ignored in the COVID-19 response: In conversation with Jenn Clamen of the Canadian Alliance for Sex Work Law Reform.* Amnesty International Canada. https://www.amnesty.ca/blog/rights-sex-workers-are-being-ignored-covid-19-response-conversation-jenn-clamen-canadian

Banerjee, D., & Burke, A. (2022, August 8). *Sex work is real work: Global COVID-19 recovery needs to include sex workers.* The Conversation. https://theconversation.com/sex-work-is-real-work-global-covid-19-recovery-needs-to-include-sex-workers-183773

Barari, S., Caria, S., Davola, A., Falco, P., Fetzer, T., Fiorin, S., ... & Slepoi, F. R. (2020). Evaluating COVID-19 public health messaging in Italy: Self-reported compliance and growing mental health concerns. *MedRxiv.* https://doi.org/10.1101/2020.03.27.20042820.

BC Centre for Disease Control. (2020). *COVID-19 and sex.* http://www.bccdc.ca/health-info/diseases-conditions/covid-19/prevention-risks/covid-19-and-sex

Benoit, C. (2015, April). *Are all sex workers victimized?* CIHR Institute of Gender and Health. https://cihr-irsc.gc.ca/e/documents/igh_mythbuster_issue5_2015_en.pdf

Benoit, C., & Shumka, L. (2015, May 7). *Sex work in Canada.* Power Ottawa. https://www.powerottawa.ca/wp-content/uploads/2019/09/2015-05-07-Benoit-Shumka-Sex-Work-in-Canada_2.pdf

Benoit, C., & Unsworth, R. (2022). COVID-19, stigma, and the ongoing marginalization of sex workers and their support organizations. *Archives of Sexual Behavior, 51*(1), 331–342.

Benoit, C., Belle-Isle, L., Smith, M., Phillips, R., Shumka, L., Atchison, C., Jansson, M., Loppie, C., & Flagg, J. (2017). Sex workers as peer health advocates: Community empowerment and transformative learning through a Canadian pilot program. *International Journal for Equity in Health, 16.* https://doi.org/10.1186/s12939-017-0655-2

Bingham, B., Leo, D., Zhang, R., Montaner, J., & Shannon, K. (2014). Generational sex work and HIV risk among Indigenous women in a street-based urban Canadian setting. *Culture, Health & Sexuality, 16*(4), 440–452. https://doi.org/10.1080/13691058.2014.888480

Blommaert, J., & Bulcaen, C. (2000). Critical discourse analysis. *Annual Review of Anthropology, 29*(1), 447–466. https://doi.org/10.1146/annurev.anthro.29.1.447

Bruckert, C., & Hannem, S. (2013). Rethinking the prostitution debates: Transcending structural stigma in systemic responses to sex work. *Canadian Journal of Law & Society, 28*(1), 43–64.

Bruckert, C., Caouette, A.-A., & Clamen, J. (2013, April). *Language matters: Talking about sex work.* Global Network of Sex Work Projects. https://www.nswp.org/sites/nswp.org/files/StellaInfoSheetLanguageMatters.pdf

Callander, D., Meunier, É., DeVeau, R., Grov, C., Donovan, B., Minichiello, V., Kim, J., & Duncan, D. (2020). Investigating the effects of COVID-19 on global male sex work populations: A longitudinal study of digital data. *Sexually Transmitted Infections, 97,* 93–98. https://doi.org/10.1136/sextrans-2020-054550

Canadian Public Health Association. (2014, December). *Sex work in Canada.* Canadian Public Health Association. https://www.cpha.ca/sites/default/files/assets/policy/sex-work_e.pdf

City of Toronto. (2020, April 3). *COVID-19: Orders & bylaws.* https://www.toronto.ca/home/covid-19/covid-19-what-you-should-do/covid-19-orders-directives-by-laws/

City of Vancouver. (2020). *COVID-19 (Coronavirus): Community support.* https://vancouver.ca/people-programs/community-resilience.aspx

Coccia, M. (2021). Effects of the spread of COVID-19 on public health of polluted cities: Results of the first wave for explaining the dejà vu in the second wave of COVID-19 pandemic and epidemics of future vital agents. *Environmental Science and Pollution Research, 28*(15), 19147–19154.

Cubides Kovacsics, M. I., Santos, W., & Siegmann, K. A. (2023). Sex workers' everyday security in the Netherlands and the impact of COVID-19. *Sexuality Research and Social Policy, 20*(2), 810-824.

Deering, K. N., Amin, A., Shoveller, J., Nesbitt, A., Garcia-Moreno, C., Duff, P., Argento, E., & Shannon, K. (2014). A Systematic Review of the Correlates of Violence Against Sex Workers. *American Journal of Public Health, 104*(5), e42–e54. https://doi.org/10.2105/AJPH.2014.301909

Duff, P., Shoveller, J., Chettiar, J., Feng, C., Nicoletti, R., & Shannon, K. (2015). Sex work and motherhood: Social and structural barriers to health and social services for pregnant and parenting street and off-street sex workers. *Health Care for Women International, 36*(9), 1039–1055. https://doi.org/10.1080/07399332.2014.989437

Fairclough, N. (1993). Critical discourse analysis and the marketization of public discourse: The universities. *Discourse & Society, 4*(2), 133–168.

Finset, A., Bosworth, H., Butow, P., Gulbrandsen, P., Hulsman, R. L., Pieterse, A. H., Street, R., Tschoetschel, R., & van Weert, J. (2020). Effective health communication: A key factor in fighting the COVID-19 pandemic. *Patient Education and Counseling, 103*(5), 873–876. https://doi.org/10.1016/j.pec.2020.03.027

Fry, H. (2020, May 13). Dr. Hedy Fry: Sex workers and COVID-19. *The Georgia Straight.* https://www.straight.com/news/dr-hedy-fry-sex-workers-and-covid-19

Government of Canada. (2020). *Canada's COVID-19 economic response plan—Overview.* https://www.canada.ca/en/department-finance/economic-response-plan/fiscal-summary.html

Guttman, N., & Salmon, C. T. (2004). Guilt, fear, stigma and knowledge gaps: Ethical issues in public health communication interventions. *Bioethics, 18*(6), 531–552. https://doi.org/10.1111/j.1467-8519.2004.00415.x

Hallgrimsdottir, H. K., Phillips, R., & Benoit, C. (2006). Fallen women and rescued girls: Social stigma and media narratives of the sex industry in Victoria, B.C., from 1980 to 2005. *Canadian Review of Sociology/Revue Canadienne de Sociologie, 43*(3), 265–280. https://doi.org/10.1111/j.1755-618X.2006.tb02224.x

Hensley, L., & Bowden, O. (2020). *Some sex workers' income has "completely dissolved" due to COVID-19. Here's how they're surviving.* Global News. https://globalnews.ca/news/6883831/sex-workers-coronavirus/

Hesse-Biber, S. N., & Leavy, P. (2011). *The practice of qualitative research* (2nd ed.). SAGE; WorldCat.org. http://hdl.library.upenn.edu/1017.12/366295

Jain, V. K., Iyengar, K. P., & Vaishya, R. (2021). Differences between First wave and Second wave of COVID-19 in India. *Diabetes & Metabolic Syndrome, 15*(3), 1047.

Jozaghi, E., & Bird, L. (2020). COVID-19 and sex workers: Human rights, the struggle for safety and minimum income. *Canadian Journal of Public Health, 111*(3), 406–407. https://doi.org/10.17269/s41997-020-00350-1

Karamouzian, M., Johnson, C., & Kerr, T. (2020). Public health messaging and harm reduction in the time of COVID-19. *The Lancet Psychiatry, 7*(5), 390–391. https://doi.org/10.1016/S2215-0366(20)30144-9

Kass, N. E. (2001). An ethics framework for public health. *American Journal of Public Health, 91*(11), 1776–1782.

Krüsi, A., Chettiar, J., Ridgway, A., Abbott, J., Strathdee, S. A., & Shannon, K. (2012). Negotiating safety and sexual risk reduction with clients in unsanctioned safer indoor sex work environments: A qualitative study. *American Journal of Public Health, 102*(6), 1154–1159. https://doi.org/10.2105/AJPH.2011.300638

Krüsi, A., Pacey, K., Bird, L., Taylor, C., Chettiar, J., Allan, S., Bennett, D., Montaner, J. S., Kerr, T., & Shannon, K. (2014). Criminalisation of clients: Reproducing vulnerabilities for violence and poor health among street-based sex workers in Canada—A qualitative study. *BMJ Open, 4*(6), e005191. https://doi.org/10.1136/bmjopen-2014-005191

Kuniya, T. (2020). Evaluation of the effect of the state of emergency for the first wave of COVID-19 in Japan. *Infectious Disease Modelling, 5*, 580–587.

Lam, E. (2020). Migrant sex workers left behind during COVID-19 pandemic. *Canadian Journal of Public Health/Revue Canadienne de Santé Publique, 111*(4), 1–2. https://doi.org/10.17269/s41997-020-00377-4

Lazarus, L., Deering, K. N., Nabess, R., Gibson, K., Tyndall, M. W., & Shannon, K. (2012). Occupational stigma as a primary barrier to health care for street-based sex workers in Canada. *Culture, Health & Sexuality, 14*(2), 139–150. https://doi.org/10.1080/13691058.2011.628411

Lewis, J. (2020, July 22). *Sex workers treated as criminals, and left without support, during COVID-19.* The Tyee. https://thetyee.ca/Analysis/2020/07/22/Sex-Workers-Without-Support/

Mandel, E., Peci, A., Cronin, K., Capraru, C. I., Shah, H., Janssen, H. L., ... & Feld, J. J. (2022). The impact of the first, second and third waves of Covid-19 on hepatitis B and C testing in Ontario, Canada. *Journal of Viral Hepatitis, 29*(3), 205–208.

Matos, B., & Haze, L. (2019). Bottoms up: A whorelistic literature review and commentary on sex workers' romantic relationships. *Sexual and Relationship Therapy*, *34*(3), 372–391.

Matos, B., & Woods, J. (2022). Carnal knowledge: Epistemic injustice and the wisdom of whores. In *Sex work, labour and relations* (pp. 151–184). Palgrave Macmillan.

McElroy, J. (2020, April 29). *B.C. government should buy hotels being used for homeless, advocates say*. CBC News. https://www.cbc.ca/news/canada/british-columbia/vancouver-homeless-hotels-bc-government-covid-19-coronavirus-1.5549370

Nan, X., Iles, I. A., Yang, B., & Ma, Z. (2022). Public health messaging during the COVID-19 pandemic and beyond: Lessons from communication science. *Health Communication*, *37*(1), 1–19.

Overs, C., & Loff, B. (2013). Toward a legal framework that promotes and protects sex workers' health and human rights. *Health and Human Rights Journal*, *15*(1). https://www.hhrjournal.org/2013/10/toward-a-legal-framework-that-promotes-and-protects-sex-workers-health-and-human-rights/

Parent, C. (2012). Regulating sex work: Between victimization and freedom to choose. In C. Parent, C. Bruckert, P., Corriveau, M. Nengeh Mensah & L. Toupin (Eds.), *Sex work: Rethinking the job, respecting the workers* (ProQuest Ebook Central). UBC Press. http://ebookcentral.proquest.com/lib/mcgill/detail.action?docID=3412869

Parliament of Canada. (2014). *An Act to amend the Criminal Code in response to the Supreme Court of Canada decision in* Attorney General of Canada v. Bedford *and to make consequential amendments to other Acts*, no. C–36. http://www.parl.gc.ca/LEGISInfo/BillDetails.aspx?billId=6635303

Patton, M. (1990). Designing qualitative studies. In *Qualitative evaluation and research methods* (pp. 169–186). Sage. https://legacy.oise.utoronto.ca/research/field-centres/ross/ctl1014/Patton1990.pdf

Pearson, J., Shannon, K., Krüsi, A., Braschel, M., McDermid, J., Bingham, B., & Goldenberg, S. M. (2022). Barriers to governmental income supports for sex workers during COVID-19: Results of a community-based cohort in metro Vancouver. *Social Sciences*, *11*(9), 383.

Peterson, J. (2020, October 25). *For Canadian sex workers, CERB was a lifeline—if they could get it*. CBC News. https://www.cbc.ca/news/canada/saskatchewan/cerb-sex-worker-access-1.5769650

Phillips, R., & Benoit, C. (2005). Social determinants of health care access among sex industry workers in Canada. In J. Jacobs Kronenfeld (Ed.), *Health care services, racial and ethnic minorities and underserved populations: Patient and provider perspectives* (Vol. 23, pp. 79–104). Emerald Group. https://doi.org/10.1016/S0275-4959(05)23005-3

Pivot Legal Society. (n.d.). *Protecting the health, safety, and human rights of sex workers*. https://www.pivotlegal.org/sex_workers_rights

Platt, L., Elmes, J., Stevenson, L., Holt, V., Rolles, S., & Stuart, R. (2020). Sex workers must not be forgotten in the COVID-19 response. *The Lancet*, *396*(10243), 9–11. https://doi.org/10.1016/S0140-6736(20)31033-3

Public Health Agency of Canada. (2020a, June 5). *Public health ethics framework: A guide for use in response to the COVID-19 pandemic in Canada*. Government of Canada. https://www.canada.ca/en/public-health/services/diseases/2019-novel-coronavirus-infection/canadas-reponse/ethics-framework-guide-use-response-covid-19-pandemic.html

Public Health Agency of Canada. (2020b, August 4). *Coronavirus disease (COVID-19): Outbreak update*. Government of Canada. https://www.canada.ca/en/public-health/services/diseases/2019-novel-coronavirus-infection.html#a1

Putnis, N., & Burr, J. (2020). Evidence or stereotype? Health inequalities and representations of sex workers in health publications in England. *Health, 24*(6), 665–683. https://doi.org/10.1177/1363459319833242

Rukavina, S. (2020, August 27). *Facing long winter during a pandemic, Montreal opens three new homeless shelters.* CBC News. https://www.cbc.ca/news/canada/montreal/montreal-temporary-homeless-facilities-for-covid-winter-1.5702208

Sauer, M. A., Truelove, S., Gerste, A. K., & Limaye, R. J. (2021). A failure to communicate? How public messaging has strained the COVID-19 response in the United States. *Health Security, 19*(1), 65–74.

Shankar, V. K., Sahni, R., Seshu, M. S., Pai, A., Murthy, L., & Sevekari, T. (2022). Sex work, COVID-19, and half-truths. *Economic & Political Weekly, 57*(19), 49.

Shannon, K., Bright, V., Gibson, K., & Tyndall, M. W. (2007). Sexual and drug-related vulnerabilities for HIV infection among women engaged in survival sex work in Vancouver, Canada. *Canadian Journal of Public Health, 98*(6), 465–469. https://doi.org/10.1007/BF03405440

Shannon, K., Kerr, T., Allinott, S., Chettiar, J., Shoveller, J., & Tyndall, M. W. (2008). Social and structural violence and power relations in mitigating HIV risk of drug-using women in survival sex work. *Social Science & Medicine, 66*(4), 911–921. https://doi.org/10.1016/j.socscimed.2007.11.008

Shannon, K., Kerr, T., Strathdee, S. A., Shoveller, J., Montaner, J. S., & Tyndall, M. W. (2009). Prevalence and structural correlates of gender-based violence among a prospective cohort of female sex workers. *BMJ, 339*, b2939. https://doi.org/10.1136/bmj.b2939

Socías, M. E., Shoveller, J., Bean, C., Nguyen, P., Montaner, J., & Shannon, K. (2016). Universal coverage without universal access: Institutional barriers to health care among women sex workers in Vancouver, Canada. *PLOS ONE, 11*(5), e0155828. https://doi.org/10.1371/journal.pone.0155828

Spittal, P. M., Bruneau, J., Craib, K. J. P., Miller, C., Lamothe, F., Weber, A. E., Li, K., Tyndall, M. W., O'Shaughnessy, M. V., & Schechter, M. T. (2003). Surviving the sex trade: A comparison of HIV risk behaviours among street-involved women in two Canadian cities who inject drugs. *AIDS Care, 15*(2), 187–195. https://doi.org/10.1080/0954012031000068335

Statistics Canada. (2020, July 10). *Labour Force Survey, June 2020.* https://www150.statcan.gc.ca/n1/daily-quotidien/200710/dq200710a-eng.htm

Toronto Public Health. (2020, August 14). *COVID-19 notification for Brass Rail Tavern (August 4, 5, 7 and 8).* City of Toronto. https://www.toronto.ca/news/covid-19-notification-for-brass-rail-tavern-august-4-5-7-and-8/

Wright, T. (2020a, April 19). *Sex workers say they have been left out of Canada's COVID-19 response.* CTV News. https://www.ctvnews.ca/health/coronavirus/sex-workers-say-they-have-been-left-out-of-canada-s-covid-19-response-1.4902772

Wright, T. (2020b, July 4). *Stop enforcing sex work laws during COVID-19, Amnesty, sex worker advocates say.* CBC News. https://www.cbc.ca/news/politics/sex-work-laws-covid-19-1.5637741

Zhang, Y. S. D., Young Leslie, H., Sharafaddin-Zadeh, Y., Noels, K., & Lou, N. M. (2021). Public health messages about face masks early in the COVID-19 pandemic: Perceptions of and impacts on Canadians. *Journal of Community Health, 46*(5), 903–912.

CHAPTER EIGHT

Neo-Vagrancy Laws in Media Discourses During Canada's First Wave of COVID-19

ELLIOT FONAREV,[1] RAVITA SURAJBALI,[2] AND JOE HERMER[3]

Abstract: The onset of the COVID-19 pandemic brought visibility to homeless people using public spaces versus those who could shelter indoors in private dwellings. This renewed attention foregrounds a legal landscape of anti-homeless legislation in Canada that criminalizes homeless people's occupancy of public spaces, contributing to housing insecurity and marginalization prior to and during the pandemic. The outlawing of the everyday presence and survival activities of homeless people in public spaces is primarily legislated in contemporary municipal bylaws, which operate as legal forms of banishment. These "neo-vagrancy" laws have origins in Victorian vagrancy law, which characterized homeless and other marginalized people as threats to public order. This chapter shows how Canadian law, policy, and media contribute to the normalization of exclusionary laws as solutions to deal with the visibility of "disorderly" homeless people in public spaces. Focusing our analysis on media coverage of neo-vagrancy bylaws during the first five months of Canada's federal COVID-related emergency public health measures, we found that most news stories reproduced policymaking frames that emphasized homelessness and disorder as the central public problem, rather than a housing crisis, such that limited solutions could be imagined. We argue that a feedback loop between law, policy, and public discourse on homelessness during the pandemic represents an acceptance of localized forms of neoliberal governance strategies, obscuring processes of dispossession and legal forms of banishment that legislate away, spatially exclude, and further marginalize homeless people—during the pandemic and beyond.

Keywords: neo-vagrancy laws, homelessness, banishment, spatial exclusion, neoliberalism, anti-homeless legislation, media discourse

INTRODUCTION

> [One] who has been banned is not, in fact, simply set outside the law and made indifferent to it but rather abandoned by it, that is, exposed and threatened on the threshold in which life and law, outside and inside, become indistinguishable.
>
> —Agamben (2002, p. 28)

The onset of emergency public health measures following COVID-19's first wave, which mandated "staying at home" and physical distancing to prevent the spread of the virus, emphasized the importance of private domestic space to rationales of state governance. But, as Canada's emergency measures at all levels of government called for the closing of public facilities, shelters, and community agencies, the pandemic exposed a glaring policy gap in adequately addressing the needs of homeless[4] people who rely on public spaces, like parks and streets, for survival and respite. Amid calls to "stay home" during the pandemic, the lives of homeless people, along with other marginalized groups, became acutely present where they were previously politically inconspicuous.

This provisional attention to homelessness during the pandemic has renewed conversations about the legitimacy of long-standing anti-homeless legislation, including municipal bylaws (Beckett & Herbert, 2008; Mitchell, 1997). Such bylaws—what we call "neo-vagrancy laws"—work to exclude, displace, and criminalize homeless and other marginalized individuals' presence and survival activities in public spaces, resulting in prohibitive fines, legal exclusionary zones, displacement, and other barriers (Beckett & Herbert, 2008, 2010; Chesnay et al., 2013; Mitchell, 1997; Sylvestre et al., 2020). These spatio-legal techniques of banishment target unwanted or "disorderly" bodies from, and reinforce a neoliberalized conception of public space, processes which obscure ongoing colonial practices of state-sponsored displacement of marginalized, racialized, and Indigenous bodies from settler space (Beckett & Herbert, 2008; Mitchell, 1997; Razack, 2014). The punitive and destabilizing implications of these measures are especially concerning for homeless people during the pandemic, who are already at disproportionate risks for both infection and death (Gaetz et al., 2014).

This chapter demonstrates how neo-vagrancy laws were presented in media discourse as a strategy to address homelessness during Canada's first wave of the COVID-19 pandemic, and addresses the implications of this coverage. We present findings from a content analysis of Canadian news articles ($n = 22$) covering changes, amendments, and proposed changes to neo-vagrancy laws that were published between March and August 2020, the first five months following the implementation of COVID-19-related emergency and public health measures in Canada. These findings present ongoing conversations within public discourse through news media and highlight the reception to anti-homeless neo-vagrancy laws in Canada during the pandemic. We suggest that while the pandemic generated public debate about homelessness, neo-vagrancy laws remained reified as an effective response to conflicts over the use of public spaces in ways that subvert homeless people's rights by punishing their survival activities, and prioritizing the interests of the consumer-citizen. We find that a feedback loop between law, policy, and public discourse reflects a hegemonic acceptance of this form of urban governance, with the consequence of limited critical coverage of law and policy-making around public space and homelessness.

BACKGROUND

By examining the form, substance, and effects of laws targeting homeless people, we emphasize how a revival of anti-homeless legislation in Canada has occurred at the provincial and municipal level over the past 30 years (Graser, 2000; Ranasinghe, 2015). These offenses target homeless and other marginalized people by prohibiting their survival activities in specific, often highly localized places and times through provincial acts or municipal bylaws. For this reason, we refer to these laws as "neo-vagrancy laws," characterized by their effect of targeting survival activities of homeless people. Neo-vagrancy laws can be categorized by offense type, depending on which outlawed behavior or conduct they capture. Offense types include loitering, panhandling, obstructing, sheltering, salvaging, resting, sleeping, and causing disorder in public spaces like parks and streets (Hermer & Fonarev, 2021). Approximately 77 % of Canadians live in a jurisdiction with at least one neo-vagrancy offense (using 2017 population statistics) (Hermer & Fonarev, 2021). In fact, there are 809 neo-vagrancy offenses nested within 511 municipal bylaws across 343 Canadian municipalities (Hermer & Fonarev, 2021). Neo-vagrancy laws, then, operate concomitantly as contemporary forms of anti-homeless legislation and regulatory features of everyday urban life.

Neo-Vagrancy Laws in Canada as a Spatial Exclusion Technique

The Canadian state has long been concerned with eliminating the visibility of poor, homeless, and other marginalized people, such as sex workers and other precarious workers, from public spaces under rationales of public order and safety (see Chapter Seven). The presence of anti-homeless legislation in Canada can be historically traced to centuries-old English vagrancy laws, which governed a host of issues including "poverty, labour, crime, religion, public health, and even entertainment and leisure" (Ranasinghe, 2015, p. 59). The 1892 *Criminal Code* of Canada wrote the "vagrant" into Canadian law, a criminalized status defined as a "loose, idle or disorderly person" that was unemployed and had no visible means of subsistence (*R. v. Heywood*, 1994). This remained virtually unchanged until the 1950s, when vagrancy law was reconceptualized: the crime of *being* a vagrant shifted to the crime of *committing* vagrancy through acts such as wandering, trespassing, begging, and loitering in public spaces (Ranasinghe, 2015). Vagrancy law then met its eventful end in the early 1970s, when virtually all sections of vagrancy in the *Criminal Code* were abolished (Ranasinghe, 2015). The disappearance of the "vagrant" and "vagrancy" in Canadian criminal law was largely attributed to reimagined legal norms attempting to correct their unconstitutionally vague form and overly broad applicability (Ranasinghe, 2015). Despite this, status-based offenses associated with the vagrant person were redefined in new terms: as features of public disorder, shifting the predominant site of legal regulation and social control from the federal to provincial and local levels of governance (Graser, 2000; Hermer & Mosher, 2002; Ranasinghe, 2015).

Urban anxieties over public disorder became especially emboldened through strategies of "broken windows" policing that emerged in the 1990s throughout North America. This resulted in greater policing in under-resourced neighborhoods because of associations between crime and scattered, untidy, or broken homes (Feldman, 2006; Hermer & Mosher, 2002; Ranasinghe, 2015). The broken windows movement heightened fears about the visibility of disorder in public spaces—in turn, minor offenses committed by "disorderly" people were perceived as major threats to the social and economic order (Beckett & Herbert, 2008; Wilson & Kelling, 1982).

Broken windows policing and the politics arising from fears of disorder gave municipal governments a "broad and flexible" mandate to use local spatial regulations to curb disorder (Beckett & Herbert, 2008, p. 8). This same broadness and flexibility had been afforded to the state in upholding status-based vagrancy laws (Beckett & Herbert, 2008). Rather than explicitly targeting individuals, these local regulations prohibited activities and behaviors considered unwanted by other urban residents or viewed as potential precursors to more serious crime (Beckett & Herbert, 2008).

Consequently, the shift from treating vagrancy as a criminal matter of individual status, (punishable federally as an offense against the state), to a spatial matter of ordering public spaces (governed locally through time-and-place specific regulations), changed the form, but not the substance of punitively socially controlling "problem populations such as the homeless" (Beckett & Herbert, 2010, p. 2). Criminologists and geographers characterize local regulation that gives legal effect to justifying the expulsion of people from public space as part of a repertoire of techniques of social control working alongside containment strategies such as incarceration (Beckett & Herbert, 2010; Roy, 2019). Such expulsion, what Becket and Herbert (2010) have called "banishment," involves governance techniques that "spatially exclude the unwanted over time," from contested urban spaces including public spaces such as parks, zoned locales, and privatized commercial areas (p. 3). This technique is justified as a means to improve urban quality of life and curb criminal behavior, yet it continues to give normative impetus to the notion that the population is split between the orderly and disorderly, or the civil and the criminal (Beckett & Herbert, 2018). This turn toward adopting a "law-and-order" approach to urban governance through localized regulation has generated a strong contemporary revival of displacing marginalized populations.

Spatial Exclusion Techniques as Repertoires of Colonial and Racial Dispossession

Like vagrancy laws, spatial exclusion techniques have been complicit in some of the most violent expressions of discrimination, targeting homeless people; Indigenous, Black, Asian, and queer people; and sex workers (Beckett & Herbert, 2010; Mawani, 2002; Razack, 2002). Beckett and Herbert (2010) demonstrated that such spatial exclusion techniques facilitate "an expulsion from the body politic" (p. 6), denying rights, intensifying the harms associated with precarious living, and reproducing territorial logics that stifle those deemed to be outsiders from the point of view of the state. Spatial exclusion disproportionately marks Black, Brown, and poor bodies as "dangerous and disorderly" and is used to exile racialized communities from urban spaces (Roy, 2019, p. 227). Roy (2019) suggests that this is a form of racialized dispossession that combines colonial logics with anti-poor sentiments and works to "secure sovereign possession" at local scales (p. 228). This not only reinforces social inequality and capitalist accumulation but is also at its core a "renewal of colonial expropriation" (Roy, 2019, p. 229).

Indeed, spatial expulsion in Canada is part of a long history and ongoing state practice of using legal and policing strategies to displace Indigenous peoples' presence from settler communities and urban cities (Mawani, 2003). These practices have resulted in what Sherene Razack (2014) called a roundabout or "periphractic space" of Indigenous peoples being "in the city but not of it" (p. 55). Colonial dispossession, including the decades-long cultural genocide and separation of Indigenous children from communities through residential schools, the displacement of Indigenous peoples across Turtle Island through legal decree and policing, and the institutional denials of Indigenous sovereignties have impacted Indigenous social orders, laws, and knowledge systems (Bear, 2000; Simpson, 2011). In turn, Indigenous resistance, resurgence, and collective strength have borne against the continued colonial occupation of Indigenous lands (Bear, 2000; Simpson, 2011). However, the cumulative impact of ongoing dispossession and settler-dominated and racially marginalizing institutions has created housing and job security challenges in urban centers where Indigenous peoples disproportionately represent street-involved people, who are especially targeted by neo-vagrancy laws (Gaetz et al., 2014). People who are Indigenous, racialized, and part of other socially marginalized groups, such as criminalized or stigmatized populations like sex workers, and undocumented individuals, are disproportionately represented in homeless populations because of the destabilizing impacts of these structures and processes that facilitate dispossession, displacement, and social control (Blomley, 2020; Gaetz et al., 2014; Harris & Leinberger, 2002). At the individual level, pathways to precarious housing and homelessness can be accelerated when in combination with structural barriers to regularized work, such as in the sex work industry (see Chapter Seven), and to secure housing, such as with victimization caused by intimate partner violence (see Chapter Three).

Spatial Exclusion Techniques as Repertoires of Neoliberal Urban Governance

Keeping in mind Roy's (2019) caution that analyses of spatial exclusion techniques using only the vocabulary of neoliberalization obscures the centrality of processes of colonial and racial dispossession in such techniques, we nevertheless consider here how spatial exclusion helps construct and reinforce hegemony around what is both welcomed and critiqued as neoliberal governance strategies at local scales. Urban neoliberalization traditionally refers to the political economy of governing through a growth-first approach to urban development, imbued with market logics of economic development, profit enhancement, and privatization (Beckett & Herbert, 2008; Peck & Tickell, 2002). Through processes of urban neoliberalization, cities that fail to successfully engage in competitive urbanism lose access to funding from higher levels of government, which are competitively distributed to cities "on the basis of economic potential and governance capacity rather than manifest social need" (Peck & Tickell, 2002, p. 395). As the welfarist role of the state is scaled back and overridden by neoliberal objectives of economic and urban development, addressing social problems becomes an exercise of legislating away the signs, but not the causes, of social inequality (Beckett & Herbert 2008; Brown, 2020; Peck & Tickell, 2002). From a welcoming point of view, enforcing order in public spaces helps fulfill city governing mandates to increase competitive urban potential. Critics suggest this approach leads to displacement of low-income urban residents through, for example, urban regeneration programs that infuse and incentivize investment to beautify neighborhoods seen as downtrodden in manners that "sugarcoat gentrification" (Smith, 2002, p. 445).

Significantly, critics suggest that the symbolic effect of this emphasis on cleaning and beautifying urban places is to mark spaces for the public, first and foremost, as consumer spaces (Feldman, 2004). This sense of public space is imagined and reinforced through the making of public spaces, such as parks, streets, and other places. The role of local law, then, is to carve out public spaces of desirability, which lack visible disorderliness. Submerging the signs of poverty and disorder thus maintains the viability and credibility of governance rationales and policy agendas informed by urban neoliberalism (Mitchell, 1997). Mitchell (1997) has called this process the "annihilation of space through law," generating a "legal fiction in which the rights of the wealthy, of the successful in the global economy, are sufficient for all the rest" (p. 305).

The archetype of the homeless person challenges these objectives and norms because, in presenting the most obvious "visual manifestations of conflict, dissent and socio-economic inequality" (Hermer, 1997, p. 191), they fail to "play their role as 'good consumer citizens'" (Brown, 2020, p. 575). The consequence is that homeless people are "sanitized from a conception of the public and the 'civic' spaces which it embodies" (Hermer, 1997, p. 191). In other words, conceptions of who belongs in public space are limited and "exclude those who offend against the capitalistic ethic of conspicuous consumption" (Hermer, 1997, p. 191). From this lens, urban neoliberalism maintains a highly exclusionary form of modern citizenship that sidelines state efforts to enhance social citizenship through individual rights-based mechanisms (Beckett & Herbert, 2008; Mitchell, 1997). Exclusionary politics operate through spatial mechanisms, which legitimate, both legally and socially, the behavior and conduct of desirable people in public spaces—namely, those who uphold a consumption ethic and own or rent private property, which tend not to be homeless people (Feldman, 2004; Mitchell 1997).

Public Health Measures During the COVID-19 Pandemic in Canada

In the wake of the pandemic, Canadian cities have had to confront the consequences of decades of inadequate attention to structural contributors of poverty with a renewed and collapsing sense of urgency. State responses and public health measures surrounding COVID-19 have largely been organized around ideas of private space. However, the ability to follow public health advice, to effectively physically distance, self-isolate, and regularly engage in hygiene practices (e.g., handwashing, mask-wearing, bathing/showering, clothes-changing, sanitization of purchased food and groceries) posed immediate and obvious challenges for homeless people who could not stay in or stay home during the pandemic. Homeless people risk increased exposure to others, including those who have COVID-19, if they have repeatedly moved between temporary shelters or if shelters are overcrowded (Public Health Agency of Canada, 2020b). Moreover, as a vulnerable population, homeless people are especially susceptible to contracting COVID-19 because of their existing disproportionate risk of having underlying health conditions compared to the general public (Gaetz et al., 2014). Although anti-homelessness advocates called upon urban governments to urgently address housing affordability crises and increase indoor shelter spaces that complied with public health distancing guidelines, cities have defaulted to law-and-order governance techniques that displace homeless people.

METHODOLOGY

Using our typology of neo-vagrancy laws, our objective was to analyze the content of news articles that discussed changes, amendments, and proposed changes to neo-vagrancy laws during the pandemic. We focused specifically on neo-vagrancy laws operating at the local level in the form of municipal bylaws, because such laws overwhelmingly exist in the form of local bylaws across Canada. Our findings emerge from a content analysis of news articles published from March 13 to August 13, 2020, which roughly captures Canada's first wave of COVID-19. This was the selected start date because it corresponds with the beginning of Canada's advanced rollout of COVID-19-related public health measures. Convenience sampling using *ProQuest's Advanced Search* database generated the sampling frame of 112 news articles. We inputted the words "homeless" and "'bylaw' or 'by-law'" and "'change' or 'amendment' or 'proposed'" into the search term engine. The inclusion criteria for news articles required that they discuss: (1) homelessness or homeless people; (2) a neo-vagrancy bylaw change, amendment, and/or proposed change; and (3) the COVID-19 pandemic. Proposed changes to bylaws were included because they capture local level debates about legislating as a tool to govern homeless people during the pandemic. Based on our inclusion criteria and controlling for duplicate news article publications in our sampling frame, we conducted a qualitative analysis of 22 unique news articles. We analyzed latent content, identifying themes, frames, and assumptions that emerged from the news articles. We concern ourselves with the representation and symbolism in the news articles, making sense of the "subtle meanings and implications of the text(s) and use a more holistic approach to understand context as well as content" (Gilchrist, 2010, p. 7). Central to our analysis is the framing of the news articles—that is, how they presented actual, amended, or proposed legislative change affecting homeless people within the context of the pandemic. Further, we pay particular attention to how media articles frame understandings of law and urban governance rationales, homelessness, uses of public spaces, and public disorder. Emergent themes are discussed in what follows.

FINDINGS

Seven key themes emerged from our analysis of the news articles. We present these in order of prevalence. The most prevalent theme, present in 77 % ($n = 17$)

of articles, underscores a law-and-order approach to resolving the public issue, requiring legislating rather than resource allocation as a political solution. The next three themes, with prevalence in 55 % (n = 12) of articles, are as follows. One theme highlights the pandemic-related public health context and its effect on neo-vagrancy laws directing homeless people's survival activities in public spaces. The next emphasizes a framing of the core public issue to be one of homeless intrusion into public spaces during the pandemic, rather than a long-standing consequence of a state-induced housing crisis. Another demonstrates how fears of public disorder underscore opinions of homelessness. The next prevalent theme, with 41 % prevalence (n = 9), appeals to a compromise between the basic civil rights of homeless people and the interests of consumer-citizens using neoliberal logics. The two least prevalent themes, present in 36 % (n = 8) of articles, relayed views of homelessness as an urban blight, and individual sympathies for homeless people.

The breakdown of news articles by neo-vagrancy offense type include: 73 % on sheltering (n = 16), 14 % on loitering (n = 3), 9 % on scavenging (n = 2), and 5 % on panhandling (n = 1). The provinces in which a bylaw change, amendment, or proposed change occurred and was discussed in media were British Columbia (n = 13), Ontario (n = 6), New Brunswick (n = 2), and Alberta (n = 1). This does not suggest that municipalities in other provinces did not review such bylaws, but that media discussion of these issues was sparse over the course of this time.

Theme One: Reflecting a Law-and-Order Political Solution to the Problem

In the most prevalent theme, most articles (n = 17) presented policy debates and discourses through a law-and-order frame, that is, one emphasizing concerns with creating order and managing disorderly spaces. Unsurprisingly, this frame was constructed through statements taken from local public officials highlighting solutions that emphasized regulating activities associated with public concerns about disorder and safety. One article, for instance, quotes an official who said that a new neo-vagrancy law (loitering bylaw) is the only option to resolve the phenomenon of sleeping on the street, and that the alternative was to do nothing. Notably, policy to prevent and address housing insecurity was not mentioned.

Fewer articles conveyed messages that emphasized a need for more public spending as an alternative to legislation. Only one news article specifically conveyed a call for increased public support rather than regulation as a response to the interests and needs of homeless people. Sometimes, public spending for more temporary or emergency shelters and social supports were highlighted. Rather than framing sides of this story around such varied policy options, the articles in this theme overwhelmingly emphasized sides of the conflict over the use of space.

Theme Two: Highlighting Pandemic-Related Public Health Agendas

The COVID-19 pandemic demonstrated how homelessness was represented in light of public health agendas. Notably, not all the coverage contained explicit connections between public health more broadly and addressing poverty and homelessness. Over half of the articles ($n = 12$) referenced arguments for relaxing law enforcement or rules against homeless populations due to the negative health impacts of the pandemic. Additionally, the news articles that touched on this theme explored the public health risks associated with homeless living less than the specific risks of being infected with COVID-19 in shelters.

Theme Three: Framing the Core Public Issue as a Homeless Intrusion into Public Spaces

Over half of the articles ($n = 12$) specifically covered anti-sheltering bylaws and sheltering activities of homeless people during the pandemic, which implies that this was a core public issue requiring political action or intervention. The news articles framed the issue in several different ways. While there was some mention of homeless encampments as a symptom or reminder of a housing crisis, the articles often framed the issue as encroaching encampments in public parks. This news coverage gave voice to sources such as neighborhood resident groups or parents of children, who perceived a visible and growing presence of encampments in close-proximity parks they frequent. These voices sometimes expressed anger toward governments over encroachments on leisure space. In addition to highlighting anxieties around encroachments to leisure and recreational public spaces, increased homeless encampments were sometimes framed as an added burden on agencies and governments, who must spend extra time and resources thinking about and responding to the issue.

Theme Four: Keeping Public Disorder at Bay

Twelve of the articles conveyed messages about the enforcement of neo-vagrancy laws (especially anti-sheltering bylaws) that emphasized law enforcement as a necessary response to growing public disorder. They conveyed the need to keep public disorder at bay such that homelessness was understood as characteristic of public disorder. These articles referred to sources who framed encampments as "crime-ridden," "stirring up controversy," and "holding the park hostage." Disorderly conduct was referenced as driving the mobilization of local action and reaction to proposed changes to neo-vagrancy laws.

Theme Five: A Compromise of Rights and Interests

Nine of the articles which covered debates over sheltering bylaws explicitly using the framing of a conflict between the rights of unhoused and homeless people to be in parks and the interests of recreational users who use the amenities of parks. The latter represented concerns of recreational park users who, especially during the pandemic, needed to access public parks for leisure and exercise while maintaining physical distancing. This coverage presented an equivalence between competing interests over this issue, referring to balance, compromise, or weighing of rights and interests of both homeless people and park users. They also drew on a variety of sources from different sides of this debate, including from city councilors, homelessness advocates, civil liberties groups, and residents or neighborhood groups who use parks. In our discussion, we consider the consequence of this sort of discourse that obscures the inequity of continued spatial exclusion and prohibitive attention to homeless people.

Theme Six: Homelessness as Urban Blight

In addition to disorderly conduct, the response to growing encampments and visible homelessness was sometimes framed as an urban blight problem, although this was less prominent. In eight of the articles, we found coverage that highlighted the anxieties of property owners about property damage and devaluation of real estate and business. These concerns, along with concerns about crime, drug use, and safety, followed more visible homelessness and encampments during the pandemic. These news articles highlighted sources concerned with the protection of property and parklands "from inappropriate use," and public outrage about "urban decay," detraction of park (leisure) users, and neighborhood "upkeep." The interests of housed residents who feared harm to their propertied interests and spaces for leisure because of proximate poverty were often given more focus, while the harms of perpetual displacement and interests of homeless people were either briefly mentioned or unexamined. This, as we discuss in theme seven, coincides with messages about regulatory bylaws that contain the actions of those deemed out of place as being a needed public good that preserves a consumer urban experience.

Theme Seven: Individual Sympathies for Homeless People

Less prominently, in eight of the articles, we also found coverage that gave favorable attention to the interests of homeless citizens and anti-poverty advocates. Often, this attention conveyed sympathies for featured individuals, exploring in narrative detail their stories or struggles, with even one "riches to rags" story. These news articles mostly fell short of identifying and connecting individual experience with systemic factors informing a national housing shortage or political neglect, instead emphasizing homelessness as a personal predicament. Other times, statistics or statements emphasized that homelessness disproportionately affects people who are racialized, Indigenous, disabled, and queer, or people who have intersecting marginalized identities, such as Indigenous women.

DISCUSSION

The renewed visibility of homeless people in public spaces during the pandemic generated debate and media attention over the legitimacy and use of neo-vagrancy laws to address homelessness, poverty, and access to shelter and services in Canadian urban settings. Our findings suggest that a feedback loop between law, policy, and media discourse at the onset of the pandemic revealed a hegemonic acceptance of urban governance strategies that subject homeless people to spatial exclusion or what Beckett and Herbert (2010) call banishment. We discuss this in greater detail and how coverage may be improved to more critically cover law and policymaking around public space and homelessness.

Competing Claims to Public Spaces

Anti-sheltering bylaws, which regulate and prohibit sheltering and encampments in parks, are the type of neo-vagrancy offense discussed most frequently in the articles—this context animates much of our discussion. We found that the interests of recreational park-users and their concomitant claim to use of public spaces for leisure was most pronounced in the media coverage. In many of the articles, neo-vagrancy laws were presented as improving the quality of life for orderly urban residents or good consumer-citizens. Views on how neo-vagrancy laws implicate the rights and agency of homeless people were mostly absent, though one article highlighted that civil liberties groups spoke against restrictive anti-sheltering bylaws, producing discourse over the legitimacy of such measures. The rights and needs of homeless people to shelter, compared to those of consumer-citizens to recreation—especially in public parks where many homeless encampments are found—were then often framed as competing claims to use of public spaces.

This purported mutual exclusivity of public space use can be seen in policy-level decisions that justify banishment, ironically using the discourse of economic development. At best, local political actors presented homelessness as a "complicated problem" to muddle through, and at worst, an "unfixable" burden on taxpayers and public servants. In one Northern Ontario town, neo-vagrancy laws targeting and criminalizing homeless people's survival activities were legitimated to protect the town's economy, one driven by "cottagers and tourist traffic." Pitting poor and homeless people's survival activities as threats to the town's economic and social priorities and tourist reputation excludes them from the town's purview while evading the issue of housing precarity, which is seen as separate from economic development. Not addressing the root and complex causes of homelessness also contributes to the perpetuation of insecurity and stigma against homeless people. This is particularly notable in this example because housing precarity within northern urban communities, where homeless and street-involved populations are disproportionately Indigenous, is a legacy and ongoing impact of colonialism. In turn, imagined policy solutions narrow to simply doubling down on the enforcement of neo-vagrancy laws against those who, by simply existing in public space, have no real avenue to avoid violating them.

This competitive framing has several negative implications. For one, when homeless people's rights to basic shelter were contrasted with park-users' interests in leisurely spaces, this demonstrated a troubling equivalency between one's basic needs and another's leisure interests, obscuring the inequities of these interests. This is important to unpack because stigmatizing and ostracizing narratives about homeless people as disorderly encroachers on consumer-citizens' spaces politicize homelessness. For example, many articles highlighted the sentiments of incensed citizens that attributed blame to politicians for failing to protect public leisure space. Meanwhile, narratives addressing the politics over a shortage of affordable housing and other structural contributors to homelessness were less prominent.

Consequently, the frame of compromise misses an opportunity for critical media discourse to address deeper social and political questions about how we define public space and why it has been normalized as leisure space. Instead, this framing reinforces tensions produced through vocabularies of neoliberalization of public space as a certain space of desirability, which pits the homeless and the housed as fundamentally at odds. Contained within this notion of public space, the presence of homeless people has been politicized as a matter of public and personal safety, creating the specter of the disorderly person that hangs over and replaces considerations of the lived experiences of safety of homeless individuals.

The Homeless Exception and Legal Banishment from Public Space

While pandemic-related public health measures including physical distancing, city lockdowns, and social gathering restrictions sharply reduced recreational or leisure visits from park users, they increased the visibility of homeless people in public spaces during the first wave of the pandemic. We found that the news media discourse presented homelessness as a problem, characterizing homeless encampments and homeless people as visible markers of public disorder symbolizing urban blight, urban decay, crime, and poverty. Homeless people, then, are understood as threats to local order, security, and safety, where their presence in public spaces during the pandemic, especially in parks, is seen as inducing urban anxieties. Representations that challenged these anxieties were less prominent in articles, and views addressing the problems of legislating away signs of homelessness as a function of keeping homeless people at the margins, were mostly absent. Yet, neo-vagrancy laws push homeless people into a state of perpetual homelessness and displacement where they are regularly forced to relocate and tear down their sheltering structures in public spaces. Like former vagrancy laws, current neo-vagrancy laws continue to "to regulate access to and movement through space" where homeless people continue to be seen as socially undesirable subjects who deserve spatial exclusion (Beckett & Herbert, 2010, p. 3).

Further, when neo-vagrancy laws carve out narrow exceptions for when, where, and how homeless people occupy and shelter in public spaces, this works to reinforce state control over spatial order and reaffirms public space as space primarily for the non-homeless. The enforcement of neo-vagrancy laws that restrict sheltering in parks erodes the rights-bearing capacity of homeless people, even when they are presented as granting exceptions to temporary overnight shelter. In fact, several articles covered debates over such amendments to neo-vagrancy laws in city parks in Vancouver and Victoria. These homeless exceptions regulate when and where homeless people, often a defined term in the bylaw, can shelter in place. Primarily, these restrictions prohibit sheltering during daylight hours or in visible sight in areas of park recreation and entertainment. As urban spatial mechanisms, these neo-vagrancy laws function to effectively target homeless people and banish them "from contested urban spaces for extended periods of time" (Beckett & Herbert, 2010, p. 3). Consequently, homeless people are banished from these spaces during the pandemic, which continues to contribute to a loss of access to stabilizing resources, namely shelter, where the deprivation of security diminishes homeless peoples' life circumstances and rights-bearing capacities (Beckett & Herbert, 2010, p. 4).

The exclusionary and discriminatory logic that extends from neo-vagrancy laws is paradoxically framed as a progressive relaxation of existing sheltering rules, or exceptions made for the well-being of homeless people. However, homeless exceptions to enforcing neo-vagrancy laws during the pandemic, such as allowing homeless encampments parks, reifies homeless people as markers of public disorder in need of heavy regulation. Amendments to neo-vagrancy law establishing time-and-place rules for temporary overnight sheltering in parks in cities like Vancouver highlight the spatial (and temporal) regulation of homeless people in public spaces, where they remain subjects of law enforcement actors, including police, municipal bylaw officers, and park rangers. As such, they remain banished targets that are forced to move daily and remain in perpetual transience.

The substance of these exceptions is to demarcate parameters for accessing and using park space in ways that are consistent with broader governance techniques of spatial exclusion, legal annihilation, and displacement of homeless people from public spaces (Beckett & Herbert 2010; Mitchell, 1997). In this framing, "public space" does not include space for survival activities of homeless people, such as having a place to live while unsheltered.

Overwhelmingly, neo-vagrancy laws further minimize the ability for homeless people to contest such use of public space. As Beckett and Herbert (2010) have suggested, there is "little evidence that these techniques reduce the individual and collective harm associated with homelessness … ," but rather "intensify the pain and harm associated with these social problems" (p. 34). Spatial exclusion also reinforces symbolic exclusion, where homeless people are treated as lesser citizens (Beckett & Herbert, 2010, p. 34). Spatial exclusion thus limits the rights-bearing capacities of homeless people, while reproducing the emotionally charged and ostracizing effects of being made banished targets (Beckett & Herbert, 2010). The result is the effective ostracization, marginalization, and banishment of homeless people from public space.

Contextualizing Systemic Causes of Homelessness

As some articles pointed out, amendments or non-enforcement of neo-vagrancy laws, such as sheltering bylaws, served as temporary fixes to ameliorating homelessness during the pandemic. Our findings showed, however, that the media discourse largely did not address systemic causes or aggravating risk factors of homelessness, including Canada's lack of affordable housing crisis, overdose crisis, and the ongoing legacies and practices of colonialism, racism, classism, social stigma, and other structural and interpersonal violence. Beckett and Herbert (2010) have highlighted that new social control techniques of banishment are "used to limit mobility and rights of those whose principal 'offence' consists of being poor, homeless, and/or of colour", further perpetuating "their economic and cultural 'misrecognition'" (pp. 34–35). Our findings showed that the disproportionate impacts of homelessness on marginalized populations were largely absent from media coverage. Those news articles that do give sympathetic portrayals of homeless people's experiences of marginalization emphasize personal histories, but could make room for social histories of marginality connecting to larger systemic and structural systems of power and state (in)action. Brief acknowledgment of the adverse effects of neo-vagrancy laws on Indigenous peoples, people with mental health issues, people with substance abuse issues, and poor people appeared in one article, but overall, the disparate health outcomes and inequities that these groups already face in the wake of the pandemic, which render them increasingly vulnerable to COVID-19, could be better included.

Moreover, while some articles mentioned experiences of homeless among Indigenous peoples, such narratives were not contextualized with reference to settler-colonialism and processes of colonial and structural violence. This risked leaving impressions of issues that conflate Indigeneity with damage (Tuck, 2009). It is important to underscore how ongoing colonialism and anti-Indigeneity impacts housing insecurity for urban Indigenous peoples at disproportionate rates across Canada (Belanger et al., 2013). In this way, Indigenous peoples may be disproportionately subject to the discriminatory effects and enforcement of neo-vagrancy laws. Neo-vagrancy laws, in connection, can be understood as part of colonial repertoires of legal and spatial practices operating to exclude Indigenous peoples from settler space (Mawani, 2003; Roy, 2019). Further, taking an intersectional perspective is necessary to capture the disproportionate effects of neo-vagrancy laws on those who racialized, queer, and disabled (Crenshaw, 1989). Future research should extend this analysis to explore if, or how, homeless people with intersecting marginalized identities are presented in media articles during the pandemic.

Limitations

Our research captures a particular historical moment, focusing on news articles published during Canada's first wave of COVID-19, from March 2020 to August 2020. Given that our study is limited to news articles published during this time and drew from a specific set of search terms, our sample size is small. Our sample is not representative of all news articles covering changes, amendments, or proposed changes to neo-vagrancy bylaws across Canada, as it was filtered using ProQuest's limited database, primarily focusing on contexts within British Columbia, Ontario, New Brunswick, and Alberta. Though this chapter finds that neo-vagrancy laws and their effects received limited media coverage during the onset of the pandemic, it is worth noting that media coverage of the law and governance of homelessness is likely to have been limited before the pandemic as well, given the marginalization of the issue in public discourses. Nonetheless, this sample offers a valuable initial mapping of media discourse on homelessness during the pandemic in Canada. As the COVID-19 pandemic continued to unfold, neo-vagrancy laws and the politics of public space and homelessness gained media attention across Canadian cities, thanks to increased local movements and homeless advocacy. Further research could examine these changes to coverage on homelessness, expanding to broader media landscapes and time periods covering later periods of the pandemic, as well as to jurisdictions outside Canada or more specific localities.

CONCLUSION

It was no surprise that the most prominent theme found in media discourse about neo-vagrancy laws people relays "law-and-order" approaches to governance. Its prevalence highlights how an urban order that relies on legal techniques of banishment via neo-vagrancy laws was normalized and impacted the politics around homelessness in public space. Banishment techniques are punitive laws that facilitate the spatial and symbolic exclusion of unwanted "disorderly" bodies from public space for the comfort of the consumer-citizen. During the pandemic, urban governance strategies continued to rely on these mechanisms to remove the signs, but not the causes of homelessness, justifying violent enforcement actions against shelter encampments in cities across Canada.

This chapter shows that early media framing of homelessness in public space precipitated these actions, highlighting the prevalence of concerns about preventing public disorder in urban spaces. This emphasis on the crisis of disorder and conflict over public space use in media coverage gave marginal space to voices highlighting the need for homelessness prevention policy, and these voices were often sublimated to the authority of public policymakers. While some sympathetic attention to homeless people presented a contrasting frame to challenge discourse that frames homelessness as a problem, it did not necessarily contest the normalizing processes using laws that outlaw, regulate, and banish disorder in public space. This highlights the interrelated role of media, policy, and law in normalizing the legislating away of homeless presence in public through neo-vagrancy laws. Without more critical attention on the policy and governance of public space, the fourth estate risks reifying techniques of urban social control that work to spatially exclude and marginalize homeless people—during the pandemic and beyond.

NOTES

1 Department of Sociology, University of Toronto.
2 Centre for Criminology and Sociolegal Studies, University of Toronto.
3 Department of Sociology, University of Toronto Scarborough.
4 We use the term "homeless" to refer to "the situation of an individual, family or community without stable, safe, permanent, appropriate housing, or the immediate prospect, means and ability of acquiring it" (Gaetz et al., 2014, p. 38), capturing unsheltered, emergency sheltered, and provisionally accommodated individuals, families, or communities. We especially emphasize those who are visibly poor and unsheltered, who lack housing and must occupy spaces that are not designed for human habitation, including public spaces such as parks, squares, sidewalks, and streets.

REFERENCES

Agamben, G. (2002). *Homo sacer: Sovereign power and bare life* (A. Hiepko, Trans.). Suhrkamp Verlag.

Bear, L. L. (2000). Jagged worldviews colliding. In M. Battiste (Ed.), *Reclaiming ndigenous voice and vision* (pp. 77–85). UBC Press.

Beckett, K., & Herbert, S. (2008). Dealing with disorder: Social control in the post-industrial city. *Theoretical Criminology*, 12(1), 5–30. https://doi.org/10.1177/1362480607085792

Beckett, K., & Herbert, S. (2010). Penal boundaries: Banishment and the expansion of punishment. *Law & Social Inquiry*, 35(1), 1–38. https://doi.org/10.1111/j.1747-4469.2009.01176.x

Belanger, Y. D., & Awosoga, O., & Head, G. W. (2013). Homelessness, urban Aboriginal people, and the need for a national enumeration. *Aboriginal Policy Studies*, 2(2), 4–33. https://doi.org/10.5663/aps.v2i2.19006

Blomley, N. (2020). Precarious territory: Property law, housing, and the socio-spatial order. *Antipode*, 52(1), 36–57. https://doi.org/10.1111/anti.12578

Brodie, J. (1994). *Politics on the boundaries: Restructuring and the Canadian women's movement.* Robarts Centre for Canadian Studies, York University.

Brown, K. J. (2020). The Banishment of the poor from public space: Promoting and contesting neo-liberalisation at the municipal level. *Social & Legal Studies*, 29(4), 574–595. https://doi.org/10.1177/0964663919889104

Chesnay, C., Bellot, C., & Sylvestre, M. (2013). Taming disorderly people one ticket at a time: The penalization of homelessness in Ontario and British Columbia. *Canadian Journal of Criminology and Criminal Justice*, 55(2), 161–185. https://doi.org/10.3138/cjccj.2011-E-46

Crenshaw, K. (1989). Demarginalizing the intersection of race and sex: A black feminist critique of antidiscrimination doctrine, feminist theory and antiracist politics. *University of Chicago Legal Forum*, 1(8), 139–167.

Feldman, L. (2004). *Citizens without shelter: Homelessness, democracy, and political exclusion.* Cornell University Press.

Gaetz, S., Gulliver, T., & Richter, T. (2014). *The state of homelessness in Canada 2014.* Homeless Hub.

Gilchrist, K. (2010). "Newsworthy" victims? *Feminist Media Studies*, 10(4), 373–390.

Gordon, T. (2004). The return of vagrancy law and the politics of poverty in Canada. *Canadian Review of Social Policy*, 54, 34–57.

Graser, D. (2000). Panhandling for change in Canadian law. *Journal of Law and Social Policy*, 15, 45–91.

Harris, C., & Leinberger, E. (2002). *Making native space: Colonialism, resistance, and reserves in British Columbia.* UBC Press.

Hermer, J. (1997). Keeping Oshawa beautiful: Policing the loiterer in public nuisance by-law 72-94. *Canadian Journal of Law and Society*, 12(1), 172–192.

Hermer, J., & Fonarev, E. (2021). *Neo-vagrancy laws in Canada.* Policing Homelessness. http://policinghomelessness.ca/

Hermer, J., & Mosher, J. E. (2002). *Disorderly people: Law and the politics of exclusion in Ontario.* Fernwood.

Mawani, R. (2002). The iniquitous practice of women: Prostitution and the making of white spaces in British Columbia, 1898–1905. In C. Levine-Rasky (Ed.), *Working through whiteness: International perspectives* (pp. 43–68). SUNY Press.

Mawani, R. (2003). Imperial legacies (post) colonial identities: Law, space and the making of Stanley Park, 1859–2001. *Law Text Culture, 7*, 98–141.

Mitchell, D. (1997). The annihilation of space by law: The roots and implications of anti-homeless laws in the United States. *Antipode, 29*(3), 303–335. https://doi.org/10.1111/1467-8330.00048

Peck, J., & Tickell, A. (2002). Neoliberalizing space. *Antipode, 34*(3), 380–404. https://doi.org/10.1111/1467-8330.00247

Public Health Agency of Canada. (2020a, June 11). *Government of Canada takes action on COVID-19*. Government of Canada. https://www.canada.ca/en/public-health/services/diseases/2019-novel-coronavirus-infection/canadas-reponse/government-canada-takes-action-covid-19.html

Public Health Agency of Canada. (2020b, June 29). *Guidance for providers of services for people experiencing homelessness (in the context of COVID-19)*. Government of Canada. https://www.canada.ca/en/public-health/services/diseases/2019-novel-coronavirus-infection/guidance-documents/homelessness.html

Ranasinghe, P. (2015). Refashioning vagrancy: A tale of law's narrative of its imagination. *International Journal of Law in Context, 11*(3), 320–340. https://doi.org/10.1017/S1744552315000178

Razack, S. (2002). *Race, space, and the law: Unmapping a white settler society*. Between the Lines.

Razack, S. (2014). "It happened more than once": Freezing deaths in Saskatchewan. *Canadian Journal of Women and the Law, 26*(1), 51–80. https://doi.org/10.3138/cjwl.26.1.51

Roy, A. (2019). Racial banishment. In T. Jazeel, A. Kent, K. McKittrick, N. Theodore, S. Chari, P. Chatterton, V. Gidwani, N. Heynen, W. Larner, J. Peck, J. Pickerill, M. Werner & M. Wright (Eds.), *Keywords in radical geography: Antipode at 50* (pp. 227–230). Wiley. https://doi.org/10.1002/9781119558071.ch42

R. v. Heywood, 1994 SCC 761.

Simpson, L. (2011). *Dancing on our turtle's back: Stories of Nishnaabeg re-creation, resurgence, and a new emergence*. ARP Books.

Slater, T. (2004). North American gentrification? Revanchist and emancipatory perspectives explored. *Environment and Planning A, 36*(7), 1191–1213. https://doi.org/10.1068/a368

Smith, N. (2002). New globalism, new urbanism: Gentrification as global urban strategy. *Antipode, 34*(3), 427–450. https://doi.org/10.1111/1467-8330.00249

Sylvestre, M., Blomley, N., & Bellot, C. (2020). *Red zones: Criminal law and the territorial governance of marginalized people*. Cambridge University Press.

Tuck, E. (2009). Suspending damage: A letter to communities. *Harvard Educational Review, 79*(3), 409–427. https://doi.org/10.17763/haer.79.3.n0016675661t3n15

Wilson, J. Q., & Kelling, G. L. (1982). Broken windows. *Atlantic Monthly, 249*(3), 29–38.

CHAPTER NINE

Flow of Inequity: Period Poverty and the COVID-19 Pandemic

LISA SMITH,[1] RIM GACIMI,[2] NEAL ADOLPH,[3] AND JANE HOPE[4]

Abstract: Period poverty is a pervasive social issue in Canada. Many women, girls, trans men, and non-binary people face barriers in accessing menstrual supplies as well as safe, secure wash facilities necessary for the maintenance of short and long-term reproductive health. Organizations across Canada have begun to tackle period poverty through menstrual product drives to get supplies to those in need, advocate for improved education, and push for broader policy changes. In this chapter, we review existing scholarly work on period poverty and then consider how the COVID-19 pandemic intensified the scope of period poverty. We examine how the pandemic has shifted the work of organizations involved in addressing period poverty in Canada by analyzing the experiences of United Way of the Lower Mainland (UWLM) and Aisle International. Four main themes emerged from our analysis: changing demographics and greater numbers of vulnerable populations placing new strains on a non-profit sector that operated beyond capacity before COVID-19; recognition of local sites for collection and distribution of goods and services to allow for social distancing; evolving supply chain management that resulted from changes in the economy; and parallels between personal protective equipment, such as face masks, and period products regarding the protection of personal and public health, safety, and mobility. This chapter concludes that understanding the flow of inequities during the COVID-19 pandemic will lead to a deeper understanding of ongoing gaps, as well as the path forward to address period poverty.

Keywords: period poverty, Canada, COVID-19, organizational responses, menstruation activism, feminist policy

INTRODUCTION

Prior to the COVID-19 pandemic, period poverty—economic barriers to accessing menstrual supplies[5]—was a pervasive and largely invisible reality in Canada and many other parts of the world. Widespread cultural beliefs and values frame menstruation as taboo. Social systems of menstrual management enforce social stigma, shame, and embarrassment. In addition, social pressure to employ costly menstrual products as a "solution" place low-income and income-insecure groups at a significant disadvantage (Wootton & Morison, 2020). In the Global North, the individual is meant to "manage menstruation" privately and bear the costs associated with doing so, without interrupting other activities, including work and school. This broader cultural context means that period poverty is part of a realm that is already cloaked in silence. Inequitable access to menstrual products can have consequences on short- and long-term reproductive health, and impact access to education (Sebert Kuhlmann et al., 2020), and full participation in the workforce (Sommer et al., 2015). In addition, period poverty is often intertwined with and connected to other forms of vulnerability and marginalization, for example, housing precarity, substance abuse, and intimate partner violence (Sebert Kuhlmann et al., 2019; Vora, 2020; Wootton & Morison, 2020; see Chapters Three and Eight). Tackling period poverty is about addressing a fundamental need for menstrual supplies, while understanding that it is part of wider systems and patterns of inequity that persist in Canadian society.

In this chapter, we discuss the broader context of the impacts of the COVID-19 pandemic on period poverty in Canada, with an emphasis on disruption to menstruators' lives and how local organizations catering to vulnerable communities have responded to these challenges since March 2020. The authors of this chapter come from three different organizations—Douglas College Menstrual Cycle Research Group, Aisle International (Aisle), and United Way of the Lower Mainland (UWLM)—which work to understand, address, and respond to period poverty in Canada more fully.

We begin this chapter with a brief primer on menstruation. We then consider period poverty in the Canadian context. Our discussion on the impacts of the pandemic on period poverty in Canada begins by looking into the larger context of the pandemic's effects on women globally. Due to a lack of scholarly work on menstruation, especially newly published work which takes into account the changes brought on by the pandemic, we rely on data provided by governmental organizations such as Statistics Canada and reports published by non-profit organizations such as Plan International and the United Nations.

Following this, we discuss preliminary data that can help gauge the scope of period poverty under the COVID-19 pandemic. We describe broad patterns of organizational response providing an in-depth look at how the UWLM's Period

Promise Campaign and Aisle shifted their work to address period poverty in response to the COVID-19 pandemic. The accounts shared by UWLM and Aisle highlight the challenge of holding the needs of those experiencing period poverty at the center, while remaining flexible and responsive to shifting terrain and widespread uncertainty.

BACKGROUND: THE PROBLEM WITH PERIODS

Menstruation is a normal recurring biological process experienced by women and girls, as well as some trans men and non-binary people. There is considerable variation in menstrual cycles for each individual; however, typically, every 28 days the blood-rich lining of the uterus sheds and flows out of the vagina over a span of five to seven days, a process called "having a period." The blood is captured with disposable pads and tampons, washable pads, menstrual cups, rags, and other materials. Periods typically begin between age 12 and 13, but can start as early as age 8, and continue until approximately age 55 (Hillard, 2002).

In North American society and culture, there have been significant changes over the past century in access to sexual and reproductive healthcare, including increased visibility of and awareness about menstrual cycle health. Nevertheless, menstruation is still strongly tied to shame and menstrual flow management is meant to be kept private and hidden (Kissling, 2006; Newton, 2016). In addition, cultural beliefs and attitudes have a profound impact on what are often perceived as individual choices in terms of "what to do with the blood" and how this work takes place (see Wood, 2020). Across the life course, many factors will impact what is used to manage menstrual flow, including lifestyle, comfort, and individual biology. Some menstruators prefer to employ disposable-single-use supplies, while others may prefer to use hormonal contraception to manage, control or suspend periods. Regardless of the supply being used, in Canadian society, a menstruator is expected to deal with menstruation in private, to pay for the supplies, and to ensure that doing so does not disrupt participation in everyday activities. Menstruation continues to be framed as an individual burden rather than a biological experience profoundly shaped by social forces (Sommer et al., 2015). Jennifer Weiss-Wolf (2017) coined the term "menstrual equity" to refer to breaking down the barriers that limit access to menstrual supplies, including cost and product safety, as well as disrupting problematic social and cultural views that reproduce a delimited view of menstrual responsibility. Her work is part of a broader global movement aimed at raising awareness about menstruation and the barriers facing menstruators.

The work of addressing period poverty is part of and connected to movements for menstrual equity (Smith et al., 2020), but is more specifically situated within broader efforts to eradicate poverty and support low-income communities (Period Promise, 2021). Those seeking to address period poverty understand it as a systemic issue impacting individuals, families, and communities. To this end, understanding period poverty means situating menstruation and menstrual inequities—including access to supplies, facilities, and reproductive healthcare—within the context of broader patterns of social inequity. To this end, socioeconomic status, as well as gender, race, geographic location, ethnic origin, and many other social identity categories are relevant. Further, this wider lens means that broader access to menstrual supplies will not necessarily support the needs of all population groups, and more specifically, may have a limited impact on the extent of period poverty; as such, a comprehensive definition of menstrual product needs, as well as associated requirements is helpful.

Sebert Kuhlmann et al. (2019) defined "adequate menstrual hygiene" as follows:

> Adequate menstrual hygiene involves access to clean sanitary materials that can be changed in private as often as necessary, access to soap and water for washing, and access to a place for the hygienic disposal of used sanitary materials or washing, if reusable pads are used. (p. 238)

As Bobel and Fahs (2020) observed, there is some danger in reproducing a narrow view of "good" menstrual hygiene as keeping clean, contained, and tidy. There is no one-size-fits all approach to managing menstrual health; yet, cleanliness and capacity to effectively manage menstrual leaks is often framed as the *only* goal (see Wootton & Morison, 2020). Bobel and Fahs caution against a narrow view of social issues related to menstruation which leaves unaddressed the "root causes" of inequity and marginalization (p. 966).

In Canada, several organizations have been leading the way in developing campaigns to address period poverty on a bigger scale, such as the UWLM's Period Promise Campaign, Oxfam, and Period Purse.[6] At the same time, the heightened profile of period poverty—which began in the early 2000s—is tied to the advocacy of corporations manufacturing and distributing menstrual supplies. Major American companies such as Kotex, Thinx, and Always,[7] all have public campaigns focused on addressing period poverty through public advocacy and distributing free menstrual supplies. In part, these campaigns reflect the pressure on menstrual supply companies to help address menstrual inequities, as well as related social issues, such as sustainability concerns associated with single-use disposable menstrual supplies. These campaigns often highlight economic barriers related to accessing period supplies, yet we argue they have a limited capacity to address period poverty in the long term. Despite contributing to broader cultural conversations about menstruation, the focus remains mostly on distributing product as the "solution" to "ending period poverty." Such a focus is too narrow and fails to speak to the root causes of period poverty, which is poverty. Further, both period poverty and poverty are deeply intertwined with other forms of systemic inequity.

In Canada, as in other parts of the world:

> Poverty, while not unique to women, remains a gendered phenomenon: in 2003, 53 per cent of lower-income women were female. Moreover, single women, Indigenous women, immigrant women, women with disabilities, senior women, and women of color are more likely than other women or than men, to be impoverished. (Siltanen & Doucet, 2017, p. 166)

Period poverty exists for many reasons; however, one of the main reasons is that period supplies are costly and are treated as a commodity to be purchased. Sebert Kuhlmann et al. (2019) found that low-income women were often unable to afford menstrual supplies along with other essentials, such as food and toilet paper. Recent research examining the extent of period poverty in British Columbia, revealed that 51 % of the study respondents had struggled to purchase product for themselves (Period Promise, 2021, p. 43). Further, 15 % of study respondents have struggled to purchase product for a dependent (p. 44). Overall, the study revealed that period poverty impacts many women and girls, and gender-diverse people, and particularly those from already marginalized communities. Broader and more comprehensive policy and sustained advocacy, both informed by rigorous and community-engaged research, are essential to addressing period poverty. We, as the authors of this chapter, are involved in such work in our respective domains. Within this context, understanding current research into menstruation, as well as the broader history of menstruation activism and the push to include menstruation as a site of political action and autonomy is key.

PERIOD POVERTY IN THE CANADIAN CONTEXT

> Several years ago, a parent shared her story of deciding whether to buy menstrual supplies or put food on the table. She chose food and was left feeling dirty and degraded by the experience. We believe there are many women who experience this but don't speak about it. When we take menstrual supplies to our food bank programs, the supplies are snapped up immediately, we never have any left at the end of the session. (Period Promise, 2020)

In a recent public talk, Chantelle Spicer, Women Student's Representative of the British Columbia Federation of Students and a key advocate for freely available menstrual supplies at post-secondary institutions in British Columbia, recounted that as a teenager she was caught shop-lifting period supplies that she could not afford and explained that her experience helped her understand the urgent need to address menstrual equity and period poverty (Spicer, 2020). Chantelle Spicer's testimony was part of *Periods, Politics and Beyond!*, an event organized by the Douglas College Menstrual Cycle Research Group, which brought together students, activists, scholars, and politicians who are working toward making menstrual supplies free and accessible in schools and public washrooms (Brito, 2020; Fuller Evans, 2020). Stories such as Spicer's have raised the profile of period poverty within Canada and elsewhere and motivated a diverse array of individuals, activists, and organizations to respond with period product drives and distribution chains within their communities. In British Columbia, many organizations collect and distribute period supplies, for example, the UWLM's Period Promise Campaign and the UBC chapter of Free Periods Canada. These groups are actively involved in knowledge mobilization, community-based research, and the push for policy change (see Khan & Oveisi, 2020). In recent months, UWLM has been involved in a comprehensive research program and Aisle has proposed a pilot program to offer reusable period supplies to 2000 low-income British Columbia students. These are just a few examples of the ways that organizations are pushing for change.

Prior to the COVID-19 pandemic, scholarly work on the nature, scope, and extent of period poverty was sparse. Despite this, period poverty has become a focal point in the global public health agenda in recent years (Sommer & Sahin, 2013), especially in the Global South (Sommer, 2013; Chandra-Mouli & Vipul Patel, 2017). Unfortunately, few studies exist that examine period poverty in the Global North (Wootton & Morison, 2020), where until recently it was widely assumed that barriers in access to menstrual supplies were not a problem (Sebert Kuhlmann et al., 2020). In the North American context, existing research focuses on cultural beliefs and attitudes (Britton, 1996), experiences of shame and embarrassment (Schooler et al., 2005), and the relationship between socioeconomic status, race, and ethnicity on knowledge about menstruation (Chenoa Cooper & Barthalow Koch, 2008). More recently, attention has turned to consider trans and non-binary people's experiences with menstruation (Frank, 2020) and broader themes of equity and inclusion within law and policy (Goldblatt & Steele, 2019; Moffat & Pickering, 2019). A rich body of scholarship is developing on the broader history, context, and culture of menstruation (Delaney et al., 1976) and period activism, as well as the challenges faced by the "mainstreaming" of menstrual activism (Bobel, 2010; Bobel & Fahs, 2020).

Two recent studies from the United States provide an in-depth account of the extent and impact of lack of access of period supplies on school attendance (Sebert Kuhlmann et al., 2020), and unmet menstrual hygiene needs among low-income women (Sebert Kuhlmann et al., 2019). The former found that students relied heavily on accessing supplies at school, and not being able to access period products at school was a barrier to attendance (Sebert Kuhlmann et al.,

2020). The latter, which aimed to document the "menstrual hygiene needs of low-income women" (Sebert Kuhlmann et al., 2019, p. 238), found that "64 % of women were unable to afford needed menstrual hygiene supplies during the previous year" and that this recurred for a fifth of the study population on a monthly basis (p. 238). In addition, participants in the study noted that it was not only about not being able to afford commercially available product, but also the costs associated with procuring product (e.g., transit costs, travel time). These studies highlight the need to advocate for increased access to supplies for low-income women, while at the same time understanding that broader policy changes need to be part of the solution. To this end, making supplies available to students at school, and more broadly in public washrooms, ought to be paired with tandem campaigns to address poverty more generally as experienced by menstruators.

Scholarly research into period poverty in Canada is sparse. Recent years have seen increased interest in menstruation as a focal point for addressing equity and in drawing issues facing women and girls into policy discussions (Scala, 2020). Up until 2015, menstrual supplies were subject to a luxury tax, which was removed after coordinated pressure from the activist group Canadian Menstruators (2015). More recently, there has been a widespread push for public schools to provide free menstrual supplies directly in school restrooms and post-secondary institutions (Dobie, 2019; Shore, 2019; Vikander, 2019).

A recent study conducted by the Douglas College Menstrual Cycle Research Group documented existing access to menstrual supplies on campus and impacts on students. While the focus of this study was not experiences of period poverty, aspects of the results speak to general barriers experienced by menstruators when navigating through public space. For example, 67 % of study participants reported employing toilet paper to address menstrual emergencies (Tribe & Smith, 2021). The study also revealed that the primary mode of menstrual supply distribution on campus was via coin-operated dispensers located primarily in women's restrooms, many of which were broken or defective. In several cases, study participants also highlighted the high cost of product on campus as a barrier to managing menstruation while pursuing studies (Tribe & Smith, 2021). Providing free products in public schools and post-secondary restrooms makes menstrual supplies part of the expected features of a publicly accessible institution. To date, British Columbia, Nova Scotia, Toronto, Whitehorse, and several other municipal and provincial jurisdictions have adopted policies requiring public schools to have period supplies freely available in school restrooms (Hong, 2019; Province of British Columbia, 2019; Province of Nova Scotia, 2019; Toronto District School Board, 2019). Anecdotally, we know that some Canadian workplaces have also made these changes, which reflects the growing awareness that free access to menstrual supplies is an important way to eliminate barriers to the full participation of women and girls in public spaces, such as workplaces and schools. While progress has been made, these changes do not directly address period poverty, and tend to paint measures that address menstrual equity as measures that benefit all, which is problematic on many levels. Furthermore, as we explain in the following section, these changes have not been adequate in addressing period poverty during the COVID-19 pandemic for a number of reasons.

THE COVID-19 PANDEMIC: WHAT HAPPENED?

March 2020 marked the start of a global health crisis in the Global North. Canada, like many countries affected by COVID-19, enforced an emergency stay-at-home-order to stop the spread of the novel virus. People were discouraged from going out and meeting with other people, while students and employees worked remotely. Some people lost their jobs and their homes, while others said goodbye to loved ones who caught the disease. Mental distress became more prevalent due to social isolation and uncertainty about the future (Rottermann, 2020). Government-sanctioned lockdowns and quarantines led to frenzied grocery store buying; news channels and social media posts abounded with stories of empty shelves and the dearth of hand sanitizer, face masks, canned food, and toilet paper (Knoll, 2020).

Absent from this narrative highlighting the lack of essential supplies during the pandemic was the fact that period supplies were also being stock-piled by some, impacting access to disposable tampons and pads in Canadian retail stores. We at the Douglas College Menstrual Cycle Research Group recorded varying levels of short supply of period products across the Lower Mainland area, with major chains often depleted of stock. In addition, several organizations whom many relied upon for a supply of essential goods, period products included, were forced to shut down for weeks or months (Vantage Point et al., 2020). The closure of safe spaces and social services meant vulnerable populations, including people who menstruate, had to fend for themselves.

The Impact of the Pandemic on Menstruators

As the virus spread across the world, some populations were hit harder than others. In Canada, like many other countries, the pandemic shed a light on existing social and economic inequities. It amplified existing experiences of poverty that is not equally shared across genders. Reports highlighted how women's and girls' lives have been disproportionately affected by the COVID-19 pandemic, from the increasing burden of home-based emotional and physical labor, to the disruption and relocation of essential services women benefit from, and higher losses of employment and social protection (Plan International, 2020; United Nations, 2020).

Plan International (2020) conducted a study in 30 countries and found that managing periods was especially difficult due to the shortages of products, price gouging, and lack of access to information about menstrual health. The study revealed these issues affected women worldwide, including from Australia, Ireland, Kenya, Nepal, and Cambodia (Plan International, 2020). In countries such as India, where many vulnerable populations tend to live in urban slums and highly dense low-income group settlements, forced lockdowns were accompanied with intense summer heat and lack of access to safe water for sanitization (Jahan, 2020). Women's need for privacy to manage their periods was quickly lost, along with access to menstrual supplies more generally. In the example of the city of Chennai, seven million individuals (of which half are female and 29 % live in urban slums) were expected to quarantine without any way to access necessities such as water, food, and menstrual products, further exasperating the deprivation, discrimination, and poverty of already vulnerable communities (Jahan, 2020).

In Canada, the economic and social impact of the COVID-19 pandemic has not affected women and men equally. Recent published data on labor force participation and financial difficulties during the pandemic show that the pandemic has exacerbated women's and minorities' financial difficulties to a greater degree than other populations such as men and non-visible minorities (Moyser, 2020; Statistics Canada, 2020a, 2020b, 2020c). Women have been disproportionately impacted for many reasons, including the fact that they were more likely to be minimum-wage and part-time workers, and that women are more likely to work in industries at a higher risk of lay-off during the pandemic (Statistics Canada, 2020b). These industries are largely low-paying, and a large portion of workers did not have workplace benefits or financial reserves to rely on for support during either short-term or prolonged unemployment. In addition, women at all socioeconomic levels were—and are still currently—pressured to take on unpaid family work, which prior to the pandemic may have been outsourced to others, such as caring for children, educating school-aged children, and performing housework (Moyser, 2020).

Nationally, women represented 70 % of all jobs lost in March 2020 in the core working demographic of people aged 25–54 (Statistics Canada, 2020a). At the same time, the unemployment rate in Canada reached the highest rate recorded since 1976, which is when government agencies began collecting data (Statistics Canada, 2020a). With that, over 1.8 million women had lost their jobs or lost at least half of their usual hours of employment in Canada, twice the losses incurred by men (Statistics Canada, 2020a).

As health measures were lifted and restrictions eased, low-wage workers, many of whom are menstruators who were already living precariously prior to the

COVID-19 pandemic, including, for example, sex workers (see Chapter Seven), struggled to recover financially. In the month of August 2020, more men than women were employed in Canada and, among low-wage earners, young women were recovering at a slower rate than young men (Statistics Canada, 2020c). In September and October 2020, young women aged 15–24 continued to see considerable job losses and reported 16.4 % fewer hours worked as compared to young men who reported 8.6 % fewer hours worked (Statistics Canada, 2020d). Thus, as Canada struggles to adapt to the ongoing COVID-19 pandemic, the preliminary reports published by Statistics Canada (2020a, 2020b, 2020c, 2020d) show that women, especially youth, low-wage workers, and those from visible minority groups, have had a very difficult year.

Plan International (2020) noted that the COVID-19 pandemic has unfairly impacted menstruators, in particular marginalized women who were already living in social and economic precarity prior to the pandemic. In other words, women were generally more vulnerable to poverty this year, which for some meant having to make a choice between food or period products. As a result, the pandemic exacerbated existing inequities, including experiences of period poverty. Period supplies, and menstrual health management more generally, remain a luxury many cannot afford. This remained true and was exacerbated during the COVID-19 pandemic. Recognizing this reality, many organizations across Canada working to address period poverty adapted to the challenges posed by the pandemic, and sought to continue their work in a difficult and shifting terrain. In the next section, we provide brief accounts of how UWLM and Aisle responded, adapted, and shifted their work to address period poverty during the pandemic.

Adapting Out of Necessity: A Closer Look at Organizational Response Under COVID-19

The disruption caused by the COVID-19 pandemic in March of 2020 was widespread and impacted all workplaces, including essential service organizations. In May 2020, Vantage Point, a British Columbia charity which connects and supports local non-profits, in association with the Vancouver Foundation and the Victoria Foundation, published an extensive report on the impact of the pandemic on the operations and program delivery of 1,119 non-profit organizations across British Columbia (Vantage Point et al., 2020). They found that organizations, including those which provide free period supplies, experienced challenges regardless of geographical location, size, or sector. Reported difficulties included a lack of personal protective equipment (PPE), the inability of many goods and services to be delivered virtually, and poor communication with members from vulnerable communities who often lack internet access (Vantage Point et al., 2020). The most pressing challenge was related to the distribution of food and essential items due to difficulties in procurement and delivery in the face of skyrocketing demand across British Columbia (Vantage Point et al., 2020). With so many Canadians relying on them for necessities, many non-profit organizations struggled with funding cancellations, lack of fundraising opportunities, low operating reserves, and massive employee and volunteer layoffs (Vantage Point et al., 2020). We look at two organizations, one in the non-profit sector and the other a consumer-packaged goods company, that adapted to the pandemic by quickly modifying how they operate.

United Way Lower Mainland's Period Promise Campaign: Redesigning Distribution Channels

UWLM, a non-profit organization, has been working on the issue of period poverty in different regions of British Columbia since 2016. Working with local governments, labor and non-profit organizations, activists, businesses, and academic researchers, UWLM is dedicated to finding solutions to period poverty and menstrual inequity through the Period Promise Campaign. Their vision is to address period poverty in the community through large-scale mobilization, research and policy analysis, education and awareness-building, and collaboration with a wide range of community partners.

Prior to the COVID-19 pandemic, UWLM ran the Period Promise (formerly Tampon Tuesday) menstrual product drives and distributed the donated supplies to non-profit groups that served clients in need. In the span of four years, UWLM collected and distributed more than 1,000,000 disposable and sustainable menstrual supplies to over 65 community organizations in British Columbia (United Way Lower Mainland, 2018, 2019). The program is successful in its outreach, collection, and impact, and has seen substantial year-over-year growth in the size of donations, number of participants, and level of commitment from volunteers (United Way Lower Mainland, 2019). Nonetheless, prior to the pandemic, these efforts and other public policy initiatives simply were not enough to fully address period poverty in British Columbia.

In March 2020, when the Canadian government placed restrictions on workplaces, UWLM, like many local organizations, experienced substantive disruptions. UWLM had to make difficult choices, one of which was to put the Period Promise Campaign and related events on indefinite hold, interrupting menstrual supply drives and contributing to a lack of accessible reproductive health services, especially those from marginalized communities. In addition, the immediate impact of the pandemic on employment coupled with directives to self-isolate, resulted in a new population of vulnerable people in need of goods and services, including food and menstrual supplies. Many individuals who had not previously relied on the non-profit sector to support their day-to-day needs now had to navigate an unfamiliar sector of community-focused services experiencing profound transitions in function and viability. Increased need, coupled with reduced services was a theme across the not-for-profit and community sector. For example, the recent research into period poverty by UWLM revealed that the majority of organizations (11 of 12) participating in the study had to reduce programming, while many also had to reduce services and supports (10 of 12) (Period Promise, 2021). Like many other organizations, UWLM needed a solution to recover and find new ways to work in the community to alleviate period poverty.

UWLM responded to the pandemic by launching the Local Love Food Hubs program, a new initiative to fund and support community organizations and their clients. Food Hubs were embedded in the community to serve as a catchment easily accessible by a neighborhood or region, allowing clients to receive goods, such as menstrual supplies, meals, food hampers, gift cards, or meal vouchers, while getting triaged to other community services. By late August 2020, more than 130 Food Hubs were established across the Lower Mainland. UWLM also worked with businesses such Aisle and Procter & Gamble to collect and distribute large amounts of tampons, pads, and reusable menstrual products. Combined with donations from the public, UWLM received more than 250,000 menstrual products, all of which were distributed to people in need through the Food Hub program.

Aisle International: Pivoting the Business Model

Formerly known as Lunapads and operating in Vancouver, British Columbia since 1993, Aisle International (Aisle) designs inclusive, reusable menstrual products that contribute to reproductive knowledge and justice. They also advocate for policy change with regards to free menstrual products as a way to eradicate period poverty. With many of their products produced and sold locally, the company is closely involved in Vancouver communities. When the COVID-19 restrictions were imposed in March 2020, Aisle experienced major disruptions to their business model, yet they realized the opportunity to make a difference to the health and safety of local communities.

The pandemic disrupted the global supply of PPE, such as face masks, gloves, and hand sanitizer. Canada, whose only land border is with the United States, had critical shipments of masks held up by United States officials (Stone & Morrow, 2020). At a time where ill-equipped healthcare workers were putting their lives at risk in order to fight the new virus, often relying on makeshift masks to protect themselves, Aisle responded by expanding their business model. Aisle began to mass produce reusable face masks to help local communities stop the spread of COVID-19.

With offices located on the edge of the downtown Eastside of Vancouver, a neighborhood characterized by poverty and substance use, Aisle's addition of reusable masks to their product line resulted from witnessing the demand in their local community. This fast transition helped Aisle stay open as a business, showing resilience at a time when 32 % of British Columbia businesses had to fully shut down production and services, and 47 % operated only partially (Canadian Federation of Independent Business [CFIB], 2020a). As of September 2020, only one third of Canadian small businesses were fully open with many at risk of closing their doors permanently due to the financial impacts of the pandemic (CFIB, 2020b). A survey of 1363 Canadian businesses found that half of open businesses reported loss of revenue due to fewer customers spending less than average (CFIB, 2020b). Although these statistics paint a gloomy picture of the British Columbia economy, swift action by businesses like Aisle provide hope that recovery is possible. Further, that responding to and working with those seeking to meet the shifting needs of vulnerable and marginalized populations is key.

Aisle's newly produced masks were first donated to local vulnerable populations and paired, when appropriate, with donations of menstrual products. In addition, Aisle began fundraising to donate reusable masks and menstrual pads more widely. It became apparent that the two products were intrinsically linked: Both masks and menstrual supplies provide safety, mobility, dignity, and are essential in supporting menstruators' access to public spaces. For example, both masks and menstrual supplies are needed for menstruating women to safely use public transport, run errands, and visit social service centers, schools, and churches. Both masks and menstrual supplies are a public health requirement, yet they are not free nor freely available. Both are expensive retail products that many vulnerable people cannot afford. Aisle actively works to address these health inequities and continues to make masks and menstrual products readily available to everyone.

NO SMALL THING: FINDING BALANCE IN SHIFTING TERRAIN

Several themes emerged as we examined how the COVID-19 pandemic shifted the work of organizations seeking to address period poverty in Canada. Changing demographics and growing vulnerable and marginalized populations placed new strains on the non-profit sector that was already operating over capacity before the pandemic. In addition, the for-profit sector had to adapt quickly to continue to meet the needs of their communities, especially if part of their mandate involved community or social justice engagement. Global shutdowns necessitated domestic solutions and brought into sharp relief the need for local distribution of goods and services to allow for social distancing. During the original province-wide shut down, period poverty was clearly tied to other forms of poverty that disproportionately affect vulnerable and marginalized populations, such as food insecurity and threats to public health and safety. While some organizations were able to partially address period poverty in the midst of pandemic challenges and have some measure of positive effect on local communities, the fact remains that period poverty continues to rise and is still in urgent need of solutions. The tendency to cordon off menstruation as a niche issue, as well as ongoing social stigma related to menstrual flow management contribute to this reality.

Addressing period poverty is an important issue reflecting multiple embodied and systemic forms of inequity affecting many people who menstruate in Canadian society. This is an issue facing women and girls, as well as gender-diverse people, from a range of communities and backgrounds. We are just beginning to understand the extent of this social issue in Canada. This research gap is compounded by the reality that menstruation continues to be relegated to the private sphere and excluded from public policy. To this end, the parallels between menstrual supplies and face masks in increasing people's health, safety, and mobility can illuminate the issue for policymakers and others who otherwise may not fully appreciate the importance of and need for freely and widely available period products in the public realm. Overall, addressing period poverty is an essential element of broader work to move gender equity forward. In addition, as it intersects with systemic patterns of inequity and marginalization, addressing period poverty can be understood as part of the deep work of supporting individual needs as they arise, and along with that, building a more just society.

The approaches taken by UWLM and Aisle offer insight into how Canadian organizations adapted quickly to the needs of vulnerable and marginalized groups experiencing period poverty, especially during times of crisis like the ongoing COVID-19 pandemic. As much as raising awareness and building broader policy change across a society is key, the responses of these two organizations speak to the importance of relationships, local communities, and quick and responsive solutions to immediate needs. At the same time, the Douglas College Menstrual Cycle Research Group, UWLM and Aisle continued to be involved during the COVID-19 pandemic in the broader work of policy advocacy to address longer-term solutions. This balancing act between attending to systemic barriers and supporting local communities and the immediacy of individual needs has always been central to the struggle for creating a more caring society that places safety, health, well-being, and equity at the center. It is also in some ways a unique feature of advocacy aimed at supporting menstruation, which continues to be pushed to the margins of policy work and responses. This past year has that the flow of inequity persists across Canadian society in so many ways; further, period poverty doesn't stop for a pandemic and neither did we.

NOTES

1 Department of Sociology, Douglas College.
2 Douglas College.
3 United Way Lower Mainland, Period Promise.
4 Aisle International, Communications Manager.
5 In this chapter, menstrual supplies or period supplies refer to anything used to support menstrual flow management, including menstrual cups, disposable liners, pads, and tampons, reusable pads. Certain forms of hormonal contraception can also be included in this list but are not the primary focus of the campaigns discussed in this chapter.
6 See https://www.theperiodpurse.com/.
7 See for example, Alliance for Period Supplies, https://www.allianceforperiodsupplies.org/, United for Access, https://www.shethinx.com/pages/thinx-giverise-united-for-access, and Always' "#EndPeriodPoverty" campaign, https://always.com/en-us/about-us/end-period-poverty.

REFERENCES

Bobel, C. (2010). *New blood: Third-wave feminism and the politics of menstruation.* Rutgers University Press.
Bobel, C., & Fahs, B. (2020). From bloodless respectability to radical menstrual embodiment: Shifting menstrual politics from private to public. *Signs: Journal of Women in Culture and Society, 45*(4), 955–983.
Brito, A. L. (2020, March 17). Period, politics, and beyond! *The Other Press.* https://theotherpress.ca/period-politics-and-beyond/
Britton, Cathryn J. (1996). Learning about 'the curse': An anthropological perspective on experiences of menstruation. Women's Studies International Forum, 19 (6), 645-653.
Canadian Federation of Independent Business. (2020a). *Your business and COVID-19: Survey #4, preliminary results as of April 5, 2020.* https://www.cfib-fcei.ca/sites/default/files/2020-04/COVID-19-survey-results-April-6.pdf
Canadian Federation of Independent Business. (2020b). *COVID-19: State of small business, key results of survey.* https://www.cfib-fcei.ca/sites/default/files/2020-09/COVID-19-survey-results-September2.pdf
Canadian Menstruators. (2015). http://www.canadianmenstruators.ca/
Chandra-Mouli, V., & Vipul Patel, S. (2017). Mapping the knowledge and understanding of menarche, menstrual hygiene and menstrual health among adolescent girls in low- and middle-income countries. *Reproductive Health, 14,* 1–16.
Chenoa Cooper, S., & Barthalow Koch, P. (2008). "Nobody told me nothin": Communication about menstruation among low-income African American women. *Women & Health, 46*(1), 57–78.
Delaney, J., Lupton, M. J., & Toth, E. (1976). *The curse: A cultural history of menstruation.* University of Illinois Press.
Dobie, C. (2019). *New Westminster school board makes history by approving period products initiative.* New Westminser Record. https://www.newwestrecord.ca/news/new-westminster-school-board-makes-history-by-approving-period-products-initiative-1.23647515

Frank, S. E. (2020). Queering menstruation: Trans and non-binary identity and body politics. *Sociological Inquiry*, *90*(2), 371–404.

Fuller Evans, J. (2020, March 6). Douglas College fair aims to create conversation about menstruation. *Vancouver Courier*. https://www.vancourier.com/douglas-college-fair-aims-to-create-conversation-about-menstruation-1.24091661

Goldblatt, B., & Steele, L. (2019). Bloody unfair: Inequality related to menstruation -- Considering the role of discrimination law. *Sydney Law Review*, *41*(3), 292–325.

Hillard, P. J. A. (2002). Menstruation in young girls: A clinical perspective. *Obstetrics & Gynecology*, *99*(4), 655–662.

Hong, J. (2019, September 17). Whitehorse high school provides free menstrual products to students. *Yukon News*. https://www.yukon-news.com/news/whitehorse-high-school-provides-free-menstrual-products-to-students/

Jahan, N. (2020). Bleeding during the pandemic: The politics of menstruation. *Sexual and Reproductive Health Matters*, *28*(1), 1801001. https://doi.org/10.1080/26410397.2020.1801001

Khan, Z., & Oveisi, N. (2020). *Let's talk about periods: A critical analysis of Canada's menstrual inequities*. Free Periods Canada, UBC Chapter.

Kissling, E. A. (2006). *Capitalizing on the Curse: The business of menstruation*. Lynne Rienner.

Knoll, C. (2020, March 13). Panicked shoppers empty shelves as Coronavirus anxiety rises. *The New York Times*. https://nyti.ms/2viIgcQ

Moffat, N., & Pickering, L. (2019). "Out of Order": The double burden of menstrual etiquette and the subtle exclusion of women from public space in Scotland. *The Sociological Review Monographs*, *67*(4), 766–787.

Moyser, M. (2020). Gender differences in mental health during the COVID-19 pandemic. *StatCan COVID-19: Data to Insights for a Better Canada (45-28-0001)*. Statistics Canada.

Newton, V. L. (2016). *Everyday discourses of menstruation: Cultural and social perspectives*. Palgrave MacMillan.

Period Promise. (2020). *United way of lower mainland*. https://www.periodpromise.ca/

Period Promise. (2021). *United way period promise research report project final report*. https://uwbc.ca/program/period-promise/#research

Plan International. (2020). *Periods in a pandemic: Menstrual hygiene management in the time of COVID-19, Report*. https://plan-international.org/publications/periods-in-a-pandemic

Province of British Columbia. (2019, April). *Provision of menstrual products* [New Public School Policy]. https://www2.gov.bc.ca/gov/content/education-training/k-12/administration/legislation-policy/public-schools/provision-of-menstrual-products

Province of Nova Scotia, Department of Education and Early Childhood Development. (2019, September 17). *Free menstrual products available in schools* [News Release]. https://novascotia.ca/news/release/?id=20190917006

Rottermann, M. (2020). Canadians who report lower self-perceived mental health during the COVID-19 pandemic more likely to report increased use of cannabis, alcohol and tobacco. *StatCan COVID-19: Data to Insights for a Better Canada (45-28-0001)*. Statistics Canada.

Scala, F. (2020). The gender dynamics of interest group politics: The case of the Canadian menstruators and the campaign to eliminate the "tampon tax." In M. Tremblay & J. Everitt (Eds.), *The Palgrave handbook of gender, sexuality and Canadian politics* (pp. 379–398). Palgrave MacMillan.

Schooler, D., Ward, M., Merriweather, A., & Caruthers, A. (2005). Cycles of shame: Menstrual shame, body shame, and sexual decision-making. *Journal of Sex Research*, *42*(4), 324–334.

Sebert Kuhlmann, A., Key, R., Billingsley, C., Shanot, T., Scroggins, S., & Teni, M. T. (2020). Students' menstrual hygiene needs and school attendance in an urban St. Louis, Missouri district. *Journal of Adolescent Health, 67*, 444–446.

Sebert Kuhlmann, A., Peters Berquist, E., Danjoint, D., & Lewis Wall, L. (2019). Unmet menstrual hygiene needs among low-income women. *Obstetrics & Gynecology, 133*(2), 238–244.

Shore, R. (2019, February 4). Vancouver mom pushes for free access to pads and tampons for students. *Vancouver Sun.* https://vancouversun.com/news/local-news/vancouver-mom-pushes-for-free-access-to-pads-and-tampons-for-students

Siltanen, J., & Doucet, A. (2017). *Gender relations in Canada: Intersectionalities and social change.* Oxford University Press.

Smith, L., Tribe, S., & Brito, A. (2020, August 2). Period equity now: Canadian need universal access to menstrual supplies at work. *Canadian Dimension.* https://canadiandimension.com/articles/view/period-equity-now-canadians-need-universal-access-to-menstrual-supplies-at-work

Sommer, M. (2013). Structural factors influencing menstruating school girls' health and well-being in Tanzania. *A Journal of Comparative and International Education, 43*(3), 323–345.

Sommer, M., & Sahin, M. (2013). Overcoming the taboo: Advancing the global agenda for menstrual hygiene management for schoolgirls. *American Journal of Public Health, 103*(9), 1556–1559.

Sommer, M., Sutherland, C., & Chandra-Mouli, V. (2015). Putting menarche and girls into the global population health agenda. *Reproductive Health, 12*(24), 1–3.

Spicer, C. (2020, March 10). *Periods, politics, and beyond!* Douglas College.

Statistics Canada. (2020a). *Labour Force Survey, March 2020.* https://www150.statcan.gc.ca/n1/daily-quotidien/200409/dq200409a-eng.htm

Statistics Canada. (2020b). *Labour Force Survey, May 2020.* https://www150.statcan.gc.ca/n1/daily-quotidien/200605/dq200605a-eng.htm

Statistics Canada. (2020c). *Labour Force Survey, August 2020.* https://www150.statcan.gc.ca/n1/daily-quotidien/200904/dq200904a-eng.htm

Statistics Canada. (2020d). *Labour Force Survey, October 2020.* https://www150.statcan.gc.ca/n1/daily-quotidien/201106/dq201106a-eng.htm

Stone, L., & Morrow, A. (2020, April 6). Ontario says 500,000 masks destined for province to be released by U.S. *The Globe and Mail.* https://www.theglobeandmail.com/canada/article-ontario-says-500000-masks-destined-for-province-to-be-released-by-us/

Toronto District School Board. (2019, August 30). *TDSB to provide free menstrual products to students* [News Release]. https://www.tdsb.on.ca/News/Article-Details/ArtMID/474/ArticleID/1347/TDSB-to-Provide-Free-Menstrual-Products-to-Students

Tribe, S., & Smith, L. (2021). Post-secondary periods: Access to menstrual supplies on campus and impacts on students. *Menstrual Research Day.* Douglas College.

United Nations. (2020). *Policy brief: The impact of COVID-19 on women.* https://www.un.org/sexualviolenceinconflict/wp-content/uploads/2020/06/report/policy-brief-the-impact-of-covid-19-on-women/policy-brief-the-impact-of-covid-19-on-women-en-1.pdf

United Way Lower Mainland. (2018, March 23). Tampon Tuesday nets over 220,000 donated menstrual products. https://www.uwlm.ca/news/tampon-tuesday-nets-220000/

United Way Lower Mainland. (2019, April 4). Period Promise campaign makes profound impact. https://uwbc.ca/stories/2019/period-promise-campaign-makes-profound-impact/

Vantage Point, Vancouver Foundation, & Victoria Foundation. (2020). *No immunity: BC nonprofits and the impact of COVID-19, Early impact summary report.* https://thevantagepoint.ca/blog/no-immunity-the-impacts-of-covid-19-on-our-sector/

Vikander, T. (2019, January 17). Vancouver mom wants free pads and tampons in all public washrooms. *The Star.* https://www.thestar.com/vancouver/2019/01/17/vancouver-mom-wants-free-pads-and-tampons-in-all-public-washrooms.html

Vora, S. (2020). The realities of period poverty: How homelessness shapes women's lived experiences of menstruation. In C. Bobel, I. T. Winkler, B. Fahs, K. A. Hasson, E. A. Kissling, & T.-A. Roberts (Eds.), *The Palgrave handbook of critical menstruation studies* (pp. 31–47). Palgrave MacMillan.

Weiss-Wolf, J. (2017). *Periods gone public.* Arcade Publishing.

Wood, J. M. (2020). (In)visible bleeding: The menstrual concealment imperative. In C. Bobel, I. T. Winkler, B. Fahs, K. A. Hasson, E. A. Kissling, & T.-A. Roberts (Eds.), *The Palgrave handbook of critical menstruation studies* (pp. 319–336). Palgrave MacMillan.

Wootton, S., & Morison, T. (2020). Menstrual management and the negotiation of failed femininities: A discursive study among low-income young women in Aotearoa (New Zealand). *Women's Reproductive Health, 7*(2), 87–106. https://doi.org/10.1080/23293691.2020.1740485

Appendix

Province or Territory	Statute	Timeline of Declarations
Alberta	*Public Health Act* (2006) and *Emergency Management Act* (2000)	Declared state of public health emergency March 18, 2020, pursuant to s.52.1 of the *Emergency Management Act* (2006), expands powers to 'take measures intended to protect public health', including the entry of any building without warrant (Emergency Management Act, 2000, s.52.6(1)(d)) and ordering immunization (Block & Goldenberg, 2020; Block, Goldenberg, & Waschuk, 2020; Block, Goldenberg, et al., 2020; Block, Loranger, & Goldenberg, 2020; Block, Smyth, et al., 2020; Public Health Act, 2006; s.38(1)(c)). Has not yet declared a provincial state of emergency under *Emergency Management Act* (2000), but notably amended the act April 7, 2020 so that provincial authorities could override local orders (Joannou, 2020).

Province or Territory	Statute	Timeline of Declarations
British Columbia	*Emergency Program Act* (1996) and *Public Health Act* (2008) (BCPHA)	Declared public health emergency March 17, 2020, pursuant to s.5 *British Columbia Public Health Act* (2008), expanding powers to issue verbal orders with immediate sanctions. Declared a state of emergency March 18, 2020, pursuant to s.91(1) *Emergency Program Act (1996)*, expanding powers to conscript persons to render assistance, and ration food or supplies. Obstruction of provincial powers imposes criminal sanctions (Emergency Program Act, 1996; s.27; Public Health Act, 20008; s.56(4)). Courts review government decisions under both legislation with considerable deference.
Manitoba	*Emergency Measures Act* (2001)	Declared state of emergency March 20, 2020 pursuant to s.10(1) of the *Emergency Measures Act (2011)*, expanding powers to "any party to do everything necessary to [...] limit loss of life", including entry without a warrant (Emergency Measures Act, 2001; s.12(1)(iii)).
New Brunswick	*Emergencies Measures Act* (2011)	Declared state of emergency on March 19, 2020 pursuant to s.12 *Emergency Management Act (2011)*, expanding powers to do "everything necessary for the protection [of] health and safety," including ordering assistance of any person in relation to the emergency (Emergency Management Act, 2011).
Newfoundland and Labrador	*Public Health Protection and Promotion Act* (2018) and *Emergency Services Act* (2018)	Declared state of emergency March 18, 2020 pursuant to s.27 *Public Health Protection and Promotion Act* (2018), expanding powers to "take measures reasonable [...] for protection of health." Scope of *Public Health Protection and Promotion Act* is broader than other provincial public health legislation. Has not invoked *Emergency Services Act* (2018), but if so, emergency powers would take precedence over *Public Health Protection and Promotion Act*, including entering private property.

Province or Territory	Statute	Timeline of Declarations
Northwest Territories	*Public Health Act* (2007) and *Emergency Management Act* (2017)	Declared public health emergency March 18, 2020 pursuant to s.32 of *Public Health Act* (2007), expanding powers to issue permits, acquire or use public and private property. Declared state of emergency March 24, 2020 pursuant to s.14 *Emergency Management Act* (2017), expanding powers to authorize conscription and "any other act to mitigate, respond or recover the effects of the emergency" (Emergency Management Act, 2017; s.17; McCarthy, 2020).
Nova Scotia	*Emergency Management Act* (1990)	Declared state of emergency March 22, 2020 pursuant to s.12(1) of the *Emergency Management Act* (1990), expanding powers to "do everything necessary for […] health and safety […] including authorizing entry without warrant […] or issuing fines" (Emergency Management Act, 1990; s.14) (McCarthy, 2020).
Nunavut	*Public Health Act* (2016) and *Emergency Measures Act* (2007)	Declared public health emergency March 18, 2020 pursuant to *Public Health Act* (2016), expanding powers to "take measures […] necessary for protection" (s.41) except to enter dwelling without warrant (s.41(4)). Has not declared a territorial state of emergency under *Emergency Measures Act* (2007). As of July 31, 2020, there are no confirmed cases of COVID-19 in the region (McCarthy Roundup, 2020).
Ontario	*Emergency Management and Civil Protection Act* (1990)	Declared a state of emergency March 17, 2020, pursuant to s.7.0.1 *Emergency Management and Civil Protection Act (1990)*, expanding powers "necessary to alleviate effects of an emergency", that remain with the Premier alone. Privacy concerns are subject to judicial review only when the declared emergency is terminated (Emergency Management and Civil Protection Act, 1990; ss.7.0.2(4)13 and 7.0.2(7)(2)). Note that the *Emergency Management and Civil Protection Act* (1990) does not include the power to conscript.

Province or Territory	Statute	Timeline of Declarations
Prince Edward Island	*Public Health Act* (1988) and *Emergency Measures Act* (1988)	Declared public health emergency pursuant to s.49 *Public Health Act* (1988), expanding powers to "issue directions to […] manage threat" and appropriate "premises for temporary quarantine facilities." Declared state of emergency April 16, 2020 pursuant *Emergency Measures Act* (1988), where emergency powers precede *Public Health Act* (1988), including order additional assistance to "carry out measures related to emergency" (Emergency Measures Act, 1988; s.11).
Quebec	*Public Health Act* (2001) and *Civil Protection Act* (2019).	Declared a public health state of emergency March 14, 2020 pursuant to s.119 *Public Health Act* (2001), expanding powers to order compulsory vaccination, mandate health documentation, or "any other measure […] to protect health" (Public Health Act, 2001; s.123(2–8)). Can be done without delay or formality. Has yet declared a provincial state of emergency under the (Civil Protection Act, 2019).
Saskatchewan	*Emergency Planning Act* (1989)	Declared provincial state of emergency March 18, 2020, pursuant to *Emergency Planning Act* (1989), allowing the Cabinet a "catch-all" power to "do all acts and take all proceedings that are reasonably necessary to meet the emergency" (McCarthy, 2020)
Yukon	*Public Health and Safety Act* (2002) and *Civil Emergency Measures Act* (2002).	Declared public health emergency March 18, 2020 pursuant to s.4.3 *Public Health Safety Act* (2002), expanding powers to "require any person provide personal information [that] enables officers to person duties" (s.4.5(1)), "detail for surveillance" or "order to disinfect persons exposed to disease" (Public Health Safety Act, 2002; s.3(2)(b-c)). Declared state of emergency March 27, 2020 pursuant to s.6 *of Civil Emergency Measures Act* (2002), expanding powers to put into operation "any civil emergency plan" and may "do all things considered advisable [to] deal with emergency" including law enforcement (*Civil Emergency Measures Act*, 2002; s.8(1)(iii)).

Note: This table was compiled in August 2020.

Notes on Contributors

NEAL ADOLPH leads United Way British Columbia's Period Promise. His work includes running collections, conducting community-based research, working with government, and establishing collaborative networks for menstrual equity advocates. A proud member of UFCW 1518, he holds a Master of Arts in History from Simon Fraser University.

SAFIA AMIRY is a researcher and activist interested in working for women's rights, gender equality, gender-based violence, and education. She has worked with many institutions for women's rights and education in Afghanistan. Her doctoral research focuses on role of education in challenging patriarchy in Afghanistan.

NAWAL AMMAR is the Dean of the College of Humanities and Social Sciences at Rowan University, New Jersey, USA. Her research focuses on justice and equity. She is a public-facing scholar, working with various national and international groups on justice and equity.

AMANDA COUTURE-CARRON is a senior strategic planner with a police service and a research fellow whose research focuses on violence against women with emphasis on immigrant women, sexual assault, and experiences with the police. She received her PhD in Sociology from the University of Toronto.

ELLIOT FONAREV is a PhD student in the Department of Sociology at the University of Toronto. He researches sociolegal inequalities, media, education, and tech.

RIM GACIMI holds a Bachelor's Degree of Arts (Honors) in Applied Psychology and is interested in intersectional studies of emotion, economic inequality, socioeconomic status, and social class.

JOE HERMER is the Chair of the Sociology Department at the University of Toronto Scarborough.

LAURIE HIGGINS, RECE, BCD, MEd is an early childhood educator in a kindergarten classroom. One of her biggest accomplishments besides being a mother to four is winning the Prime Minister Award of Excellence, which recognized her teaching philosophy to provide an equitable space for all.

JANE HOPE was the marketing and communications lead for Vancouver-based B Corp Aisle International from 2016 to 2021. When not working, she lives in East Vancouver with her oddball cat.

SHANNON HUTCHESON is a PhD candidate at McGill University in the Department of Integrated Studies in Education. As an international educator who has worked in the United States, France, and Canada, her research focuses on international education, with a lens on equity for international students.

MICHELE PICH is the Assistant Director of the Shrieber Family Pet Therapy Program and an Adjunct Professor of Law and Justice Studies at Rowan University, holding graduate degrees in Clinical Psychology, and Criminal Justice. Her research includes victimization, substance use, corrections, policing, and animal-assisted interventions.

IRADELE PLANTE is a lawyer with a master's degree in public health in service to southern Albertans with family disputes, civil litigation, and estate planning. When not working, she is either on a bike or planning a bike trip.

WILLIAM T. SMALE, Professor of Education at Trent University, received his PhD in Educational Administration and Leadership from the University of Alberta in 2001. His research interests include school law, educational administration, and early school leaving.

LISA SMITH is a Faculty Member in the Department of Sociology at Douglas College. Her areas of research and teaching include, social and political aspects of sexual and reproductive health, the menstrual cycle, and gender-based violence and the post-secondary context.

RAVITA SURAJBALI is a PhD student at the Centre for Criminology and Sociolegal Studies at the University of Toronto. She researches the legal and institutional governance of sexual violence on campus in Canada.

KIMIA TOWFIGH, BCL/JD, 2021, is a lawyer and graduate of McGill University's Faculty of Law. She has supported the iMPACTS project since 2020. Her research interests include sustainable development, immigration policy, and tax law.

SARAH TOWLE holds a Master of Science in Family Medicine and Bioethics from McGill University. She has expertise in knowledge translation/mobilization, health equity, and sexual health.

ALEXANDRA M. ZIDENBERG, PhD, is an Assistant Professor at King's University College at Western. Her research examines the nexus between forensic psychology and human sexuality, focusing on topics like sexual violence, zoophilia, bestiality, multiple perpetrator sexual offenses, and children under 12 with concerning sexual behaviors.

www.ingramcontent.com/pod-product-compliance
Lightning Source LLC
Chambersburg PA
CBHW061715300426
44115CB00014B/2694